CONFLICTS

IN A NUTSHELL

THIRD EDITION

By

DAVID D. SIEGEL
Distinguished Professor of Law
Albany Law School of Union University

and

PATRICK J. BORCHERS
Dean and Professor of Law
Creighton University School of Law

D0465837

THOMSON
—— ∗ ——™
WEST

Mat #40367635

COPYRIGHT © 1982, 1994 WEST PUBLISHING CO.
© 2005 Thomson/West
          610 Opperman Drive
          P.O. Box 64526
          St. Paul, MN 55164–0526
          1–800–328–9352

Printed in the United States of America

ISBN 0–314–16066–3

 TEXT IS PRINTED ON 10% POST CONSUMER RECYCLED PAPER

Still for Sheela and Rachel

*

PREFACE

Conflict of laws as I see the subject now is not conflict of laws as I saw it in law school. It has to do with obtaining a view of the whole, for only with the whole view can all the pieces be fitted in. When everything finally fell into place for me, some of the pieces that once looked awfully big turned out to be almost invisible. And others, hardly noticeable earlier, turned up with prominent places in the broad picture.

Teaching conflicts along with both federal and state practice has been my law school activity over the years, but for the "whole view" I am equally indebted to the other side of my professional life: writing for and conducting lectures and seminars with judges and lawyers, which requires one constantly to relate the theoretical to the practical. Undertaking these responsibilities alongside law teaching, I soon learned that not only need neither be sacrificed for the other; each in fact colors and balances the other. It teaches the teacher to blend theory and practice at all times, and for me its ultimate lesson has been that the chasm between the classroom and the courtroom can be closed, or in any event reduced to a narrow gap—a gap that the student, now the young lawyer, can cross without breaking a leg.

This Nutshell is designed as an introduction and review tool for students and as a quick refresher and reference tool for lawyers. It is conflict of laws as I see it in perspective, with stress on the things that a broadened vantage point tells me are important. It tries to avoid the occasional pitfall of the enthusiastic teacher: the attempt to do too much, often with the consequence of doing too little. And it tries to avoid the occasional pitfall of the harried lawyer: preoccupation with a rule's content to such an extent that sight is lost of its purpose, with the consequence of a lost opportunity, and perhaps a lost case.

I try to reduce each topic to workable size, so that if an answer is not in hand, it will at least be within reach. It would please me if a law student or practicing lawyer going through this book were to come out with the feeling that conflict of laws is negotiable after all; and it would delight me if each of them were to feel as if addressed as the other.

The temptation to expand at many points was great, and at some junctures of choice of law—the most challenging of the conflicts family—almost irresistible. I resisted. I have kept it always in the front of my mind that this is a Nutshell. I trust that the reader who at some points may want more will remember that, too. The reader who wants more will find helpful the brief bibliography in § 11.

Included prominently in that bibliography is the work of Patrick J. Borchers, Dean at Creighton University School of Law and a former colleague of mine here at the Albany Law School. Accepting my invitation to assume prime responsibility for future editions of the Nutshell, Dean Borchers updated this one at many points. In recognition of his efforts, I have added his name as co-author, and with our combined efforts we hope this little book will be as current a tool in the subject as the space of a "nutshell" can provide.

We both acknowledge our debt to Conflict of Laws itself. It weaves its way in and out of every subject the law knows, keeping the mind alive and making the labor of writing about it a labor of love.

DAVID D. SIEGEL

North Egremont, Massachusetts
April, 2005

*

OUTLINE

*

TABLE OF CASES

References are to Pages

TABLE OF CASES

TABLE OF CASES

TABLE OF CASES

CONFLICTS

IN A NUTSHELL

THIRD EDITION

*

CHAPTER I

INTRODUCTORY

A. PRELIMINARIES

§ 1. Introduction

In its broadest sense, the phrase "conflict of laws" covers every case and situation with which two or more jurisdictions have had some contact. If a case is entirely between or among parties from the same state, and that state is where the claim or controversy arose and is otherwise the only one with any nexus to the case, no reference to conflicts principles is required. But inject any foreign element at all, and the law school course known as "Conflict of Laws" will make some room for the case that involves it.

In its narrow sense, a "conflict of laws" describes a case that has had contacts with two or more jurisdictions, and in which the laws of these several places differ with respect to some issue that has arisen in the case. The very fact of the difference will make it necessary for the judge to choose among the competing laws, and on this choice the whole case may hang. This area is more accurately described as the "choice of law" realm, and although it is often the only reference meant by a "conflict of laws", choice of law is in fact only one

1

of three major subjects embraced by the "Conflict of Laws" course as it is generally structured in American law schools. Europeans, by the way, prefer the term "Private International Law" to describe what we in the United States call "Conflict of Laws": the domain of rights, duties, and disputes between and among persons from different places. What we understand domestically as "International Law"—the realm of rights, duties, and disputes between and among sovereign states themselves and the sphere in which mankind has devised war as the ultimate dispute-settlement device—is called "Public International Law" by the Europeans.

§ 2. Approach of This Book; Citations

While we will try in the brief space of this Nutshell to take as practical an approach as possible to all questions presented—to the end that the interests of the client not become completely submerged in the academic—there are a number of junctures at which an understanding of theory and background is indispensable. This is notably the case in choice of law, the favorite playground of commentators and the beneficiary (or victim?) of much scholarship. Because limitations of space necessarily curtail treatment, we must occasionally be allowed a citation to secondary as well as primary sources to which the reader can turn for a more complete fabric begun with a few threads here.

To conserve space, a case will be cited only by the plaintiff's name, often with even the name abbreviated, followed by only a few letters to identify the court and the year. Enough will be supplied to identify the case in the Table of Cases, where the complete case name and citation can be found. Erie v. Tompkins would be cited: Erie (USSC 1938); a Fifth Circuit Court of Appeals citation in the federal system would identify the court as CA5. Other citations, whether of cases, statutes, or other materials, will be self-explanatory.

It is the hope of this book to give the reader a perspective on the conflict of laws. We seek to break the subject down into manageable components and thereby divest it of its mystery. Then, to the extent that a given matter or problem in one conflicts setting has some influence on or relevance to another, the two will be stitched up with a cross-reference, usually with just an abrupt parenthetical citing the other's section number.

B. PRINCIPAL CONFLICTS SUBJECTS SUMMARIZED

§ 3. Three Major Conflicts Realms

There are three major subdivisions of the "Conflict of Laws". "Choice of law", for which "conflict of laws" is often used as a synonym, is only one of them, albeit the most difficult and challenging. Another is jurisdiction. The third is the recognition and enforcement of judgments. In the chronological order in which these three subjects are likely to be met in practice, jurisdiction comes first, choice of law second, and judgments last. We'll do them in that order. The next few sections set forth an introductory perspective on each of these major conflicts realms.

§ 4. Jurisdiction; Introductory Note

Conflict of laws is usually studied in the second or third year of law school, and it sometimes comes as a surprise to the student that much of its subject matter has already been taken up, at least in outline form, in first year. This is surely the case with "jurisdiction". Most law schools have a civil procedure course in the first year and one of its studies is likely to be "longarm jurisdiction". Longarm jurisdiction is used when the defendant is a nondomiciliary of the forum state: if the defendant has nevertheless had certain minimum contacts with the state, the state can entertain personal jurisdiction over that nondomiciliary defendant in respect of that claim even if she is served with the court's process outside the state. The study of what will satisfy as "minimum contacts" sufficient to warrant this kind of extraterritorial jurisdiction is often part of the syllabus in the first year course. But the simple fact that the defendant is a domiciliary of a state other than the forum means that the forum is no longer the only state interested, and that means in turn that the case falls under the "conflict of laws" banner. Every time a state presumes to entertain jurisdiction over a nondomiciliary, it must have some basis for doing so. A study of these bases and of connected jurisdictional problems is a conflicts study.

In rem jurisdiction is a subdivision of personal jurisdiction based on the presence of property in the forum state and also has an important place on the conflicts front. The study of jurisdiction is in Chapter III, covering §§ 19 through 54.

§ 5. Choice of Law; Introductory Note

The most volatile of the three principal conflicts subdivisions—and the one to which "conflict of laws" is referring when used in its narrow sense—is choice of law. Whenever two or more states have a connection to a case and an issue arises as to which their respective laws differ, a choice of law must be made. The importance of the issue will vary, but more often than not when a genuine "conflict" is at hand, the choice is likely to mean the life or death of the claim. A simple and common example that arose in a number of cases during the formative years of the 1960's and 1970's, as will be seen in better context when choice of law is examined in depth later on (Chapter IV), is where cars from one state collide in another and one of the states has a "guest-host" statute that bars a passenger from recovering against the host-driver. Which state's law applies can determine whether the passenger wins or loses a tort suit.

Each forum makes its choice based on choice of law rules that it formulates for itself, usually through case law. Statutes play an occasional but relatively infrequent role. The various choice of law rules that the states have devised are a fascinating study, sometimes posing more questions than answers. Disagreement abounds about what is right to do and how to do it.

The law-choosing process that a court goes through in a case with multi-state contacts is often said to be undertaken only for "substantive" issues. As far as procedure is concerned, each forum follows its own. To the extent that a right seeks implementation in a foreign forum, it will have to take that forum's procedure as it finds it. Much attention is therefore spent on determining whether a given issue is "substantive" (so as to be put through a law-choosing process) or "procedural" (so as to avoid it). The substance-versus-procedure controversy, an active one on the conflicts front, is addressed in §§ 62 and 102.

Rules of choice of law are best studied within the framework of individual substantive areas: contracts, torts, property, etc. Each has its own housing in the choice of law chapter. Family law, especially with respect to divorce, has spawned a case law so profuse that it has been given a chapter of its own (Chapter VII).

It is also likely that choice of law has already been met by the second year of law school. The same course, first year procedure, that offers an introductory dose of jurisdiction will probably have treated Erie v. Tompkins (USSC 1938) as well. Erie holds that when the basis of a federal court's jurisdiction is not the federal nature of the right asserted ("arising under" jurisdiction) but merely the fact that the parties come from different states ("diversity of citizenship" jurisdiction), the federal court must deem itself just another state court and must therefore apply the forum state's law, whether statutory or decisional, just as would the state court sitting in the building next door. Since Erie applies only to substantive issues, however, its study has likely geared the student up for substance-versus-procedure contests. Better than that, it has already offered some exercise in choice of law, because the Erie realm is very much a choice of law realm and for that reason has also been given its own chapter (Chapter V).

Erie choice of law questions are sometimes referred to as "vertical" choice of law questions. This is because the choice is between sovereigns that are not equal. The federal government is "supreme" over the state governments by virtue of the constitution. So, if one thinks of the federal government as "above" the states, then the choice is vertical. Choice of law questions in the state-to-state sense (illustrated by the guest statute example above) are "horizontal" because the choice is between sovereigns at the same level.

§ 6.   Choice of Law; Constitutional Introduction

By and large the states are on their own in shaping their choice of law rules. There are few supervening restrictions. The few come from the federal constitution, but the source from which one would perhaps most expect governance and limitation—the full faith and credit clause of Article IV—

has been construed to play little role in determining state choice of law obligations. The clause is virtually dictatorial in requiring recognition of judgments among the states (see § 110 et seq.), but while its language could as well have been applied to choice of law as to recognition of judgments (it addresses "public acts" as well as "judicial proceedings", see §§ 56, 110), the U.S. Supreme Court has mostly given it sway only over the latter. It has been held, when two states have a nexus to a case, that the full faith and credit clause does not require the one that happens to be the forum to apply the other's law to substantive issues, else each would have to apply the other's and each would therefore become the forum only when the plaintiff thought the other's law the more favorable.

The due process clause has the leading choice of law role, and plays the role negatively. It does not tell a state what law to apply; it merely tells the state that it may not choose the law of a jurisdiction having no significant relationship to the case. If two or more states have relationships through one set of contacts or another, due process is satisfied to have the law of any of them govern, and the choice is therefore left to the forum state. Studying state preferences in this regard is the stuff of choice of law.

§ 7. Choice of Law; Different "States"

By a conflict of laws involving different "states" is meant not only states of the United States, but also sovereign nations and their political subdivisions, or any combination of them. Thus the word "states" in this book can usually be taken in its international sense of including nations, unless the context obviously suggests otherwise.

Nor need a conflict of laws problem involve different sovereigns. A conflict can occur within subdivisions of a single sovereign. That is of course the case in the United States, where each state is sovereign within the separate sovereignty of the United States—the phenomenon that accounts in large measure for the Erie v. Tompkins (USSC 1938; Chapter V) realm—and it can be found as well between mere municipal subdivisions of a single sovereign unit. For example: In the absence of an issue's resolution by a state legislature or by its highest court, courts or agencies in different districts or departments or counties (etc.) of the same state may come up with different resolutions of a given issue. If the case has a connection to several such units, a conflict of laws problem, or at least one calling for analogous resolutions, is at hand.

§ 8. Choice of Law; Introductory Choice of Forum Note

Because choice of law rules differ from forum to forum, it behooves every lawyer to give some consideration, in a multi-state dispute that will have to go to court, to the possibility of arranging for suit outside his own bailiwick. A lawyer not admitted to practice in the most appropriate forum may lose control of the case, or will in any event have to retain someone to act as counsel. Still, an analysis of the substantive issues in the case along with the choice of law rules applicable in the several forums that might offer jurisdiction—and this means that jurisdictional opportunities must also be researched and considered—may indicate that the client's best chances are in a court elsewhere. It is a lawyer's duty to consider that. It comes under the caption of "choice of forum". Unfortunately, the lawyer sometimes overlooks it, to the detriment of the client. Whatever the extent of the preliminary researches—and these may involve jurisdictional issues, substantive issues and choice of law issues—and whatever the difficulty of their resolution and the subtlety of their interplay, it is unforgivable for a lawyer to bring suit in her own state for having overlooked that the client's interest would be better served by suit elsewhere. A later part of this book (§ 86) is therefore devoted to "choice of forum" issues, with appropriate illustrations.

§ 9. Recognition of Judgments

The third and last of the major conflict of laws subjects is the recognition and enforcement of judgments. While often treated in law school classes before choice of law is taken up, this subject is met last in the chronological order of litigation and so we assign it that position in this book (Chapter VI).

It is here that we find the flesh of the federal constitution's full faith and credit clause, which has an extensive case law as applied to judgments. The clause applies, however, only to the judgments of American courts (state, federal, District of Columbia and territorial, see § 110). It has no application to the judgments of foreign nations, where the states are pretty much on their own in determining whether or not to offer recognition. When they offer it, they are giving the foreign judgment what we call "comity" (§ 109).

A number of questions come up in the recognition of judgments, involving interesting issues of res judicata and enforcement, but they have a comparatively orderly set of answers. This is rather in contrast to the choice of law realm. The difference may be traced to the United States Supreme Court's consistent—and demanding—construction of the full faith and credit clause as applied to judgments.

§ 10. Domicile as Conflicts Subject

Domicile is a giant subject in the conflict of laws and usually occupies its own chapter in casebooks on the subject. But from this the impression should not be drawn that domicile is just another subdivision of conflicts, vying with jurisdiction, choice of law, and recognition of judgments to make the trio a quartet. The trio stands. As frequently as one meets domicile, the meeting is always on the terrain of one of the big three, especially the first two. Domicile furnishes a basis for judicial jurisdiction in several ways, involving both in personam and in rem jurisdiction (§§ 28 and 43). And when it comes to listing the elements that will determine a choice of law, domicile figures prominently. Because of its influential role in conflicts, domicile's various ingredients are best collated and noted early so they can then be available for use throughout. Hence the assignment of Chapter II to domicile.

C. BACKGROUND AND MATERIALS

§ 11. Evolution of Conflicts; Brief Bibliography

The shrinkage of the world with the growth of rapid travel and communication accounts for the dramatic recent growth of conflict of laws as a legal subject. The existence of separate legal units always posed potential conflicts issues, but it is only through travel or communication that a person passes—literally or figuratively—through one such unit and reaches a second one. Before technology facilitated travel and sped up communication, conflicts problems existed in numbers too small to touch ordinary people. Certainly they lacked the influence they have today on a law school curriculum. Now, with thanks in varying measure to the Internet, train, car, plane, wire, and airwave, among other things, they touch us all.

The United States is natural terrain for conflict of laws. Sovereigns abound, more than 50 of them (including the District of Columbia, Puerto Rico, the Virgin Islands and other non-state components of the U.S.), each with its own laws, and over them is a super sovereign, the federal government, with the federal constitution allotting powers among them and, through the courts, overseeing their exercise. Add to that the fact that the United States has been the leader in the technology of rapid travel and instant communication, and it is no wonder that in the conflict of laws the United States has been at the center of developments.

It is in the law reviews that one often finds the major writings on conflict of laws. But there are several textbooks and like works that students and lawyers may find helpful. One of these, Scoles, Hay, Borchers and Symeonides's Hornbook on Conflict of Laws (West 2004) is in its fourth edition. Another is American Conflicts Law by McDougal, Felix and Whitten, which is in its fifth edition. Russell J. Weintraub's Commentary on the Conflict of Laws is in its fourth edition (2001). Famous writings of a somewhat older vintage include The Choice–of–Law Process (Mich.U.Press 1965) in which David F. Cavers probes choice of law theory, and Brainerd Currie's Selected Essays on the Conflict of Laws (Duke U.Press 1963).

A work of major influence in choice of law today is the Second Restatement of Conflicts published in 1971, to which reference will be made frequently in this book.

A major historical work on conflicts in this country is Story's Commentaries, first published in 1834. The First Restatement of exactly a century later (1934), chiefly the work of Professor Beale, has been superseded by the more flexible thinking of the Second, but still wields influence and is often helpful for historical perspective.

In consulting any of the authorities cited, or any other in respect of an issue of choice of law, the principal thing to be wary of is the arbitrary rule and the short answer, which is usually its by-product. The venerable legions on any side of a complex choice of law problem can often be matched—and battled to a standstill—by the venerable legions on the other side.

CHAPTER II

DOMICILE

A. ROLE OF DOMICILE

§ 12. Domicile Defined

As generally used in American jurisprudence, a "domicile" is a person's home. It is to be distinguished from other terms describing an individual's relationship to a particular place, and since there is no absolute definition of any of these terms binding on one and all, it is often necessary to challenge each term in its particular context to find out what it means. Among the other terms are "residence" and "citizenship". Often a statute will use one word when it means one of the others. Sometimes even judicial opinions will interchange the words, especially when nothing of consequence turns on them. The case law arises when something of consequence, usually money or property, does turn on them.

The general rule is that a person can maintain as many residences in as many states or nations as he pleases, and can afford, but that only one place can qualify as that person's "domicile". This is because the law must often have, or in any event has come to insist on, one place to point to for any of a variety of legal purposes (§ 13).

15

A person's "domicile" is almost always a question of intent. A competent adult can, in our free society, live where she pleases, and we will take her "domicile" to be wherever she does the things that we ordinarily associate with "home": residing, working, voting, schooling, community activity, etc.

One resides in one's domicile indefinitely, that is, with no definite end planned for the stay. While we hear "permanently" mentioned, the better word is "indefinitely". This is best seen in the context of a change of domicile (§ 15).

In the United States, "domicile" and "residence" are the two major competitors for judicial attention, and the words are almost invariably used to describe the relationship that the person has to the state rather than to the nation. We use "citizenship" to describe the national relationship, and we generally eschew "nationality" (heard more frequently among European nations) as a descriptive term.

In international conventions, to several of which the United States is a party, the term in vogue is "habitual residence". This term is a favorite of treaty drafters probably because nobody is quite sure what it means. Apparently it's something more than mere "residence" but not quite domicile, necessarily. A 1990 House of Lords decision, C. v. S., described a habitual residence as being a place where a person had lived for an "appreciable period of time" with a "settled intention" to take up "long-term residence". Note the wiggle room here.

"Appreciable period" clearly means something more than a few days, but whether it's a few weeks, or months, or years is anybody's guess. Note here the distinction from domicile, which can switch instantly, while habitual residence does not. And while domicile requires an intent to remain "indefinitely", habitual residence requires only an intention to be there "long-term".

In at least one important context, however, "citizen" describes the person's relationship to the state and borrows "domicile" rather than "residence" for analogy. One of the bases on which a federal court can entertain jurisdiction of a claim is that it is "between citizens of different states" (Const. Art. III, § 2). In that context "citizen" means that the person is a citizen of the United States and a domiciliary (not a mere "resident") of a particular state. (Morris, USSC 1889.)

The domiciles of special categories of persons (e.g., infants, corporations, etc.) are discussed in § 14.

§ 13. Relevance of Domicile

Domicile puts in many appearances in the conflict of laws, especially in the first two of the three major realms: jurisdiction and choice of law. It has less of a function in the third one, recognition of judgments, but it becomes relevant there, too. If, for example, P has a valid judgment against D from a court of other than D's domicile, and can't enforce it in the forum of rendition, P is wont to turn to D's domicile, where D likely has property, and take steps to obtain a domicile-court judgment based on the foreign one so as to make it enforcible against that property. More on that will be seen in the chapter on judgments (Chapter VI).

Also to be seen later in more appropriate context are the many important roles domicile plays in jurisdiction and choice of law, but a few of these can be summarized here for introductory purposes. The White case treated in § 15 illustrates the rule that a decedent's personal estate is distributed according to the law of the state in which he was domiciled when he died. The Dorrance cases discussed in § 16 involve the rule that a decedent's domicile at death is also the state entitled to tax her gross estate. These are but two examples of the many one meets in the choice of law realm, and from one vantage point they may be seen as overlapping the subject of jurisdiction as well. (A state wouldn't be able to apply its own tax laws to a case, for example, if it hadn't somehow obtained jurisdiction in it. The fact that the decedent is a domiciliary would offer jurisdiction, if nothing else would.)

In the more common choice of law situation, in which the parties are from various states and the facts involved may have arisen in still another—the meat of choice of law as so often met in contract, tort, succession, and property cases—domicile plays a weighty role in determining whose law to apply to a given issue. Domicile is by no means the only element weighed on the choice of law scale, but it is one of the heaviest. Indeed, if all of the parties are domiciled in the same state, there is a likelihood that that state's law will apply to significant issues in the case even if the conduct involved occurred and the cause of action therefore arose elsewhere. Babcock v. Jackson (N.Y.1963) is a famous example of this in the tort area (§ 78). There are counterparts in other areas.

On the jurisdictional side, a defendant's domicile in the forum is itself a basis for the exercise of personam jurisdiction against him by a domicile court (§ 28). In rem jurisdiction is also a beneficiary of domicile, this time when the plaintiff is a forum domiciliary. In matrimonial actions, for example, the plaintiff's acquisition of a domicile in the forum state may enable that state to divorce the plaintiff even though the defendant spouse is not a forum domiciliary and the forum court has obtained no personam jurisdiction over the defendant. The theory here is that the local domicile of either spouse is sufficient to bring the marriage itself into the forum—call it the "marital res"—and the presence of the marital res enables the court to dissolve the marriage without personal jurisdiction of the defendant spouse (§§ 43, 125).

When jurisdiction is clearly present and does not depend on domicile at all because some other jurisdictional basis is present, domicile may nevertheless be relevant in determining whether the court should exercise the jurisdiction, such as in an application of the forum non conveniens doctrine (§ 53).

Analogous to the function of domicile in jurisdiction and choice of law but in reality distinct from it is the "residence" requirement one often finds as a precondition a state imposes before it will permit a person to vote, or receive welfare payments, or maintain an action of some kind, usually a matrimonial action. The requirement that the plaintiff show local "residence" for a stated period before bringing suit is in this instance a condition precedent to the maintenance of the action rather than a basis on which to rest jurisdiction. Residence requirements as a precondition to the exercise of matrimonial jurisdiction vary among the states from weeks to years. Iowa's one-year period for divorce was upheld in Sosna (USSC 1975).

Domicile is also a basis for various kinds of taxation (in addition to the estate tax already mentioned).

§ 14. Domicile of Various Categories of Persons

In § 12, domicile was given its common application to a competent, adult, natural person. If a guardian or committee or like person is appointed by a court to take charge of an incompetent person, the court can direct domicile changes or the person appointed may be generally empowered by the law of the particular state to effect them (Rst.2d § 23).

A minor has its parents' domicile, and if the parents are separated the general rule today is that a minor has the domicile of the parent with whom it actually lives. If custody of the minor has been the subject of a court order, the order can include directions about domicile changes. When the child comes of age, it can change domicile like an adult. An orphan has the domicile of the person, usually a relative, who is caring for it, or that of a guardian appointed for it if a court has acted. An out-of-wedlock child is generally deemed to have its mother's domicile (Rst.2d § 22).

Old common law notions about a married woman's having only her husband's domicile have been pretty much abandoned, but if the wife and husband are living together at least a presumption will arise that her domicile is the same as his. If for any purpose the wife in fact takes a separate domicile, she will usually be deemed to have whatever domicile she has actually taken, without regard to motive, and this attitude is by no means of only recent vintage. (E.g., Commonwealth v. Rutherfoord, Va.1933.) A wife's change of domicile need not be shown to have been made, as was once so, for the sole purpose of bringing a matrimonial action.

A person in public life who must go where the government tells her to can obtain a domicile in her place of assignment if she intends to make it home, but will not be deemed to have made the change if she intends to return to her earlier home when the stint of public service is over. A person in military service does not ordinarily acquire domicile at the place to which he is assigned for the reason that he has no say in the assignment. But if he lives off base, and especially if his family is with him, and evinces an intention to make the assigned place his home, it can be deemed his domicile.

A prisoner ordinarily can't choose a domicile because a crimp has been put in his freedom of choice (Rst.2d § 17).

As a general rule, students away at a university, seminary, or like place of learning do not obtain domicile there, and thus retain the one they left. States often have statutes so providing, usually to prevent such persons, deemed to have too little stake in local government, from participating in their elections. But a student's showing that she has severed parental ties and that her residence in the school community is as much a home as she has, may overcome this rule and obtain the privileges of domicile. (Ramey, EDNY 1972.)

To the extent that a corporation's domicile must be fixed, it is the state of its incorporation (Bergner, Mass.1898). In measuring diversity of citizenship for federal jurisdictional purposes, a statute, 28 U.S.C.A. § 1332(c), gives a corporation two citizenships: that of its state of incorporation and that of the state (if different) in which it has its principal place of business. This increases the chance that a corporation's citizenship will be the same as an opposing party's and thus decreases the prospect that there will be diversity jurisdiction (§ 22), which was Congress's intent.

Ubiquitous national corporations are of course subject to regulation and taxation based on activities carried on in the states they enter; that doesn't depend on domicile.

B. CHANGING DOMICILE

§ 15. Change of Domicile

Perhaps the best way to understand domicile is to see how one changes a domicile. The general rule is that two things must concur for a person to effect the change: he must physically reach the new place and have, when he does, the intention of making it home. A well known case (White, W.Va.1888) illustrates. A parcel of land straddled the border between West Virginia and Pennsylvania. On the West Virginia part was the main house, belonging to M's brother, and on the Pennsylvania part was a smaller house. M, who lived elsewhere in West Virginia at the time, wanted to move to the Pennsylvania house. He and his wife started for it, passed from West Virginia into Pennsylvania, reached the house and unloaded their things. But it was damp and they decided to stay for a while at the brother's West Virginia house. They went to it promptly. M died there shortly afterwards, before they could go back to the Pennsylvania house.

Under West Virginia law M's wife would take all of M's property; under Pennsylvania law, certain others would share the personal estate with the wife. The certain others claimed that M died with a Pennsylvania domicile, and were upheld. M had physically reached the Pennsylvania house, the objective fact that is the first part of the domicile-change rule, and the court found that at that moment M also had the intent to make it his home, the subjective fact that is the second requirement. M thus acquired the new domicile of Pennsylvania and lost the old West Virginia one. (The rule is that the old domicile adheres until a new one is obtained [Jones, Iowa 1921], so that everyone will have one, and only one, domicile at all times.) It made no difference that M almost immediately afterwards went to the West Virginia house, because, when he reached that house physically, he did not intend to make it home but only to stay for a short while. Hence prong two was missing, and the Pennsylvania domicile, secured shortly before, remained.

The judges are practical about the rule. When a person does not himself reach the new place but does as much as he can under the circumstances, he may be held to have achieved the new domicile. Hence a ship's captain whose wife moved to the new place (with his approval) while he was at sea was also held to have achieved the new domicile (Bangs, Mass.1873). Similarly, when a person is prevented from leaving his domicile by circumstances not of his doing and beyond his control, he may be relieved of consequences attendant on domicile at that place. In Roboz (USDC D.C.1963), a federal statute was involved which precluded the return of an alien's property if he was found to be domiciled in Hungary prior to a certain date. It was found that Hungary was Nazi-controlled at the time in question and that the persons involved would have left Hungary (and lost domicile there) had

they been able to. Since they had been precluded
from leaving because of the political privations imposed by the very government they wanted to escape (the father was in prison there), the court
would not hold them to have lost their property
based on a domicile that circumstances beyond their
control forced them to retain.

§ 16. Evidence of Domicile Change

The courts will usually consider any evidence
tending to reflect on whether there has been a
change of domicile, even including subjective, self-
serving declarations of intent by the person involved (Rst.2d, note following § 20). The issue is
one of fact and is decided as such. The burden of
proof is usually on the one asserting that there has
been a change.

When acts and words conflict, the acts will usually control. In the final analysis, the decision is up to
the highest court that the issue can be taken to. In
the well-known Dorrance cases, one in Pennsylvania (1932) and one in New Jersey (1934), there were
conflicting findings of domicile, both of which sur-
vived—at a cost of millions each—for want of any
review by the United States Supreme Court. Mr.
Dorrance was one of the financial wizards (and
beneficiaries) behind the Campbell's Soup Company, and in the Dorrance cases Pennsylvania and
New Jersey each took a look at Dorrance's estate
and smacked their lips and said "Mm, Mm, good!"
Dorrance had big estates in both Pennsylvania and
New Jersey, the former being the bigger and more

frequently used. The Pennsylvania court, listing the numerous things one does out of one's home base, found Pennsylvania to be the state in which Dorrance was domiciled when he died and hence the state entitled to a full estate tax under state law. New Jersey, whose tax officials were not parties to the Pennsylvania litigation and hence not bound by its holding, found just the contrary: that New Jersey was Dorrance's domicile when he died. New Jersey stressed Dorrance's declarations of New Jersey domicile. Each state levied a full inheritance tax of some $17 million, leaving the heirs with less than $100 million to share. The United States Supreme Court, containing its compassion, denied certiorari to the New Jersey decision, the later of the two. With no court—with say over both the New Jersey and Pennsylvania supreme courts—willing to intervene, Dorrance ended up richer than he thought, in domiciles if not in money.

Both Dorrance cases can be looked to for their extensive discourses on the evidence that may be considered on a domicile question.

In a similar case in which four states demanded estate taxes based on conflicting claims of domicile and the four together would have depleted the estate entirely, one of the states, Texas, brought an original U.S. Supreme Court action against the other three, Florida, Massachusetts and New York, and the Supreme Court entertained it and found Massachusetts to be the domicile (Texas v. Florida, USSC 1939). Texas probably would have liked to play that one over. It got a chance of sorts in a later case when the Supreme Court allowed jurisdiction in California v. Texas (USSC 1982), because the taxes threatened to bankrupt the Howard Hughes estate. The case, however, settled.

An interpleader effort, seeking in a federal court to join the tax officials of all states concerned so as to obtain a domicile adjudication binding on all, seems to be an appealing possibility. The Eleventh Amendment, however, blocks this route because it deprives the federal courts of jurisdiction in actions directly against states and state officials where state funds are at stake. (Cory v. White, USSC 1982). Several states, however, have signed onto a Uniform Act that allows for binding arbitration of the decedent's domicile at death when domicile is disputed.

§ 17.   Whose Law Governs Domicile?

It may happen that among the several states involved in a given case the definition of domicile will differ, or differ in some material particular important to the case at hand. The rule is that the forum will apply its own concepts of domicile (Rst.2d § 13). The forum will do this even if the standard applied results in a finding that A, one of the parties, is a domiciliary of State X, and that A would not be deemed a State X domiciliary by State X's own standards. The bottom line in these matters is that each forum applies its own choice of law rules to cases before it having foreign elements, and where a person is domiciled is deemed in essence a choice of law question. The reason why each forum applies its own choice of law rules to cases before it is that the court must obviously start somewhere and no place other than the forum can even be deemed relevant until something in the forum's own law makes it so.

In the usual situation in which a forum choice of law rule has been applied and has required the judge to choose the law of another state in respect of a given issue, the law chosen will be that which the other state applies to local cases having no foreign elements. When the forum state looks to foreign law, it will most often look to its "internal" law, a word used to exclude and distinguish choice of law rules. A kind of chaos can result if State F, the forum, were to consult the choice of law rules of State X, only to find that State X's choice of law rules say to apply State F's choice of law rules. This chaos is called "renvoi" in the conflict of laws, and it merits a separate section (the next one) and a slow-motion build-up.

C. "RENVOI" INTRODUCED

§ 18. Renvoi

Every state has its "internal" law, the usual body of statutes, rules, regulations, and the like (and in common law countries, cases), substantive and procedural, which its courts automatically look to and apply in cases having no foreign parties or elements. Every state has in addition a body of "choice of law'' rules, usually evolved in common law countries through case law but sometimes addressed by statutes as well, by which its judges determine whose law to choose for a given issue when, because of competing contacts, several states are involved.

Consider a case with foreign elements, and assume that a choice of law rule of the forum (State F) has told the judge to apply State X law to a given issue. Let us hope that this reference is intended to be to the internal law of State X, from which we can then extract the principle governing the issue at hand and apply it to close out the case.

But suppose that in respect of the particular issue the forum's choice of law rule directs the judge to apply not the internal rule of State X, but the ''whole law'' of State X, that is, State X's choice of law rules as well. When this happens, a giant step is taken towards a ''renvoi'', but we are not there yet. If the applicable rule in State X's batch of choice of law rules says to apply State X's internal law to the issue at hand (or even State F's internal law or any other place's internal law), there should be no problem. The final pointer being to a body of internal law, we can find there the rule of law applicable to the issue and we can apply it, once again closing out the case.

But now assume that because it gives different credits to different contacts than State F does, the relevant choice of law rule of State X, to which we have been referred by the relevant choice of law rule of State F, sends us back to the choice of law rule of State F. A deja vu is all we experience when we get back there: since the State F choice of law rule is the one that originally sent us to the State X choice of law rule, a return to the State F choice of law rule will only send us back to the X rule, which will send us back to the F rule, etc., in a kind of circular perpetual motion that will never give us an internal substantive rule to apply to the case.

This is a true "renvoi", although the term is often used to describe any case in which the relevant forum choice of law rule refers to the choice of law rules of some other place, even though the latter's choice of law rule will not necessarily lead back to the place of beginning. If it leads to some other place, thereby avoiding the cycle, it is not a true "renvoi".

Renvoi is more a phenomenon of the classroom than the courtroom today for the reason that most choice of law rules, when they refer to foreign law, aim at the internal law of the foreign place. But there are a few instances in which reference is to the whole law of the place chosen, setting the stage for a potential renvoi. This is notably the case with issues affecting real property. If an issue concerning State X real property arises in a State F action, State F law, whether statutory or otherwise, will often be found to dictate that the issue be resolved exactly as a State X court would resolve it (§§ 70, 95). This means applying State X choice of law rules.

A case in point is Schneider (NY Surr.Ct.1950), involving a New York domiciliary who left real property in Switzerland and tried to dispose of it in his will in a manner allegedly unsatisfactory to Swiss law. It was held that under New York choice of law rules the court had to look to Swiss choice of law rules. The court did. But the Swiss choice of law rule said that if the owner is a foreigner, his domicile law should be applied. This meant a reference back to New York law, but it was found to mean a reference to New York internal law, thus leading to a governing rule (which validated the disposition, and of course avoided a true "renvoi").

A case that did involve a renvoi is Annesley (Ch. 1926), in which England was the forum but France the country in which the decedent died domiciled. That is, she was a French domiciliary by English standards, English (forum) law governing that issue. The ultimate issue was how to distribute the decedent's personal property. The English court found in its own rules an instruction to apply "domicile" law to the issue, and in this instance an intention to apply the whole law of the domicile. Hence the English court looked to how France would handle the case. It divined that France would look to the law of the decedent's nationality, which was English, and divined further that the French reference would be to the whole English law, including the very same choice of law rule that had brought about the first channel crossing. Alphonse and Gaston were at it again. In its final divining, the Annesley court said that France would "accept"

the renvoi (which incidentally is a French word
meaning a sending back or returning), that is, that
on the second trip a French court would deflect the
English thrust from French choice of law to French
internal law. French law was found to govern. "Divining" is a fair word to describe how the judge
managed to find such detailed instruction in the
laws of both England and France in the Annesley
case. Seldom is the law clear when these convoluted
trails are negotiated, and as often as not there is
little hard evidence to explain the conclusion finally
reached. It is something like Dorothy Parker's response when told that Calvin Coolidge was dead.
"How can they tell?" she asked.

When we meet choice of law in the comfort of its
own chapter later, and cases are discussed in which
foreign law was chosen, the choice will be found in
most instances to lead directly to the internal law
(sometimes called the "municipal" law or "local"
law) of the foreign state. If in such a case it can be
shown that the foreign state itself, under its own
choice of law rules, would not have applied its own
law, but rather another state's, how can it be said
that State F has applied State X "law" if State X
would not have applied it had the case been brought
there? This question goes to the very heart of choice
of law policy and is discussed in § 87.

CHAPTER III

JURISDICTION

A. INTRODUCTION

§ 19. Jurisdiction, Introductory

Before a court can render an effective judgment it needs "jurisdiction", which in this context refers to a state's dispute-resolving power exercised either through its court system or through some quasi-judicial body, like an arbitration panel or administrative board. Jurisdiction can be initially divided into two broad categories:

1. jurisdiction of the subject matter, and

2. jurisdiction of the person.

A further subdivision of the second category is in rem jurisdiction, which is itself broken down into subcategories (§ 41).

The topic of jurisdiction is one of the three main branches of the conflict of laws, becoming relevant whenever a court attempts to exercise power over any person not domiciled and served with process within the borders of the state that created the court. The several groupings of jurisdiction are the subject of this chapter.

We are talking here about "judicial jurisdiction", the heading under which all of the branches and twigs of this chapter fall. One occasionally hears in the conflict of laws the phrase "legislative jurisdiction". It belongs to the choice of law chapter, but it may be helpful to describe and distinguish it briefly here:

The law of a given state may not be applied to an issue unless the state has such contacts with the issue, or with the parties in respect of the issue, that it strikes the mind as fair to subject the parties to that state's rule of law. A different conclusion could alter the rights of the parties with a rule of law that none of them could fairly have anticipated (§ 56). When a state does have a nexus sufficient to permit its law to be applied, we speak of it as having "legislative jurisdiction". It means nothing more than sufficient contacts for choice of law purposes.

"Judicial jurisdiction", on the other hand, is concerned with how a court gets the power to entertain a case. Judicial jurisdiction, to use different words, gives the court the case; legislative jurisdiction becomes relevant only afterwards, when the merits are reached.

B. CATEGORIES OF JURISDICTION

§ 20. Subject Matter Jurisdiction

This refers to a court's ability to entertain a particular kind of case. A court derives its subject matter jurisdiction from the constitution and laws of the sovereign it serves, and if it can't find there its power over a given case, then it lacks "subject matter" jurisdiction. The term is to be distinguished from "personal jurisdiction", which is concerned with whether the court, however competent over the subject matter, is able to make its judgment binding as against a given person.

"Personal jurisdiction" and its several subdivisions is a much larger realm than "subject matter" jurisdiction for the reason that the latter is not often a problem, at least not in the courts of the states. There is usually no difficulty in determining the kinds of cases a given state court can entertain.

An illustration of an issue of subject matter jurisdiction would be a case brought in a lower court for a sum of money higher than that which the applicable state law permits the court to entertain. If a given lower court has jurisdiction up to $3000, for example, an action brought there for more than that is said to be beyond its "subject matter jurisdiction". But before it is concluded that the lower court is utterly helpless in the case, the lawyer must investigate other matters. The court may have at least enough power to entertain an application to transfer the case to the more appropriate higher court, or an application by the plaintiff to reduce the demand and thereby permit the case to stay where it is. These and like possibilities depend on forum law.

Issues of subject matter jurisdiction also arise when a special category of case is brought in a court other than one specially devised to handle it. A state may have waived its sovereign immunity (§ 49) and allowed itself to be sued like a private person, for example, but only in a specified court, often called a "court of claims". If that's the case, an attempt to sue the state in some other court is likely to meet the barrier of subject matter jurisdiction.

Another example: A state may have conferred jurisdiction of divorces and the like ("matrimonial actions") on only one court, whether denominated a family court or something else. An attempt by a different court, such as a lower court with restricted civil jurisdiction, to entertain the divorce would be futile; the court would lack "subject matter" jurisdiction.

The federal courts face problems of subject matter jurisdiction more frequently than the state courts (§ 22).

§ 21. "General" Versus "Limited" Jurisdiction

Within the broad framework of "subject matter" jurisdiction, courts can be further categorized. One dichotomy separates civil and criminal jurisdiction. Another separates original from appellate jurisdiction, the former describing the courts in which an action is commenced and the latter the courts to which the case may afterwards be appealed.

Under the heading of "original" jurisdiction there can be a further separation into the categories of "general" and "limited" jurisdiction. A court of "limited" jurisdiction can entertain only the classes of cases specifically listed in the constitution, statutes, or other legal sources of the sovereign establishing the court. A court of "general" jurisdiction is one that has been given just about all the jurisdiction the particular sovereign has to give.

Note the qualifying words, "just about all". Since "general" is almost invariably juxtaposed with "limited", it is tempting to assume that "general" means "unlimited". It doesn't. If a state has withheld any given category of case from its court of supposedly "general" jurisdiction, that alone bars the word "unlimited" from describing the court.

No state, moreover, can confer on any of its courts jurisdiction of any matter that has, under competent federal legislation, been conferred exclusively on the federal courts. Patent infringement suits, for example, may be brought only in the federal courts (28 U.S.C.A. § 1338). A state court's inability to entertain any matter of exclusively federal cognizance will also, by itself, deny the word "unlimited" any use as a synonym for "general". (Federal jurisdiction is a separate topic in the next section.)

In this regard we meet yet another pair of jurisdiction categories: "exclusive", juxtaposed with "concurrent". Bankruptcy matters, for example, are of exclusively federal cognizance. But when two or more courts can entertain a given case—the choice of forum usually being with the plaintiff in that instance—we speak of those courts as having "concurrent" jurisdiction. Every case, for example, brought in a federal court based on the diversity of citizenship of the parties rather than on the federal nature of the case is under the "concurrent" category: the plaintiff didn't have to sue in a federal court; he could have sued in an appropriate state court instead.

Each state will usually be found to have created one court of "general" jurisdiction. "Superior Court" or "District Court" are names it often has; in New York the misnomer of "supreme court" applies to it (the highest court in New York being its "Court of Appeals"). This court of "general" jurisdiction is the court on which the state constitution or legislature has conferred most if not all of the judicial jurisdiction the state has to confer. In addition to this court there are likely to be other courts, and in some states many other courts, with narrower assignments: family courts, probate or surrogate's courts, courts of claims, land courts, etc., with those or other names, designed to entertain cases of a particular category: family disputes, matters relating to decedents' estates, claims against the state, claims involving land, and the like. And there may also be courts that entertain ordinary money claims at lower reaches, including a "Small Claims Court". All of these are courts of "limited" subject matter jurisdiction.

Just as "general" can't be equated with "unlimited", so must we be careful not to equate "limited" with "impotent". The word "limited" merely means that the court's power has been restricted to certain categories of cases. If the case fits the category, the jurisdiction may be potent indeed, as anyone imprisoned by a criminal "lower" court can attest.

The "general" versus "limited" pairing is sometimes applied even to appellate courts. That application offers the best evidence of all that "limited" and "impotent" are not synonyms. The jurisdiction of the U.S. Supreme Court, for example, is severely "limited"; for the most part it entertains only cases extruded through the elaborate judicial machinery of the lower federal or state courts. Once its jurisdiction attaches, however, the Supreme Court's decision is binding on all other courts in the country.

While within each state court system the usual structure is one court of "general" jurisdiction—the state's main trial court—with all other courts being "limited", the situation is different in the federal system. There the main trial court is also one of limited jurisdiction (§ 22).

§ 22.   Federal Subject Matter Jurisdiction

Because of our federal system, in which more than 50 sovereigns function within the framework of a national sovereign, the federal court structure is unique in that its principal trial court, the U.S. District Court, is a court of limited rather than general jurisdiction. The state is left to supply the "general" court. The federal constitution permits Congress to confer on federal courts of its creation only such jurisdiction as is outlined in section 2 of

Article III. Hence the source of these federal limitations is the constitution itself.

Even within the federal system, however, one can find courts of general jurisdiction. Areas within the jurisdiction of the United States that lack their own sovereignty, and thus a court system of their own, must depend on the federal legislature for a complete court system: the District of Columbia and the few remaining territories of the United States are in this category. For them, Congress has the power (from Article I of the constitution for the District and from Article IV of the constitution for the territories) to create courts of general jurisdiction. But Congress has no such power with respect to the states, for which reason all of the federal courts sitting within the states, including the district courts, must trace their powers to those within the limits of Article III and are hence courts of "limited" jurisdiction.

This is one reason why issues of subject matter jurisdiction arise more frequently in the federal system than in state courts. Another is that for a variety of reasons, federal jurisdiction is often preferred by a plaintiff who has a choice of forums. Taken together, this means that more cases near the subject matter jurisdiction borderline appear in the federal than in the state courts.

One of the major sources of federal subject matter jurisdiction is the diversity of citizenship of the parties. It authorizes federal suit even though the dispute involves no issues of federal law. The statute that authorizes this jurisdiction, however (28 U.S.C.A. § 1332), requires that there be more than $75,000 in controversy. A plaintiff near that figure and who wants federal jurisdiction will try for it, while a defendant who prefers that the state courts hear the case may try to get it dismissed from federal court on the ground that it can't support a judgment for more than $75,000.

The major source of federal jurisdiction is that the case "arises under" federal law, the phrase the constitution itself uses (Article III, § 2). Unless it so arises, there is no subject matter jurisdiction under this caption, and whether it does or does not is often the subject of a dispute between the parties to a federal action.

For these and other reasons, the study of "subject matter" jurisdiction is a more extensive one in federal than in state practice. Indeed, a law school course on federal courts is likely to be devoted in the main to subject matter jurisdiction, with a correspondingly smaller time allotment left for mere procedure, rather the reverse of what usually occurs in a course studying the state courts.

Personal as opposed to subject matter jurisdiction in the federal courts is discussed in a later section (§ 46). Admiralty jurisdiction, on which there are some special points to make, is also taken up in a later section (§ 97).

C. PERSONAL JURISDICTION IN GENERAL

§ 23. Personal Jurisdiction, Introductory

How a court obtains the power to bind the parties to its judgment is a question of personal ("in personam") jurisdiction. When it arises, the issue almost always concerns the defendant, who is usually brought within the court's jurisdiction against his will. There is no problem about the plaintiff, who is deemed to be within the court's personal jurisdiction as soon as she commences an action in the court.

In rem jurisdiction (§§ 41 to 44) is a branch of personal jurisdiction for the reason (among others) that it is almost invariably turned to only when in personam jurisdiction is not available.

In the United States, all exercises of personal jurisdiction by a court must satisfy the due process clause of the federal constitution. This means that the U.S. Supreme Court, as the ultimate custodian of the constitution and its application, has the final say about how far a court may go in exercising personal jurisdiction. Jurisdiction has been addressed in a number of cases to reach the court, but barely a dozen of them contain the fundamental guideposts. These, to be treated at various junctures of the ensuing sections, are cited over and over throughout the country, in both state and federal courts. Stress will first be on state courts, after which an additional section (§ 46) will tie together the several essentials that govern personal jurisdiction in the federal courts.

Personal jurisdiction is divided into "basis" and "notice" for the reasons set forth in the following section. After that will come in rem jurisdiction and at the end a discussion of doctrines and principles that restrict jurisdiction, or, more accurately, the exercise of jurisdiction, including forum non conveniens, enticement, immunity, and the impact of the interstate commerce clause. Incidentals will be addressed along the way, like the procedure for raising and preserving jurisdictional objections.

§ 24. Due Process Requirements

Since the federal constitution's due process clauses (contained in the 5th Amendment as a restriction on the federal government and in the 14th as a restriction on the state government) sets limits on the exercise of judicial jurisdiction, an appropriate starting point is to ask what the due process clause requires. The usual answer is: notice and an opportunity to be heard. An example can test that proposition and make an important point:

Suppose that D, after a day's work, is having a light beer at a pub in Pittsburgh, Pennsylvania, where he lives. P, on an adjoining stool, becomes bellicose and picks a fight with D. A few months later D is served in hand, in Pittsburgh, with a summons and complaint. It turns out that P is suing D for assault, that P lives in Delaware, and that the papers are for an action P has commenced in Delaware. The complaint details a claim based on the pub incident of a few months earlier, and the summons advises D that he has 30 days in which to respond. Since D has been given both notice and an opportunity to be heard, an application of the principles usually associated with the due process clause would indicate that all has been done that needs to be done in order to subject D to Delaware jurisdiction. And yet we know that Delaware has not obtained jurisdiction.

What Delaware lacks on these facts is a foundation for its jurisdiction, what we call a "jurisdictional basis". By what right does Delaware presume to act against a defendant who has no connection with Delaware, and in respect of a claim that arose in Pennsylvania? Unless there is a nexus of some kind that can be shown to tie together the state, the claim, and the defendant (Shaffer, USSC 1977), a court cannot subject a nondomiciliary defendant to jurisdiction against his will.

This "basis" requirement comes from the same place as the notice and opportunity requirements: the due process clause. Hence, the demands of due process are not really two, but three:

1. notice,

2. opportunity to be heard, and

3. jurisdictional basis.

For purposes of this study, it is best to separate and study basis before turning to the notice and opportunity requirements (which are treated together). There are a number of permissible jurisdictional bases on which a state may rely, and the assumption during their study will be that good notice has been given and poses no problem. The notice and hearing requirement is a shorter study and will be turned to afterwards (§ 47).

§ 25. Interplay of Jurisdiction and Full Faith and Credit

The full faith and credit clause (Const. Art. IV, § 1) is at the heart of "recognition of judgments", the third of the three main subtopics of conflict of laws (treated in this book in § 108 et seq.), but a brief note about it is helpful here, under jurisdiction.

The clause has been construed to require every state to accept as valid, without reinvestigation on the merits, every judgment rendered by a court of another state, provided only that the rendering court had jurisdiction. This immediately manifests an important interplay between these two major conflicts realms. As a general proposition, we may say that every time a jurisdictional point is studied, and resolved in favor of jurisdiction, the conclusion also answers—in the affirmative—the question of whether the resulting judgment is entitled to full faith and credit. That is so, in any event, whenever both F–1, the rendering court, and F–2, the court in which recognition is sought, are both subject to the federal constitution. The jurisdictional requirements that F–1 must satisfy are the same as those that F–2 must examine in assessing whether F–1 had jurisdiction: the standards associated with the federal due process clauses. Under this view, jurisdiction and full faith and credit are coterminous in American courts.

If one of the courts is that of a foreign country, however, full faith and credit does not apply and the judgment must rely on the loose-limbed doctrine known as "comity" (Hilton v. Guyot, USSC 1895). There, F–2 decides for itself whether to recognize F–1's judgment, and a jurisdictional basis recognized and used by F–1 but not satisfactory to F–2 may result in F–2's rejection of the F–1 judgment even though it is obviously valid in F–1 (Schibsby, Qns. Bench 1870). This points up the potency of the full faith and credit clause and its national application within the United States. It enables a full faith and credit conclusion to be drawn every time a jurisdictional point is resolved in favor of jurisdiction.

Variations on this theme, including questions about default judgments and the application of the res judicata doctrine to jurisdictional issues, will be met in the Judgments chapter (Chapter VI).

D. JURISDICTIONAL BASIS

§ 26. Service Within State as Jurisdictional Basis

At common law, a court acquired jurisdiction of a defendant in a civil case when the sheriff physically seized the defendant and brought him to court pursuant to a famous writ, the capias ad respondendum, obtained by the plaintiff. The writ has long since been abandoned, as noted in International Shoe (USSC 1945), but a residuum of it is that if the defendant is personally served with a court's summons while physically within the territorial area of the court, the court obtains jurisdiction of the defendant by virtue of that service alone (Nielsen, Minn.1963). The defendant may be a nondomiciliary only temporarily within the state and the claim may have arisen elsewhere (Rst.2d § 28). The local service still suffices. Local service, in other words, is its own jurisdictional basis. It is only when service is made on the defendant outside the state, or by a substituted means, that a "basis" for jurisdiction, separate and distinct from service, must be found.

For a time it was thought that service on the defendant within the state was the only way to obtain personal jurisdiction, which brought about an expanded use of in rem jurisdiction (Pennoyer, USSC 1878; Harris, USSC 1905; § 44). This narrow view of personal jurisdiction was afterwards abandoned in a progression of events culminating in "longarm" jurisdiction (§ 31 et seq.), but in-state service persists as an independent jurisdictional basis. Indeed, the U.S. Supreme Court has renewed its approval of this traditional basis for jurisdiction as still satisfactory to federal procedural due process. (Burnham, USSC 1990.)

At least one court has even extended this territorial jurisdiction skyward, holding that a defendant served on an airplane flying over the state was reached jurisdictionally even though the plane trip started and was to end elsewhere and did not even include a local landing (Grace, USDC Ark.1959).

Since longarm and other bases of jurisdiction are available today and permit service of process outside the state when there are contacts sufficient to satisfy due process, the need for a category of jurisdiction premised on nothing more than local service on a transient defendant can stand some reinvestigation. But for the time being local service continues to be a common jurisdictional "basis" and the lawyer should inquire into whether it is still relied on locally. Constitutional issues that might otherwise be met in attempted exploitations of this basis against a transient defendant can be and often are avoided by the application of a "forum non conveniens" rule, which can dismiss a case for want of local contacts notwithstanding the technical presence of "jurisdiction" (§ 53), and with the Burnham case, noted just above, the constitution is not likely to be heard from on this subject for a while.

Note that this is the only instance in which service, the notice aspect of due process, and jurisdictional basis overlap. In other instances, notably in cases of longarm jurisdiction, basis is a separate inquiry, and service of process, which is usually made outside the forum state, fulfills only the notice part of due process.

§ 27. Corporate "Presence" Doctrine

In determining whether a natural person is present within the state so as to be amenable to local service of process under the jurisdictional principles discussed in the prior section, we need only follow the contours of that person's body through her legs and down to her feet to see whether they are planted on local terrain (or on the floor of an aircraft flying over it, as in Grace [USDC, Ark. 1959]). When the defendant is a corporation, it supplies no body and makes this kind of tracing impossible. To enable us to analogize a corporation to an individual for this jurisdictional purpose, the corporate "presence" doctrine, sometimes called the "doing business" test, evolved.

If the corporation is carrying on business in the state on a regular, day-to-day basis, it is as physically present within the state as would a natural person be who is standing there. This makes it just as amenable to state jurisdiction as the natural person would be (Tauza, NY 1917). The only step needed now is to see to it that the corporation is served with process, which is usually effected through some corporate or state official, as local law may dictate.

Under this test, the regular "presence" of the corporation within the state is the jurisdictional basis, and it supports jurisdiction even of claims not arising locally, i.e., claims having no relationship to the state (Perkins, USSC 1952). This has come to be called "general" jurisdiction, as opposed to "specific" jurisdiction. "General" jurisdiction supports jurisdiction of any claim against the defendant; "specific" jurisdiction supports jurisdiction only of a claim arising out of the defendant's local conduct (Helicopteros USSC 1984). "Specific" jurisdiction, more recently adopted terminology, is a subject treated below.

Reliance on "general" jurisdiction of this kind, with its need to gauge the quantum and regularity of local corporate activity, is called for only when no other is available. If the corporation has agreed to local jurisdiction in a filed certificate formally applying to do business in the state, for example, such as one designating a state official to receive process in the corporation's behalf, that itself may be deemed a basis for jurisdiction on the theory of consent or agency (§ 29; Sondergard, CA8, cert. den. 1991). Some courts hold, however, that this will not do for an unrelated claim if the corporation, although authorized to do local business, is not in fact doing it regularly (Sandstrom, CA1 1990).

The availability of longarm jurisdiction (§ 31 et seq.), meaning that the claim itself has a state nexus through a local act of the defendant even though the defendant is not regularly within the state, will also obviate reliance on the corporate "presence" doctrine. Hence reliance on the doctrine is not ordinarily needed when the corporation, although a foreign one, is licensed to do business in the forum state, or when the claim has a local nexus. The doctrine is also superfluous when the defendant is a domestic corporation, which is usually deemed present in the state of its creation.

Although need of the corporate "presence" doctrine and the "doing business" test through which
it is implemented arises in only a small fraction of
the cases, it is a tribute to the quantum of litigation
today that their number is high. There are many
cases that test "doing business".

When the issue arises, it is a question in each
case of whether the corporate activities amount to
the regular doing of business. The yardsticks are
similar from state to state, but not necessarily identical. It behooves the lawyer to check into the local
case law to see how much corporate activity is
required, in both quality and quantity, before the
court will stamp "doing business" on the result.

The courts of a given state may hold that mere
sales and promotion of the corporate product is not
sufficient (e.g., Fisher, Cal.1959), but that an additional something else may turn the trick, such as
maintaining an office and paid staff in the state.
The maintenance of a one and a half room office
with only a handful of employees, who carried on
promotional activities and took and forwarded airline reservations, was held to be the doing of business in Bryant (NY 1965).

Usually the physical manifestation of the corporation, such as through a branch office, is the key to a
"doing business" finding, but the Internet may be
changing that. The creation of a "virtual store" on
the Internet, with nearly all the features of a brick
and mortar one, was found in Gator.com (CA9,

2003) to subject the owner to general jurisdiction wherever the Internet could be accessed. The holding in that respect was later withdrawn as moot, however (Feb. 15, 2005, opinion en banc 398 F.3d 1125), keeping this arguable but controversial issue off the table for the nonce.

Employees are the corporation's agents, and it would of course be through corporate agents that the corporation's overall local activities are measured. But the defendant corporation of which jurisdiction is sought may be carrying on its local activities not directly through employees, but through yet another corporation or several of them. The principles to keep in mind in that case are those of agency. If it is concluded that X corporation is present locally, whether through regular licensing or its own doing business, and that its local activities manifest that it is acting merely as an agent or department of D corporation—the one of which jurisdiction is sought—the court can conclude that D corporation is present through X corporation. So finding, it can subject D to the court's jurisdiction just as if its presence had been spelled out through the activities of directly paid employees.

It may also happen, and it often will in cases like these, that there is an interlocking ownership of the several corporations involved. D owns X, or A owns both, or the like. It has been said that interlocking ownership will not alone spell out doing business against D corporation (Cannon, USSC 1925), but if there is also some indication of agency activities on the facts, the additional fact of interlocking ownership may take on added significance "because it gives rise to a valid inference as to the broad scope of the agency" (Frummer, NY 1967). In the Frummer case, the London Hilton hotel was found to have a New York presence because a local Hilton reservation service, involved in an interlocking ownership, was found to be acting as the hotel's agent in New York. When something like that happens, the impact may be heavy: since the reservation service in New York was doing for the London Hilton what it did for all the other Hiltons, all the others would presumably have a local New York presence as well.

Note that the inquiry throughout is not about the local presence of a corporate official, but of the overall "corporate" presence. Unless the aggregate of activity being carried on for the corporation qualifies (and quantifies) for a corporate presence, jurisdiction of it will be lacking. Local service on even a high officer of the corporation does not give jurisdiction of the corporation itself if the other jurisdictional requisites are not met. Unlike a partner in respect of his partnership, a corporate officer does not carry the corporation around with him wherever he goes. If he is on a private mission unrelated to corporate business, or on but a piece of corporate business which does not have enough other pieces with which to add up to a regular corporate activity, "presence" jurisdiction of the corporation does not result.

For the reason that a partner does carry her partnership about with her, so that service on a partner gives jurisdiction of the partnership when the claim arises out of partnership business (Sugg, USSC 1889) even if it does not arise locally, the corporate "doing business" test has not usually been applied to partnerships, or, for similar reasons, to natural persons or unincorporated associations, although an occasional case (e.g., ABKCO, NY App. Div.1976) will make such an application.

§ 28. Domicile as Jurisdictional Basis

If the defendant is a domiciliary of the forum state, its courts can entertain jurisdiction over him no matter where he is served with process (Milliken, USSC 1940). Of course, one who is domiciled in a state is more often than not a resident of that state as well and can be found there physically for service, invoking the presence basis for jurisdiction and obviating resort to domicile. Domicile is nevertheless a distinct basis, and from time to time a helpful one, as where the defendant is temporarily outside the state when served.

When using this basis, the moment of service counts. It is at that time that the defendant should have a forum domicile. Domicile at some time in the past will not suffice, at least not in respect of a claim also lacking in forum contacts.

It will usually take a statute or rule to exploit this domicile jurisdictional basis. The plaintiff's lawyer should seek one out if need arises.

The theory underlying this basis is that as a domiciliary, the defendant owes a set of obligations to the state, including the duty to respond to its judicial process. And process for this purpose is not restricted to a summons or other action-commencing paper. A subpoena also qualifies as process (it subjects a witness, as opposed to a party, to the court's jurisdiction and to punishment for contempt for disobedience), and if the forum wishes to require its domiciliaries to return to the state to give needful testimony in a pending proceeding, it can subject them to the extrastate service of its subpoenas. By analogy, citizenship can be exploited as such a basis, as it was in Blackmer (USSC 1932), in which service of a federal subpoena on a United States citizen abroad was upheld in connection with local criminal proceedings.

Whether a state wishes to go this far in respect of either an action-commencing summons or a testimony-seeking subpoena is of course a matter of local option. Some states permit the extrastate service of a summons but not of a subpoena.

§ 29.　Agency as Jurisdictional Basis

A defendant can subject herself to the jurisdiction of a state's courts by designating a local person to be her agent for service of process. The service on the agent is then the equivalent of service on the defendant, who is thus brought within the jurisdiction of court.

There are two broad categories of agency: express and implied. A common example of an express agency is that which results when a domestic corporation, or a foreign one fulfilling the licensing require-

ments of the forum, files a certificate or like paper
with a state office designating a state official, such
as the attorney-general, secretary of state, or like
person, to be the corporation's agent for service of
process. The statute so prescribing may prescribe
the method of service as well.

A state statute may allow any person to designate an agent for service on a voluntary basis.
(The corporate designation just mentioned is usually mandatory, a condition of the corporation's being allowed to do local business.) The designation
may earn a statute of limitations advantage for the
designor. A state provision that tolls (stops the
running of) the statute of limitations during the
defendant's absence may become inoperative if the
defendant has a local agent for service.

In some places the clerk of the court may be
designated as a process-service agent in behalf of a
given person, such as in probate proceedings where
the duly appointed personal representative of a
decedent's estate may have to agree to the clerk's
agency before being allowed to qualify for letters
testamentary or of administration. This facilitates
actions against the estate if the personal representative should not be physically available for service.

The clerk of a court may become an implied
agent, i.e., automatically be deemed the agent of a
party under specified circumstances, as where a
nonresident plaintiff has to be served in connection
with an action the defendant wants to bring. This
can become important if the defendant has been

sued in a lower court whose counterclaim jurisdiction does not cover the defendant's claim, and where the nonresident plaintiff can't be served in the state because he does not physically appear in the local proceedings or is under some kind of immunity (§ 49). Indeed, the local lawyer retained by the nonresident plaintiff may be statutorily deemed his implied agent for this purpose (Adam, USSC 1938).

Probably the best known of all the implied agencies for service is under the nonresident motorist legislation. A typical statute of this kind provides that any person operating a vehicle in the state, or owning one being driven in the state with permission, is deemed to have designated a specified state official as agent for service with respect to any claim arising out of an in-state accident in which the vehicle is involved. Service under such a statute should be made in strict accordance with its terms. Typically, the statute requires service on the state official within the state by a prescribed method, along with a mailing of the summons to the defendant, outside the state if need be. These statutes, of importance in tort cases, have been constitutionally upheld (Hess, USSC 1927).

Similar statutes may be found governing boats, planes, and other vehicles as well as cars.

The nonresident motorist legislation was a giant step on the road to general "longarm" jurisdiction, but while the latter permits service outside the state (§ 31), the act of "service" that obtains jurisdiction under the motorist statutes is technically the service on the state official, which takes place within the state. This is homage to the prevalent notion of the Pennoyer case (USSC 1878), applicable when the motorist statutes first came in, that only service within the state can secure personal jurisdiction. The additional requirement of a mailing to the defendant is important, and today perhaps indispensable to the notice aspect of due process, but it was the within-the-state service on the state official that held the jurisdictional magic. Today, although nonresident motorist statutes stand on the books and continue to be invoked, they will often be found to overlap equally serviceable general longarm statutes, which means the plaintiff has a choice (§ 37).

The mailing (to the defendant) requirement may be imposed on the state official when the agency is express, because that official will usually be found to have the defendant's address listed in her office. Under the implied agencies, it is more common to require the plaintiff to carry out the mailing step, if there is one, so that it becomes the plaintiff's burden to determine the defendant's address.

§ 30. Consent as Jurisdictional Basis

A person can consent to the jurisdiction of a court, such as in a contract between the parties in which they consent to the jurisdiction of the courts of State A for any dispute arising out of or in connection with the contract. This is a basis distinct from agency, but sometimes the two may overlap, as where the contract also provides for service to be made on a specific person within the designated state. That occurred, for example, in the National Equipment case (USSC 1964), a key one recognizing this category of jurisdiction.

The contractual conferral of jurisdiction is also more a phenomenon of arbitration than of litigation. Arbitration is an ever growing source of dispute resolution, but since a contract is its principal source of jurisdiction, the array of conflicts problems one meets in litigation has fewer counterparts in arbitration. The several conflicts points to note in respect of arbitration involve choice of law and the recognition of judgments more than they do jurisdiction, and all are tied together later (§§ 75, 120).

Another form of consent jurisdiction involves the confession of judgment, a device a state can set up to enable one person to take judgment against another merely by filing certain papers in the court; the ritual of summons service and the formalities of litigation are dispensed with. The problem here is that sometimes due process also becomes a casualty, which has prompted many of the states to review these procedures and to impose rigid safeguards upon them if they retain them at all. The lesson to the lawyer who would pursue the confession route against an adversary is to carry out statutory requirements to the letter.

Even that may not help if the statute is lax in its demands and due process is thereby violated. A prime source of conflict on this score is the statute that authorizes what is loosely termed a "cognovit" instrument. A cognovit is a confession of judgment, but in many quarters it has come to connote an instrument, usually a promissory note or the equivalent, in which the borrower or credit buyer agrees that in the event of a default in his obligation anyone may be designated his lawyer to confess judgment in his behalf. Sometimes there is not even a stated restriction as to where the judgment may be entered, thus giving the creditor the whole world to choose from as to both person (to sign the formal confession papers) and place (which may not even be related to the case). A judgment so predicated may be resisted in a second forum as violative of due process, perhaps even being found not to qualify as a judicial proceeding—of the kind to earn full faith and credit—at all (Atlas, NY 1969).

It is the waiver of notice in these instruments that brings on the due process objection, but the waiver does not make the instrument void on its face. If the contract is not one of adhesion (i.e., the take-it-or-leave-it kind tendered to a person having no bargaining power) and the confessor is a self-sufficient person who knows her rights and waives them deliberately, due process will not be a barrier. So held D. H. Overmyer Co. (USSC 1972), in which the confessor was a substantial corporation.

§ 31. Longarm Jurisdiction, Introductory

When a defendant is not physically present in the state and is not one of its domiciliaries, but has "certain minimum contacts" with the state and a claim has arisen out of those contacts, the courts of that state can exercise jurisdiction over the defendant no matter where he is served with process. This is known as "longarm" jurisdiction. It is the final rejection of the Pennoyer (USSC 1878) notion that the only way to get in personam jurisdiction over an unwilling defendant is to have him served with process while he is physically within the state.

There were longarm rumblings before 1945, when the International Shoe case (USSC) was handed down. The earlier nonresident motorist statutes were a step (§ 29), and permitting a domiciliary to be served outside the domicile (Milliken, USSC 1940; § 28) was another. But the apocalypse was International Shoe, whose oft quoted language has made it the wellspring of longarm jurisdiction. It is the International Shoe case that permits a state to take jurisdiction of a defendant as long as the defendant has had:

> sufficient contacts or ties with the state of the forum to make it reasonable and just, according to our traditional conception of fair play and substantial justice, to permit the state to enforce the obligations which appellant has incurred there. . . .

The defendant must have had "certain minimum contacts with [the state] such that the maintenance of the suit does not offend 'traditional notions of fair play and substantial justice'."

The subquoted language in the foregoing is from Milliken (USSC 1940), the overall quote from International Shoe, which adds that: "[w]hether due process is satisfied must depend rather upon the quality and nature of the activity in relation to the fair and orderly administration of the laws which it was the purpose of the due process clause to insure."

On its facts, the International Shoe case sustained Washington state's jurisdiction of an out-of-state company whose local salesmen solicited business and took orders. The claim was for unpaid contributions to the state's unemployment compensation fund; it arose out of the defendant's limited local activities and hence satisfied this concept of "longarm" jurisdiction.

For longarm jurisdiction, International Shoe was the writing on the wall, but it took a few years for the states to read it. Only gradually did they begin to assemble this new jurisdictional equipment, which requires statutory implementation. But when they did, they were a parade, and longarm statutes are standard today.

There are two basic kinds of longarm legislation. One sets forth specific subject matter categories, such as "transaction of business", "commission of a tortious act", and the like, and authorizes jurisdiction only in respect of a claim falling under a delineated category. Illinois, a pioneer in longarm jurisdiction, has such a statute (Ill.Ann.Stat., ch.110, § 2–209); New York has, too (NY Civ. Prac.L. & Rules 302), modeled on the Illinois statute. This kind of statute requires the court to decide two things in each such case in which the defendant contests jurisdiction: (1) Does the defendant's activity fall under the statute? and (2) If it does, does it satisfy the "traditional notions of fair play and substantial justice" inherent in the due process clause?

The other kind of longarm statute poses only the second question. Instead of enumerating activities and authorizing longarm jurisdiction with respect to them, the statute goes all the way, authorizing jurisdiction in any situation that satisfies due process. California's (Cal.Code Civ.Proc., § 410.10) can illustrate:

A court of this state may exercise jurisdiction on any basis not inconsistent with the Constitution of this state or of the United States.

Cases involving longarm jurisdiction abound today, but there are only a handful of U.S. Supreme Court cases setting up the guideposts. While International Shoe was a red carpet in 1945, and McGee in 1957 a further invitation, the next five cases placed a restraining hand on what the Supreme Court felt to be an excess of enthusiasm. These five were Hanson in 1958, Shaffer in 1977, Kulko in 1978, and World–Wide Volkswagen and Rush, companion cases handed down in 1980. Shaffer and Rush involved in rem jurisdiction but contain language relevant to in personam jurisdiction as well.

The McGee case of 1957 concerned an insurance policy. It sustained California jurisdiction over a foreign life insurer that had no contacts with California except for the single policy that its predecessor had issued to a Californian, who mailed his premiums from there. But the claim concerned that single policy and longarm jurisdiction was therefore upheld. (Some states have longarm statutes specifically addressed to insurers, and in jurisdictionally generous terms [e.g., NY Ins.L. § 1213].)

The McGee case appeared to some to suggest so generous a reach for longarm legislation that hardly a year later, in the 1958 Hanson case, the Supreme Court reminded the bar that although the McGee case noted "the trend of expanding personal jurisdiction over nonresidents ... it is a mistake to assume that this trend heralds the eventual demise of all restrictions on the personal jurisdiction of state courts."

The court rejected Florida's attempted jurisdictional exercise in Hanson, which involved complicated trusts and estates issues and is separately treated in the next section. Discussion of longarm jurisdiction in diverse situations is distributed among the sections that follow this one. The important World–Wide Volkswagen case is taken up in § 35, on longarm jurisdiction in "products" cases, and the Shaffer and Rush cases in § 44, on quasi in rem jurisdiction.

The defendant need not have been physically present in the forum state to face longarm jurisdiction. It is sufficient if she acts through an agent. But there must be a legitimate agency. In the case of a corporate defendant, the lawyer is sometimes tempted to assume an agency merely because another corporation, owned principally or wholly by the defendant corporation, is present within the state. Even complete ownership may not suffice if the activity of the local corporation can't be shown to have been performed in the direct service of the parent (Conn, RI 1969). These matters, addressed here under the caption of "longarm" jurisdiction, are analogous to those discussed in the corporate "presence" test (§ 27), but with a big difference in quantum. There the topic was continuous corporate activity; here the investigation centers on just one act or set of acts carried on by one corporation for another. Continuous corporate activity supports jurisdiction of any claim against the defendant, which has come to be called "general" jurisdiction; in the longarm category under discussion here, there is support only for a claim arising out of the defendant's local act, also known today, as previously noted, as "specific" jurisdiction, terminology the U.S. Supreme Court recognized in Helicopteros (USSC 1984.) Longarm jurisdiction also extends to activities outside the state that produce consequences within it, as §§ 33–36 illustrate.

If the would-be longarm defendant dies before suit is brought (or during it), the action can be commenced (or continued) against his nonresident personal representative. A defendant cannot elude longarm jurisdiction by dying. This is a step away from the general rule that precludes one state from exercising jurisdiction over the foreign-appointed representative of a deceased nondomiciliary.

§ 32. Jurisdiction of Estates; No Magic in Probate

Some lawyers assume that a court administering a decedent's estate has virtually unlimited jurisdiction to affect interests in property left by the decedent. Perhaps the root of this assumption is that the administration is usually undertaken by a court of the decedent's last domicile and most if not all of the decedent's property is likely to be physically present there. "In rem" jurisdiction (§ 41), the conclusion goes, therefore offers whatever jurisdiction is needed. That would be true if the subject property were all within the domicile state. But if it is not, the assumption is wrong. Certainly a tangible outside the domicile offers no "in rem" jurisdiction to a domicile court to determine interests in it, and the same is true of paper tangibles like promissory notes, bank accounts, bonds, and stock certificates located outside the state. If their situs is beyond the state, the alleged ownership of such property by a local domiciliary does not magically re-situs them in the domicile (De Lano's Estate, Kan.1957).

And if there is no in rem jurisdiction on which a probate court can act, then, in order to adjudicate interests in the foreign property, the court would need in personam jurisdiction of every person whom it would bind with an adverse judgment. These additional points about probate jurisdiction are introduced here, in the midst of longarm treatment, because Hanson v. Denckla (USSC 1958), a major decision on longarm jurisdiction, makes them relevant.

The property involved in Hanson was securities, which, at the times in dispute, were conceded to have a Delaware situs. This of course deprived Florida of any "in rem" jurisdiction with respect to interests in the securities and meant that in personam jurisdiction had to be relied on.

Mrs. Donner in the Hanson case, at the time a Pennsylvanian, set up a Delaware trust of securities and delivered the securities to the Delaware trustees. The income she directed to herself, also keeping for herself a power of appointment to determine who would have the remainder. She afterwards moved to Florida, where she purported to exercise the power in an inter-vivos instrument. This gave $400,000 to other Delaware trusts, set up for the children of daughter X. Mrs. Donner executed her will at the same time, and in its residuary clause she gave all in trust for two other daughters, Y and Z. After Mrs. Donner's death several years later, a Florida action was brought by Y and Z. Since Y and Z were the estate's residuary beneficiaries, the more the estate could get the more Y and Z would get. The aim of the action was to have the court declare void the inter-vivos exercise of the appointment power (Y and Z contended it could be exercised only by will), thus invalidating the $400,000 transfer to X's side of the family and swelling the estate by that amount.

The jurisdictional issue was whether the Florida court could bind all parties with its judgment. The U.S. Supreme Court ruled that Florida did not have jurisdiction over the Delaware trustees, persons who were indispensable parties even by Florida's own law. Since the trustees had no contacts at all with Florida, they could not be subjected to its jurisdiction. Mrs. Donner's Florida exercise of the appointment power through which the Delaware trustees obtained the subject property was a "unilateral activity" on her part which could not be ascribed, for jurisdictional purposes, to the trustees. The language used by the Supreme Court at this point in the Hanson opinion is widely quoted. Stressing the want of Florida contacts by the trustees, the court said that

> it is essential in each case that there be some act by which the defendant purposefully avails itself of the privilege of conducting activities within the forum State, thus invoking the benefits and protections of its laws.

There were four dissents, so that the rejection of jurisdiction in Hanson was by the closest possible Supreme Court margin. What appeared most to bother the majority was its view of the potential impact of a decision upholding jurisdiction. They apparently deemed the Delaware trustees the gratuitous recipients of a gift from Mrs. Donner, voluntarily sent, or at least arranged for, from Florida. Now, after Mrs. Donner's death, Florida administers her estate and claims jurisdiction to—in effect—get the gift back. To uphold such jurisdiction might mean that a probate court, by virtue of its status as that alone, has all the jurisdiction it needs to get back property voluntarily given away by a decedent as gifts during her lifetime. This would in turn mean that anyone accepting a gift from anyone else would be subject, upon a claim to get the gift back, to the in personam jurisdiction of the probate court of wherever the donor happens to be domiciled when she dies. The dissent responds that Florida in Hanson had "substantial connections" with the case beyond its mere status as the decedent's final domicile.

One point that emerges firmly from Hanson is that a court does not obtain in personam jurisdiction of everyone merely because it is administering a decedent's estate and the argument is over what the estate contains. A court in this category, whether denominated a "probate" court or anything else, is subject to the same jurisdictional principles that govern other courts; it enjoys no advantage. It needs either in personam jurisdiction of all the parties, or, if interests in only designated property are at issue, jurisdiction of the property ("in rem" jurisdiction). If it has neither, its judgment cannot bind those of whom jurisdiction is lacking.

There is no jurisdictional magic in probate courts.

§ 33. Longarm Jurisdiction in "Business" Cases

One category found in some of the states' longarm statutes offers jurisdiction if the claim arises out of the defendant's "transaction of business" in the state. These will usually be found to generate much case law as the judges examine the facts of each case to determine whether the "transaction" arises from local contacts of the defendant sufficient to satisfy the "minimum contacts" standard of the International Shoe case (USSC 1945). The case law in this category of jurisdiction is prodigious, and all of it is relevant not only in states having a specific "transaction of business" longarm statute, but also in those states that have the "all the way" statutes (mentioned in § 31), which authorize the exercise of jurisdiction whenever due process would support it. Every sustaining of jurisdiction under a special "transaction" statute is ipso facto a statement that due process is also satisfied.

The burden of the lawyer is to consult the case law on the local statute for examples that bind, and the case law on similar statutes in other states, if more is needed, for analogies that persuade. Opinions may vary from state to state even in respect of statutory standards that appear to be the same, and while a statutory construction that sustains jurisdiction in one state will not necessarily mean a similar sustaining construction in the other (see § 35, comparing the Gray and Feathers cases), it will show that at least some courts think due process is satisfied with it. A few examples of "transaction" constructions will help.

Where D was a foreign leather manufacturer that made P its distributor, but never entered the state, all business being done outside the state or by correspondence and D sending its product f.o.b. its European base to P, who bought the product outright for resale (no agency or consignment arrangement here), D was found not to have transacted local business and P's suit for fraud (claiming that D gave P an exclusive distributorship without intending to honor the commitment) was dismissed for want of jurisdiction (Kramer, NY 1966). But when D sent employees into the state, first for contract-negotiation purposes and then to assist in the installation of expensive equipment purchased by P from D, jurisdiction was sustained under the same "transaction" statute (Longines, NY 1965). The sending of employees into the state was a "purposeful" (Hanson, USSC 1958) act entitling the state to assume jurisdiction of the actor on a related claim.

In gauging the permissible reach of the due process clause in commercial transactions, the U.S. Supreme Court has taken a more generous view of longarm jurisdiction than it has in accident cases. Burger King (USSC 1985) is the major indicator. The fast food giant has its base in Florida, and under a Florida longarm statute purporting to assert jurisdiction of anyone who "[b]reach[es] a contract in this state by failing to perform acts required by the contract to be performed in this state", Burger King was allowed to obtain Florida jurisdiction over a Michigan franchisee who never set foot in Florida. Among the obligations the franchisee undertook in Michigan, however, where it had its operation, was to send periodic payments under the franchise agreement to Florida. The court held this a major ingredient in satisfying due process.

Relying on Burger King, a federal court of appeals sustained New York jurisdiction over two California individuals in another franchise case, holding that with contacts even greater than those that sufficed in Burger King (however sparse they might otherwise seem), they "reached into New York to obtain the benefits of selling seven franchises [computer software stores] to be operated in the state". Misrepresentations and omissions in behalf of the now bankrupt corporation for which the defendants purportedly acted were claimed. The main negotiations had apparently been made at a California meeting and in telephone calls to New York, but the statements were also allegedly contained in franchise registrations and ads in New York. (Retail, CA2 1988.)

This generous view of longarm jurisdiction in cases of intentional conduct, like Burger King (a commercial case) and the Calder and Keeton cases (involving intentional torts; § 36), may be contrasted with the more restrictive view taken when accidents are involved. (See § 35.)

The factual variations in the reported cases are as diverse as commerce itself and the investigation is for that reason a sui generis one in all cases, profiting mainly if not exclusively from decisions of the highest local authorities that set forth the basic guideposts and from decisions of all levels if their fact patterns are especially close. The judges will often sigh in ennui when another such inquiry is at hand. One federal judge—state longarm statutes, by virtue of a federal adoptive rule (see § 46), apply in the local federal courts as well—opened an opinion with the unhappy lament that he had to render "another decision in the interminable line of cases applying" the local longarm statute (Orient, SDNY 1969).

This lack of enthusiasm was a candid revelation of how many judges (and many law teachers as well) feel about the largely factual inquiries that longarm cases involve. They seldom offer the occasion for a challenging legal analysis, or an opportunity to resolve a thorny point of law, but, exciting or not, longarm jurisdiction is of inestimable moment to the parties in every case. If it is sustained, the plaintiff can sue in the forum of his choice, no mean attainment, as every trial lawyer will attest. If it is rejected, the plaintiff will have to pursue the defendant elsewhere, probably much more to the defendant's tactical advantage. For the lawyer, the jurisdictional rejection probably means that he will have to retain counsel to bring suit elsewhere, with the obvious loss of all or in any event a large part of the fee. Hence the occasional drudgery of a longarm inquiry is likely to be more than offset if, perchance, the jurisdiction is sustained and the plaintiff's choice of forum therefore upheld.

This brief digression is occasioned by the fact that although everything that has been said applies to all categories of longarm jurisdiction, and under the general as well as the specific groupings, the "transaction of business" specimen is an especially prolific source of sui generis cases.

The "transaction of business" criterion, moreover, while its very name suggests that it aims at commercial cases (and, indeed, it embraces those en masse), has been construed in some places as supporting jurisdiction of noncommercial claims as well. It has been applied, for example, in actions involving torts (e.g., Singer, NY, cert.den. 1965) and separation agreements (e.g., Van Wagenberg, Md.1966).

One problem shared by all longarm categories is who has the final say about whether longarm jurisdiction that F–1 has upheld satisfies due process? Is F–2 bound by the determination if the judgment seeks recognition there? These matters are addressed in § 39.

The states' longarm statutes present a broad variety of phrases designed to obtain jurisdiction in situations analogous to those one finds under the "transaction of business" heading, and in some instances their purpose is to be even more expansive. Shipping goods into the state (Pa., 42 Pa. C.S.A. § 5322[a][1][iii]), entering into a contract to furnish goods or services in the state (Mont., Rev. C.Mont., Tit. 25, Ch. 20, Rule 4B[1][e]), promising the plaintiff "anywhere" to perform a service in the state (Wis., Wis.Stat.Ann. 801.05[5][a]), contracting anywhere to supply goods or services in the state

(NY Civ.Prac.L. & Rules 302[a][1]), or "services or things" within the state (Mass., Mass.Ann.L.C. 223A, § 3[b]), are some examples.

Whatever the statute at hand, and of course when one of the all-the-way statutes (§ 31) is involved as well, the plaintiff's lawyer must in consultation with the client consider the economic stakes of attempting to acquire longarm jurisdiction locally in the particular case. If the amount is small and jurisdictional resistance from the defendant is expected, the longarm effort may prove economically unwise even if it should succeed. Also to consider is the issue of where a judgment against the defendant can be enforced, and the cost of converting a local judgment (which assumes that longarm jurisdiction will succeed) into a judgment of a place where the defendant has assets against which to levy execution on the judgment.

The rise of business over the Internet has given rise to a blizzard of cases considering how to apply to the virtual world jurisdictional concepts rooted in the physical world. An influential case, Zippo (USDC Pa. 1997) attempted to place these electronic forms of doing business on a sliding scale. If a defendant's virtual connection with the forum is "active", i.e., he "contracts with residents of a foreign jurisdiction that involve the knowing and repeated transmission of computer files over the Internet," then the defendant is "doing business" and is subject to in personam jurisdiction. On the other hand: "A passive Web site that does little more than make information available to those who are interested in it is not grounds for the exercise personal jurisdiction."

Of course, there's a lot of room between the "active" and "passive". The Zippo court, however, anticipated this: "The middle ground is occupied by interactive Web sites where a user can exchange information with the host computer. In these cases, the exercise of jurisdiction is determined by examining the level of interactivity and commercial nature of the exchange of information that occurs on the Web site."

One might complain that this "active versus passive" test is a bit loose in the joints. But as we've seen, this is a problem common to many jurisdictional issues, not just Internet ones.

§ 34.　Longarm Tort Cases, Generally

The commission of a tortious act within the state is often a basis for longarm jurisdiction. It meets little resistance when the defendant or the agent through whom he acts is physically within the state when the act causes damage, whether to person or property, and, indeed, the nonresident motorist statutes (§ 29) are precursors of longarm statutes that predicate jurisdiction on tortious conduct within the state.

An example of a tort case that faces easy longarm jurisdiction under either a specific "tortious act" statute or one of the all-the-way statutes (that assumes longarm jurisdiction whenever a due process analysis would permit it) is the assault that D commits on P in the forum. There the tort is direct and entirely self-contained within the forum: both the tortious act and the resulting injury occur there. But now assume that the assault was the product of a conspiracy hatched outside the forum. If the out-of-state conspirators send a hireling into the forum to do their dirty work, they will not necessarily have the comfort of thinking themselves immune from forum jurisdiction. Indirection is not always insulation. In the example, the conspirators might face jurisdiction even had the assault not come about. If the conspiracy itself is the tort, and its out-of-state planning had in-state objectives, longarm links may be found.

Personal injuries in "products liability" cases are a profuse litigation generator in the sphere of "indirect" longarm tort jurisdiction, and have therefore been allotted a separate section, following. Defamation is another and also has a separate section (§ 36).

There are various forms of indirection. It does not save its appearance exclusively for a product or defamation case. It can involve something like ordinary driver negligence at the wheel. In Cornelison (Cal.1976), for example, the defendant was a Nebraskan engaged in interstate trucking that periodically reached into California, but the accident that gave rise to the claim occurred in Nevada. The facts that the victim was a Californian, that the accident occurred near the California border, and that the

defendant, though at the moment of the accident in
Nevada, was on his way to California, were cited by
a majority (4–3) of the California Supreme Court to
uphold jurisdiction even though neither the negligent act nor the resulting injury occurred in California. Given the closeness of the Cornelison vote, one
wonders whether one of the majority of four would
have voted differently had the Supreme Court's
World–Wide case (§ 35) been on the books at the
time. In World–Wide, a retailer and regional distributor of whom jurisdiction was rejected had no specific forum involvement (the forum was Oklahoma),
while in Cornelison the defendant had. Therein may
lie a distinction with a jurisdictional difference.

There have been longarm endeavors to reach
physicians who have prescribed for an individual in
one state, allegedly resulting in damage to the
plaintiff in another. A long geographical stretch
tends to negate jurisdiction. In one case, for example, a Hawaiian driver who passed out at the wheel
in Hawaii, injuring another Hawaiian, the plaintiff,
claimed that her faint was caused by medication
given to her by a doctor in Virginia. The Hawaiian
suit against the Virginia doctor was rejected for
want of sufficient Hawaiian contacts with him (Kai-
lieha, Hawaii 1975).

Even in cases involving neighboring states, courts
have not always allowed jurisdiction. The New York
Court of Appeals refused to hail a Vermont doctor
before the Empire State's courts in a claim brought
by one of his New York patients, citing the only

marginally interstate nature of his practice. (Ingraham, NY 1997).

Examples are almost limitless. The annotations on the desired forum's longarm statute are the reservoir of ideas for the plaintiff's lawyer whose tort case has spread-out contacts. They may offer the hope of jurisdiction in a number of often arising situations, such as fraud, drug, and lost-business cases in which the representation, manufacture, or inducement may have taken place elsewhere but with the intention of bringing about a result in the forum, either alone or in combination with other places. By virtue of the adoption of state longarm bases by the Federal Rules of Civil Procedure (see § 46), federal cases have also become a ready source of longarm ideas and should not be overlooked.

§ 35. Longarm Jurisdiction in "Products" Cases

Prolific inhabitants of the longarm tort reports are the physical injury cases involving product defects. They swell the annotations. Some of them specifically articulate the "tortious act" as a distinct jurisdictional basis. The Illinois statute (Ill. Ann.Stat., ch. 110, § 2–209[2]) is one; New York's (NY Civ.Prac.L. & Rules 302[a][2]), modeled on Illinois's, is another. Each was given a starkly different construction, however, when applied to a case in which an injury occurred within the state but the defendant's tortious conduct occurred outside. In Gray (Ill.1961), an Ohio valve manufacturer sold valves to a Pennsylvania radiator manufacturer, whose finished product went through the stream of commerce to a buyer in Illinois, where an injury occurred because the valve was bad. A broad construction was given the "tortious act within this state" language and Illinois jurisdiction was sustained over the Ohio defendant. Quite a long arm, that one; it had to extend from Illinois into Pennsylvania and then bend at the elbow to reach into Ohio. But it did. On analogous facts and on an identical statute, New York rejected jurisdiction, holding that the statute is not satisfied if only the injury is shown to have occurred in the state; the tortious "act" itself—negligence or some other element of liability connected with the manufacture— must occur within the state (Feathers, NY 1965).

These cases fall within the jurisdictional portion of an area law known as "products liability". In its principal sense, the substantive one, the subject determines whether a defendant—usually a manufacturer but perhaps alternatively a wholesaler, jobber, dyer, packer, or other person treating the product—is liable for an injury the product causes. As in the Gray case, the defendant may have been associated with only a component of the finished product, but the component is alleged to be the thing at fault. Before the issue of substantive liability can be adjudicated, the court must obtain jurisdiction, and so a great jurisprudence has grown up around statutes that subject manufacturers and like persons to jurisdiction in such cases. Gray is such a case.

Gray reached out under a "tortious act within the state" statute. New York would not, whereupon its legislature enacted a remedial statute designed to exercise jurisdiction even when the "tortious act" is committed outside the state but results in injury within, as long as the defendant is shown to derive substantial revenue from the consumption of its product in the state or in interstate commerce. In the latter instance the requirement of foreseeability was also imposed by New York. The foreseeability element is not an infrequent one in these longarm statutes, and it has also been an element in cases construing all-the-way longarm statutes (those which do not spell out categories but allow jurisdiction whenever due process would).

Foreseeability was an element in Erlanger (CA4 1956) in a North Carolina statute that laid jurisdiction on the "production, manufacture, or distribution" of goods by a defendant anywhere if the defendant could be said to have the "reasonable expectation that those goods are to be used or consumed in this State". Plaintiff's agent in *Erlanger* bought goods in New York, whence they were shipped f.o.b. to North Carolina, whose jurisdiction was rejected with the court citing the example of the trepidation a California tire dealer would feel at selling tires to a driver with Pennsylvania plates. Were jurisdiction sustained, said the Erlanger court, the Californian in the hypothetical would have to defend a damage suit in Pennsylvania if a defect in the tires should cause injury there.

As the years went by after Erlanger, which was a 1956 decision, state courts and the federal courts at both district and circuit level addressed a myriad of tort cases and many sustained jurisdiction on a variety of fact patterns analogous to the example volunteered (and rejected) in Erlanger. To be sure, some declined jurisdiction if all that could be shown was that the damage-causing item was put into the stream of commerce elsewhere, as Vermont did (O'Brien, 1963) when some glass in a can of beans packed in New York produced a Vermont injury, but others, such as Illinois in the Gray case, sustained such jurisdiction.

In a sense, these jurisdictional activities in products liability situations were taking place in darkness because in the almost quarter century after Erlanger, and, for that matter, in the more than a third of a century since longarm jurisdiction got its major leg-up from the International Shoe case (USSC 1945), there was nothing about longarm jurisdiction from the U.S. Supreme Court in a tort case. The entries were taxes (in International Shoe itself), insurance (in the 1957 McGee case), and a trusts and estates dispute (in Hanson in 1958). But nary a word about how long the arm could stretch in a tort case. From most quarters, the assumption was that long was the word, and hence the Erlanger case of 1956 with its head-shaking, tongue-clicking reservations about these new-fangled longarm statutes became in the ensuing years a kind of ancient curmudgeon barely tolerated by other decisions, many of which, sustaining longarm tort jurisdiction, would not even afford it honorable mention.

Then came the development that lifted Erlanger out of senility and put it on a pedestal as a prophet: the U.S. Supreme Court decision in World–Wide Volkswagen in 1980. Here, for the first time, the Supreme Court, favorably citing the Erlanger case among others, spoke not only to tort cases in general, but to one involving in almost a classic way a products liability situation with several defendants and a range of different activities. There were four defendants; two were held to jurisdiction and two were let out.

World–Wide involved an Oklahoma statute that authorized jurisdiction of a "tortious injury in this state [caused] by an act ... outside this state" if certain other contacts were also present. Plaintiffs were a couple who bought an Audi automobile in New York from R, the dealer, and were on their way to Arizona in the car when it was involved in an accident in Oklahoma. Plaintiffs sued in Oklahoma and sought jurisdiction over R, the dealer; over D, the regional distributor of Audis whose territory took in New York, New Jersey and Connecticut; over N, the national importer of Audis; and over M, the German Volkswagen company that makes them. N and M did not contest Oklahoma jurisdiction, and language in the Supreme Court's opinion suggests that jurisdiction of them would have been sustained even if they did. The manufacturer and the importer were involved in activities national in scope, intending Oklahoma involvement in general, if not with respect to this car in particular. "The forum State", said the court, "does not exceed its powers under the Due Process Clause if it asserts personal jurisdiction over a corporation that delivers its products into the stream of commerce with the expectation that they will be purchased by consumers in the forum State."

But the regional distributor and the retailer did not fit that requirement, held the court, and hence jurisdiction of them was rejected. Arguments about the mobility of the car and the reasonable expectation that car sellers know that it will be wandering all about the land—including arguments seeking special jurisdictional treatment on the ground that the car is a dangerous instrumentality—were rejected by the Supreme Court. Even the regional distributor's involvement in interstate commerce did not avail the plaintiffs: it was restricted to three Northeastern states and did not take in Oklahoma.

World–Wide was both good news and bad news for tort plaintiffs. The good news was that manufacturers and distributors with broad geographical markets are likely to be held to jurisdiction for the damage the product does anywhere in the area of distribution (Oswalt, CA5 1980). Given the fact that accident-causing defects are more often than not laid substantively at the doorstep of a car's manufacturer, perhaps the World–Wide news holds more good than bad. But should the injury-causing act be that of the dealer or retailer, which can well be the case with a car or similar item that the dealer does things to before the sale is completed, plaintiffs injured by that doing will have to seek the retailer at its base. This has repercussions in warranty and similar cases of strict liability: although the retailer and other persons along the chain of manufacture may bear substantive liability for an injury that occurs elsewhere, under World–Wide the victim may not be able to get jurisdiction of all of the tortfeasors at the same place, a serious tactical disadvantage in litigation.

The World–Wide case refers to a "stream of commerce". It included a statement designed to show that minimal jurisdictional contacts, lacking with respect to the retailer and regional distributor, were present, and supported jurisdiction, against the manufacturer and national distributor. As noted earlier, the court said that the forum "does not exceed its powers under the Due Process Clause if it asserts personal jurisdiction over a corporation that delivers its products into the stream of commerce with the expectation that they will be purchased by consumers in the forum State."

The Supreme Court afterwards came close to rejecting the "stream of commerce" test in 1987, however, in Asahi (USSC 1987), in which a motorcycle accident in California was allegedly caused by a defective tire tube and its valve. While California jurisdiction over the tube manufacturer, a Taiwanese company selling its product by the thousands in California, was sustained, jurisdiction over the Japanese valve manufacturer, from which the Taiwanese company bought the valve assemblies and which it tried to implead, was rejected. Jurisdiction with respect to only an indemnification claim between the two companies—and two foreign companies to boot—was at issue in Asahi, however, and a majority of the court stressed that point. Perhaps a different view would prevail if the injured plaintiff were the one seeking jurisdiction of the valve manufacturer.

The Supreme Court could not find, however, a majority position with regard to what constitutes a product reaching the forum state in the "stream of commerce". Four justices led by Justice O'Connor concluded that the mere resale of it was insufficient unless accompanied by further proof of purposefulness, such as advertising in the forum. Four justices led by Justice Brennan thought just the opposite: resale alone is ordinary enough to show a purposeful connection. And Justice Stevens was content to leave the resolution of the question in splendid equipoise, where it remains today.

§ 36. Longarm Jurisdiction in Defamation Cases

Libel and slander cases pose thorny jurisdictional problems because with modern communications media they can reach across the globe in a few days (or sometimes a few seconds), and because they are often intertwined with free press and free speech issues.

The problem is at its most delicate when freedom of the press is involved. A newspaper of broad circulation, for example, may face a generous longarm statute in a state in which it sells only a few hundred copies, thus being exposed to that state's choice of law rules, which can lead to perhaps vindictive results when the merits are reached if the defendant publisher is not beloved in the forum. This prompted one federal circuit (New York Times, CA5 1966) to hold that greater contact with the forum is necessary for jurisdiction in libel than in other tort cases because of First Amendment considerations. Another circuit held jurisdiction unaffected, libel or no, but looked for salvation to rules insulating responsible publishers from overbroad liability as a matter of substantive law (Buckley, CA2 1967). The Buckley case suggests as an alternative a stricter application of forum non conveniens rules (§ 53) in First Amendment cases, instead of a limited reading of jurisdiction under the 14th Amendment's due process clause. The two would seem to come to the same thing, since the restrictions would still be for the U.S. Supreme Court to set as the ultimate custodian of both amendments.

As a matter of constitutional law, the Supreme Court has indeed set the rules, and generously. Two major cases on the subject, concerning national publications, Calder (USSC 1984), involving the National Enquirer, and Keeton (USSC 1984), involving Hustler Magazine, are in point. Not only the publication itself, but also the individuals writing and editing for it, were found to be within the jurisdictional reach of the forum, which in each case was one of many states in which the publications were sold and circulated but not one in which any of the writing or editing was done. The generous reach allowed the longarm statutes involved in those cases (California's and New Hampshire's) suggest that the Supreme Court views differently, and more expansively, longarm efforts aimed at intentional as against unintentional torts. (The more restrictive approach the Court takes to unintentional tort situations is noted in § 35.)

Here again the Internet raises its head. While Keeton and Calder involved physical publications, the Internet has made it possible to spread poison far and wide with just a few clicks of computer keys. The Supreme Court cases would seem to lead to the conclusion that jurisdiction in such cases could be literally worldwide. The lower courts, however, have not been quite so enthusiastic in lengthening the longarm here. Consider, for example, the Virginia prison warden who claimed to have been libeled by a Connecticut newspaper that referred to his facility as a "cut rate gulag." The newspaper had almost no physical circulation in the warden's home state, but its webpage, where the article also appeared, certainly could have been accessed in Virginia. Nevertheless, the Fourth Circuit denied jurisdiction in Virginia, citing the largely Connecticut-local content of the paper. (Young, CA4 2002).

Choice of law in defamation cases is treated in § 88.

§ 37. Other Longarm Categories; Overlaps

Many states have as a longarm category the claim arising out of the "ownership, use or possession of any property, whether real or personal'' (e.g., Wash., R.C.Wash.Ann. 4.28.185[c]), or just real (e.g., Ill., ch. 110, § 2–209[3]), in the state. These do not generate as profuse a case law as other categories do. A claim arising out of a piece of property, especially real property, is usually so intimately connected with the forum that it offers little opportunity for the defendant to defeat jurisdiction. And if the property is unrelated to the claim, then the Supreme Court's decision in Shaffer v. Heitner (USSC 1977), makes clear that the property alone will not do for establishing jurisdiction (see § 41).

There would have been more need for longarm jurisdiction in marital actions were it not for the availability of a category of in rem jurisdiction that supports divorces and separations (see § 43). But the in rem theory does not support jurisdiction for the alimony or support aspects of matrimonial litigation, or money demands in actions independent of matrimonial claims, such as support proceedings in children's and family courts. Hence one finds longarm statutes offering jurisdiction for support and other economic purposes in matrimonial and family litigation when the breadwinner is not, or is no longer, a local domiciliary (NY Civ.Prac.L. & Rules 302[b]).

Accepting a position of responsibility in a domestic corporation or one with its principal office in the state is found as a longarm basis (e.g., Mich., M.S.Ann. § 27A.705[6]).

It will often happen that the same conduct will expose a defendant to jurisdiction under more than one local longarm statute. That would be the case, for example, in car accidents in states having an all-the-way or tortious-act longarm statute, because the state is also likely to have a separate nonresident motorist statute that would also offer jurisdiction.

Even within the verbal framework of a special longarm statute there may be categories that overlap. An absent landlord in whose building a hall defect injures a plaintiff may face jurisdiction because the claim arises out of the transaction of business, the ownership of real property, or the commission of a tort, each of which may be a separate category under the applicable longarm statute. A plaintiff in this position should ordinarily cite and rely on all available bases.

Should there be separate statutes, with a separate scheme of process service obtaining for each, the plaintiff would do best to effect service pursuant to the instructions of the statute she deems it soundest to rely on for basis.

A situation may also arise in which a nondomiciliary defendant can logically be subjected to jurisdiction under two different "basis" statutes, but, because of the technical language of each, he claims to be touched by neither. In one case, for example, the defendant was a forum domiciliary at the time he performed an act that fell under the forum's longarm statute. But before the action was brought against him he had moved from the state. Plaintiff argued that the defendant was subject to both "domicile" and "longarm" jurisdiction in the forum. The defendant answered that "domicile" jurisdiction requires that the defendant be a domiciliary at the time of suit, which he no longer was; and that the forum's "longarm" jurisdiction would not touch him because it applied in terms only to a "nondomiciliary", that this had reference to status only at the time of the act complained of, and that since he was a forum domiciliary at that time the longarm statute wouldn't reach him either.

An ingenious argument, but it failed. There is no such absurd gap. The longarm statute, phrased for a "nondomiciliary" because there is ordinarily no problem obtaining jurisdiction over a defendant with a local domicile, will just be extended to that person when there is. (State v. Davies, NY 1966.)

§ 38. Appearance as Jurisdictional Basis

Appearing in an action without raising a jurisdictional objection may be deemed a consent to personal jurisdiction, even if there was no service made on the defendant or no basis for jurisdiction at all. So, for example, when P sues A and B but serves only A, B learning of the action and taking part on the merits, B submits to jurisdiction.

How an appearance is effected and a jurisdictional objection raised and preserved in a given court system is a matter of local option (§ 48). In the federal courts, for example, the defendant raises a jurisdictional objection by either moving to dismiss based on it or by including it as a defense in the answer (FRCP12). Participating on the merits without doing either waives the objection and submits the defendant to jurisdiction.

There are several categories of appearance. A "special appearance" is one made for the sole purpose of contesting jurisdiction. It has declined in use, and since a "general appearance" is a phrase used only to differentiate a special appearance, it, too, is not as frequently heard a terminology today as it once was.

There are several other things capable of reducing the scope of a court's jurisdiction, and these may sometimes be described in terms of an "appearance".

When jurisdiction is predicated solely on a "longarm" statute—i.e., is limited only to a particular claim arising out of the local act of a nondomiciliary who has been served outside the state—the defendant may be apprehensive that if he appears in the action the plaintiff will then exploit the appearance by amending the complaint to assert additional claims that do not have local contacts and would otherwise lack a jurisdictional foundation. A state statute with the design of encouraging longarm defendants to appear and defend may insulate them from such amendments. The appearance by the defendant would thus be "restricted" to the longarm claim alone, whether or not actually called a "restricted appearance".

If an action is predicated on in rem jurisdiction alone, that is, jurisdiction based on the local presence of a thing, or "res", but without any basis for personal jurisdiction of the defendant (in rem jurisdiction is studied in § 41 et seq.), the applicable local law or rule may permit the defendant to defend with the understanding that the resulting judgment will be allowed effect only with respect to the res but will not bind the defendant in personam. This is a kind of "limited" appearance, though it may go by a different name, or lack a name altogether.

It may also be permissible for a defendant to qualify her appearance by stating in an appropriate pleading or paper that it is made with respect to only a stated claim. Assuming that forum law allows this, the qualification may bar jurisdiction of an unrelated claim. In Einstoss (NY 1970), for example, D's appearance in F–1 was qualified to say that it was in respect of P's claim only. When it was nevertheless invoked by a co-defendant as a basis for an unrelated cross-claim, the resulting judgment in favor of the co-defendant was held to be invalid and was denied recognition in F–2.

E. ADJUDICATING JURISDICTION

§ 39. Final Say as to Jurisdiction

If P bases his F–1 action on longarm jurisdiction, effecting service on nondomiciliary D outside the state, and D maintains that F–1 lacks the "minimum contacts" needed to satisfy due process, who decides the jurisdictional issue and to what extent is the determination binding?

Suppose, for example, that D, serenely confident that F–1 lacks jurisdiction, defaults; does not even bother to appear in the action. P puts in his proof ex parte, including such proof as P has of D's jurisdiction-satisfying contacts, and P is upheld, D being absent all the while and not being heard because of his default. P gets a default judgment, purporting to adjudicate jurisdiction as well as the merits. If D has property in F–1, the next thing that P is going to do is take steps to enforce the judgment out of D's local property. Unless D acts, the enforcement will proceed. May D now move, in F–1, to vacate the default judgment on grounds of lack of jurisdiction?

He may. If the alleged defect is jurisdictional, and D has not yet been heard on the matter—which is always the case if D has defaulted—the judgment is theoretically void, and D is entitled to show the court as much. Due process permits D one day in court even on a jurisdictional issue and a default means that D has not had that day in court yet and can seek it by motion to vacate the judgment after its entry.

Note that it is only the jurisdictional objection that remains open by virtue of the default. The merits do not. Hence, should D's jurisdictional attack, when he finally makes it, fail, the merits adjudication stands as binding and D has, with the default, forfeited his day in court on the merits. If jurisdiction is found to exist, an opening of the default so as to permit D to defend belatedly on the merits is a matter of judicial discretion and subject to F–1's rules about what it takes to invoke that discretion.

D's default in F–1 enables him, if he wishes, to save the issue of F–1's jurisdiction for adjudication in a different court (F–2). So, for example, if D has no property in F–1, and P must take the F–1 judgment to F–2 for enforcement (where D does have property) and take steps to convert it into an F–2 judgment, D may at that time show the F–2 court that F–1 lacked jurisdiction. Since D did not appear in F–1, the issue of F–1's jurisdiction, although F–1 has found in favor of its own jurisdiction (explicitly or by implication), does not bind F–2. If D is willing to default in F–1 and have F–2 adjudicate whether F–1 had jurisdiction, he may do so. It is a gamble, however, because if the F–2 holding is that F–1 did have jurisdiction—and F–2 is bound to apply reasonable standards of proof in determining the facts on which the jurisdictional conclusions depend (Williams II, USSC 1945)—D will now face a final judgment which he has given up the right to contest on the merits.

Quite a different result obtains when D appears in the F–1 action, even if only to contest jurisdiction. The appearance subjects D to whatever adjudication F–1 makes on the jurisdictional point, so that if F–1 sustains jurisdiction, and that holding survives such appellate steps as may be taken in F–1, F–2 is bound under the full faith and credit clause to recognize F–1's sustaining of its own jurisdiction and must then, of course, recognize the F–1 judgment on the merits (Sherrer, USSC 1948; see § 124).

In the default situation, in which F–2 is permitted to assess on its own whether F–1 had jurisdiction, the legal principles applicable to the assessment are generally those emanating from the federal due process clause. The supervening principles of due process, which govern both F–1 and F–2, are the ones F–2 will apply. But it may of course happen that the two courts will disagree about what due process permits, especially in the absence of an all-fours precedent from the U.S. Supreme Court. Indeed, whenever F–1 renders a judgment, by default or otherwise, it represents, implicitly if not expressly, that it has jurisdiction satisfactory to prevalent standards of due process; and whenever F–2 refuses to recognize the F–1 judgment, it is saying just the contrary. Unless the F–2 adjudication to the effect that F–1 lacked jurisdiction is able to press through to review by the U.S. Supreme Court court, which has the ultimate say about federal due process, the F–2 determination, as the most recent, will as a practical matter prevail, as it did in Conn (Utah 1959), in which Utah refused to recognize an Illinois judgment.

All of this discussion overlaps the recognition of judgments segment of the conflict of laws, pointing up once again the intimacy of the relationship between that subject and jurisdiction.

§ 40. Continuing Jurisdiction

Once a court has obtained in personam jurisdiction of D, the rule is that the court has it for all purposes in the action right through to final judgment. But what about post-judgment measures of one kind or another?

The initial jurisdiction adheres for purposes of appeal (Fitzsimmons, Tenn.1891), and for purposes of local enforcement of the judgment (Rst.2d § 26). In tort cases in which joint tortfeasors A and B have been brought within the court's original jurisdiction in P's action, the jurisdiction will support a later judgment by A against B for contribution (Ohlquist, NY Sup.Ct.1932). These are examples of "continuing jurisdiction".

The importance of continuing jurisdiction is plainest in marital actions, where the initial jurisdiction continues so as to enable the court to modify (raise or lower), with post-judgment applications, such alimony and support awards as the judgment directed the defendant to pay on a weekly, monthly or some other basis, or to render a judgment for arrears accumulated under that judgment (Haas, Minn.1969). The same is true to some degree of custody decrees (Sampsell, Cal.1948), but here the lawyer should inquire into the Uniform Child Custody Jurisdiction Act, which addresses jurisdictional as well as merits issues (§ 130) and has been adopted throughout the United States.

In some situations, jurisdiction is not necessarily exercised in one action and concluded in one judgment, but in a series of proceedings. This may occur, for example, in the administration of a decedent's estate. The court that appoints a personal representative of the estate may deem its jurisdiction of her retained indefinitely, so that, should she leave the state, the state's jurisdiction of her will nonetheless continue for estate-connected measures, such as her removal or a direction that she account. It was in such a context, in fact, that the Supreme Court offered its major pronouncement on the doctrine of continuing jurisdiction. (Michigan Trust, USSC 1913).

F. "IN REM" JURISDICTION

§ 41. In Rem Jurisdiction, Introductory

In rem jurisdiction describes a court's power to adjudicate interests in a thing, a "res". It is the presence of the res in the jurisdiction, and hence in the actual or constructive custody of the court, that grounds this category of jurisdiction. In rem jurisdiction has usually been exploited only when in personam jurisdiction of all interested persons was not available. During the reign of Pennoyer (USSC 1878) and its premise that only service of process within the jurisdiction could afford in personam jurisdiction of a party, in rem jurisdiction took on added importance as at least a limited substitute. If the action involved a particular property, and that property was in the state, or if the action involved a money claim against a person who had any property at all within the state, in rem jurisdiction offered aid.

In rem jurisdiction should be divided into three categories, which we can call:

1. strictly in rem;

2. in rem; and

3. quasi in rem.

These are not rigidly defined categories, and, indeed, the Restatement (Rst.2d, note preceding § 56) groups under "quasi in rem" jurisdiction what the above list separates into categories 2 and 3, but for clarity the above three serve best. (When all three categories are to be referred to collectively in this chapter, we will sometimes simply say "rem" jurisdiction without a modifier.)

Categories one and two have this in common: they both involve an action in which P is after the particular thing. Rather than seeking a general money judgment, P wants possession of the particular item of property, or to establish his ownership, lien or other interest in it, or to exclude D from some interest in it.

The difference between one and two is that under "strict" in rem jurisdiction—the Restatement calls it "in rem"—the action is brought against the thing itself and the resulting judgment binds the whole world, whether notice was given to a particular person or not. This is a rare basis of jurisdiction; it plays hardly any role in state practice, except perhaps in actions to register land titles. The Restatement says that it applies in probate proceedings, i.e., those involving the administration of decedents' estates (Rst.2d, note preceding § 56), but this is perhaps too sweeping a view; it does not apply, in any event, in disputes over property between the estate and third persons (§ 32).

Strictly in rem jurisdiction is most prominent in admiralty actions in the federal courts, where an action may be brought directly against a vessel. Such actions are in federal jurisdiction exclusively and are not embraced within the "saving to suitors" clause (28 U.S.C.A. § 1333). The clause enables an admiralty plaintiff to choose a state or federal forum (i.e., offers concurrent jurisdiction) for most other admiralty actions (§ 97).

In category two, denominated "in rem" on the above list, the action, as in category one, addresses interests only in the particular res, but its judgment binds only those who are named as parties to the action and who are notified of it. This is a more common in rem category, embracing such actions as foreclosure of a mortgage or other lien on real property or personal property, actions for specific performance, actions to recover land or chattels, and the like. There is no need to draw out the list; as long as the property is in the state and all P is seeking is to affect interests in the property, this category of jurisdiction does the whole job.

Category three, denominated "quasi in rem" on the above list, is one in which the plaintiff is seeking only a general money judgment against the defendant, involving no property in particular. But because the plaintiff can't obtain in personam jurisdiction of the defendant, the plaintiff looks about the state for any property the nondomiciliary defendant may have there. If property is found, the plaintiff tries, through appropriate judicial process—whether called attachment, sequestration, garnishment, trustee process, or any other name—to seize it and bring the property within the jurisdiction of the court. Then the defendant can be notified wherever she may be, and, even should she default, the resulting judgment is enforcible out of the seized property.

This "quasi" in rem jurisdiction was dealt an almost lethal blow by the U.S. Supreme Court in the Shaffer case in 1977. The long prevailing view had been that the presence of any of a defendant's property within the state would support a money action against him no matter how lacking relationships might be among the claim, the res, the defendant and the forum. Shaffer reviewed and rejected that notion. It imposed instead a set of "contacts" or "nexus" requirements akin to the "minimum contacts" required by International Shoe for personal jurisdiction (§§ 31, 44).

The need of in rem jurisdiction is vastly reduced by the advent and expansion of longarm ("specific") jurisdiction, a development that is of course a factor in Shaffer's curtailment of quasi in rem jurisdiction.

In the past, in the present, and to whatever extent it may be used in the future, in rem jurisdiction bound and will bind the parties only with respect to the res before the court. (See Combs, § 42.) There is nothing in American jurisprudence or in its underlying English rudiments that offers in personam jurisdiction—otherwise absent—merely because some piece of the defendant's property has been found locally. There is nothing of the idea one occasionally found in civil law countries that the seizure of an item of the defendant's property, such as clothing, offers plenary in personam jurisdiction of the owner. There was such a case back in the 1960's, for example, involving the skier, Jean–Claude Killy, sued in Austria for maintenance of a child he was accused of fathering. Apparently a piece of his underwear was seized (Ski News Int'l, Feb. 3, 1968), and was made to do full jurisdictional service even though a careful examination revealed that the underwear did not contain Jean–Claude at the time of seizure.

A final introductory point should be made to disabuse ourselves of the sometimes heard notion that notice is dispensed with in rem cases. It is not. Personal or at least substituted service of a kind that would satisfy the notice phase of the due process requirement (§ 47) "cannot be dispensed with even in the cases of judgments in rem with respect to property within the jurisdiction of the court" (Griffin, USSC 1946). The Supreme Court has made clear in a line of cases beginning with Mullane v. Central Hanover Trust Co. (USSC 1950) and including in rem cases (Schroeder, USSC 1962) that notice to the affected parties does not depend on the form of the action. Notice must be in all events "reasonably calculated" to actually inform interested parties of the pendency of the proceedings. Notice by publication or other form unlikely to inform is unconstitutional unless necessary as a last resort.

§ 42. "In Rem" Jurisdiction

A good illustration of an in rem case is Combs (Ky.1933), in which D owed money to P, a Kentucky resident. The debt was a lien on Arkansas property belonging to D. Wanting to clear his property of the lien, D brought an action against P in Arkansas, where the court, upon constructive service on P, rendered a judgment extinguishing the lien on the property. This the court could do on an in rem foundation based simply on the fact that the property was in Arkansas. But the court went further, purporting to adjudicate how much money D still owed P on the debt. This it could not do vis-a-vis P because it was a doing that needed in personam jurisdiction, which the court did not have over P. Hence, when P sued D in Kentucky on the debt, the Arkansas judgment, although binding upon P to the effect that it cleared the lien on the Arkansas land (to whatever extent that might again come in issue), could not bind P in respect of whether a debt was due P from D, or how much it was for. The Kentucky court was free to make a new adjudication of that matter.

Would Arkansas in a case like Combs be deemed to have in personam jurisdiction today? That kind of question often arises on reviewing old in rem cases. With the expansion of longarm personal jurisdiction, the fact patterns of the old in rem cases that either rejected jurisdiction or confined the judgment to its impact on local property tempt the reader to reconsider the facts to see whether, today, there would be longarm jurisdiction and hence support for a full personal judgment.

The review is worthwhile, but it will often be incomplete. An intimate and thorough inquiry into the defendant's and the transaction's contacts with the forum is needed for longarm jurisdiction, and in the in rem cases of the past, when longarm jurisdiction was unknown, such an inquiry was not usually undertaken. Still, it is quite likely that a transaction resulting in a lien on local property will also, upon closer scrutiny, present a set of contacts from which longarm jurisdiction can be spelled out. Each time that happens, in rem jurisdiction becomes more antiquated.

Obsolescent though it may be—surely a plaintiff with longarm personal jurisdiction over all parties would prefer it to the limited judgment that mere in rem jurisdiction can earn—this category of "in rem" jurisdiction is not obsolete. If perchance longarm jurisdiction is lacking, "in rem" jurisdiction can still serve. For this reason it is important to remember that the restrictions imposed by the Shaffer case (USSC 1977; § 44) do not apply to the "in rem" jurisdiction under discussion here, but only to the "quasi in rem" jurisdiction defined in

§ 41 and to be expanded upon in § 44. This is an important point, because as used in the Restatement, "quasi in rem" embraces both items, necessitating a U.S. Supreme Court reference in Shaffer to the fact that it is only the second kind that is addressed and curtailed: the "quasi in rem" jurisdiction as we defined it in § 41, applicable in actions seeking only money.

An interesting use of in rem jurisdiction appears in a federal statute that allows for the cancellation of Internet domain names that infringe on trademarks. This practice of so-called "Cybersquatting" is difficult to remedy, because the registrants of these Internet domain names are often unknown and impossible to locate. The statute, however, gives them a "location" where registered and courts have upheld this exercise of in rem jurisdiction apparently in part because there is no realistic alternative. (Harrods Ltd. v. Sixty Internet Domain Names, CA4 2002).

Land has been a frequent generator of in rem cases. The presence of the land within the jurisdiction offers an in rem jurisdictional foundation in any case in which the plaintiff is seeking an interest in the land and nothing more. When B and S contract (anywhere) to buy and sell a piece of land located in State X, the courts of X can decree specific performance to B against S even if S is beyond in personam jurisdiction, as long as all B wants is the land (Garfein, NY 1928). But when S is the plaintiff and B the nondomiciliary defendant-buyer, State X cannot, on an in rem foundation, grant specific performance because what S wants is money and an ordinary money judgment requires in personam jurisdiction (Prudential, So.Car.1930). To the extent, however, that B has obtained any lien on the property or any equitable title to it as a result of the contract, the in rem jurisdiction will of course suffice to extinguish the lien and divest the title.

In the converse situation, where State X has in personam jurisdiction of the defendant seller (S) but the land is elsewhere, the in personam jurisdiction suffices for a specific performance decree (Massie, USSC 1810). The court will direct S to make a deed to the land, satisfactory in form to the law of its situs, under penalty of contempt, i.e., the court can jail S until she complies. Ironically, though, the State X court cannot make the deed itself or direct its clerk or a sheriff or other state official to make it in S's behalf and expect to bind the situs state with the deed. A court can do that with respect to local real property, if duly authorized by applicable local law, but not in respect of foreign real property (§ 118). This is obviously hard to justify: why should a deed made by S under the coercion of a foreign court be any more valid than one made by someone designated to be S's agent by the same court and with the same in personam jurisdiction of S?

It is thus plain that while in personam jurisdiction of an individual suffices to direct her to perform an act outside the state—another significant example would be where a party before the court is directed to obtain and disclose to the court records it keeps out of state (U. S. v. First Nat'l, CA2 1968)—in rem jurisdiction does not. If the res is all the court has, its directions can affect only interests in the res, and its holding will have no effect on anything else.

§ 43. Marital Status as "Res"

If either party to a marriage is a domiciliary of the state, the marriage itself—in this context sometimes called the "marital res" or "matrimonial res"—is deemed to be present in the state and will support a divorce even if the other spouse is beyond in personam jurisdiction (Williams II, USSC 1945; Rst.2d § 71). When this category of in rem jurisdiction is relied on, it is invariably the plaintiff spouse who is the forum domiciliary and the defendant spouse the absentee. (Were matters reversed, and the defendant the domiciliary, there would be in personam jurisdiction for the divorce and help from in rem jurisdiction would not be needed.)

This is an often used jurisdictional basis in divorce actions. It is the jurisdictional phenomenon that supports the so-called "ex parte" divorce, which is a divorce in which the plaintiff spouse goes to and establishes domicile in the forum state, thus giving that state divorce jurisdiction even if the defendant spouse, a nondomiciliary, refuses to appear. (If the defendant does appear, the resulting divorce is called "bilateral". See § 124.)

Does this "marital status" jurisdiction fall under the "strictly in rem" or just the "in rem" category, per the list set down in § 41? It is probably somewhere between the two. Almost the whole world is bound to recognize the divorce; its binding effect is not restricted to the parties. Hence it can't be "in rem" jurisdiction, number 2 on the list. But since there are some nonparties who may be permitted to attack the judgment, such as a child of the marriage—the persons who can attack the divorce are determined by the law of the rendering court—the judgment does not absolutely bind the whole world and hence forfeits a place in category 1, the "strictly in rem" category. If we had to find a niche for it among the three enumerated categories of § 41, perhaps its appropriate number would be 1.005 or thereabouts. The niche is not important, but as many a former spouse can attest, the jurisdiction is.

§ 44. "Quasi in Rem" Jurisdiction

This category of rem jurisdiction, number 3 on the list contained in § 41, is the one in which the plaintiff is seeking an ordinary money judgment rather than asserting a pre-existing interest in specific property. (Note again that under the more technical definition, the one expounded by the Restatement, "quasi in rem" jurisdiction embraces both categories 2 and 3 on the § 41 list.) It holds that if a nondomiciliary defendant of whom personal jurisdiction is lacking nonetheless happens to have property in the forum state, the state can, through the issuance and execution of appropriate process, effect a seizure of the property. The seized property then becomes the jurisdictional "basis" of the action. The property seizure ordinarily precedes the commencement of the action—indeed, the Pennoyer case (USSC 1878) says that it must—after which the defendant is duly served. Then, even if the defendant fails to appear and a default judgment is entered, the judgment is enforcible against the seized property. Of course, the judgment has no effect beyond that and is entitled to recognition (and res judicata effect) in other states only to the extent that it affected interests in the res (Benadon, NY App.Div.1960). This may mean that if the amount of property seized is insufficient to pay the entirety of P's claim, a second suit may have to be brought against D for the balance wherever D is subject to personal jurisdiction. D will of course be credited in that action with whatever P obtained in the first one, the quasi in rem suit.

This category of jurisdiction had been relied on to a considerable degree for a century when the U.S. Supreme Court reviewed it in light of more modern jurisdictional principles, and abrogated it almost entirely. This it did in the Shaffer case (1977), and the nation's courts, both federal and state, have been struggling since that time to determine just how much is left.

Quasi in rem jurisdiction of this genre did not require that any relationship be demonstrated between the property seized and the claim asserted, between the claim asserted and the forum state, or between the defendant and the forum. Adequate by itself was the fact that the defendant had property of some judicially seizable kind in the state. It is this want of forum relationship that Shaffer alights upon, introducing in respect of quasi in rem jurisdiction a minimum contacts requirement similar to that which International Shoe (USSC 1945) devised for longarm personal jurisdiction. No longer may a money action be sustained on a claim and against a defendant wanting in appropriate state contacts, merely because the defendant happens to have some property in the state. A thread must hold the three elements of claim, defendant, and state together.

The facts of Shaffer involved a corporate derivative action brought in Delaware. Jurisdiction as against certain directors and officers was based on the seizure of stock they owned in the corporation. But the Delaware jurisdictional statute did not require that either the individuals or the claim have any relationship to the state, and quasi in rem jurisdiction was therefore rejected.

A high if not the highest water mark of Supreme Court recognition of quasi in rem jurisdiction had been reached in the 1905 case of Harris v. Balk. P lived in Maryland and had a money claim against D of North Carolina. G, also a North Carolinian, owed D money. P wanted to sue D in Maryland but there was no in personam jurisdiction of D. P waited until G happened through Maryland and had G served there with an attachment, "seizing" the debt that G owed to D to use as a quasi in rem basis for P's claim against D. G paid this debt to the sheriff to the credit of P's claim, and then, when D sued G on the debt in North Carolina, G's payment of it on the Maryland attachment was allowed by the U.S. Supreme Court as a complete defense.

An important aspect of the Harris case is the "situs" it affixes to the intangible "debt" that G owed to D. It was deemed a transitory obligation, following G, the debtor, on all his rounds. In this respect Harris is probably still good law to some degree, but that point will be probed further in § 45, dealing with the situs of intangibles.

In its principal aspect—that of using unrelated local property of a nondomiciliary defendant to ground jurisdiction of a claim wanting in forum contacts—Harris is almost completely overruled by Shaffer. In only a few situations, acknowledged in the Shaffer opinion, may the quasi in rem jurisdictional notions of Harris and like cases still do service.

One is where the minimal contacts imposed as requirements in Shaffer are present in the case. A quick response to this is that if the case shows such contacts, in personam (longarm) jurisdiction is present and quasi in rem jurisdiction is not needed. But perhaps a set of "contacts" inadequate for outright in personam jurisdiction may nevertheless suffice for the more limited quasi in rem jurisdiction in a given case. That is the present posture of some courts. In Intermeat (CA2 1978), for example, P sold beef to D, an Ohio corporation not within New

York in personam jurisdiction. D sold much of its product—several million dollars worth—to New York buyers, however, and one of these, the A & P, owed D money which P attached in New York. The test is "narrower" for quasi in rem jurisdiction than for in personam jurisdiction, said the court in sustaining the quasi in rem jurisdiction. Enumerating several contacts which in the aggregate were assumed by the court to be insufficient for in personam jurisdiction, the court held that they nevertheless sufficed for the more limited quasi in rem jurisdiction that P was asserting.

Long before Shaffer, a thoughtful California case (Atkinson, Cal., cert. den. 1957) appeared to weigh local contacts and then to allow a kind of quasi in rem jurisdiction based on them, while suggesting that they might not suffice for in personam jurisdiction. Pursuant to certain collective bargaining agreements, California employers sent money, earned by their California employees in California, to a New York trustee for certain purposes, and the employees sought to stop the practice. California was found to have sufficient contacts to bar the employers from sending any more money out of California but not enough to support an in personam judgment against the absent New York trustees to get back the money that had already been sent to them in the past. Although Atkinson was deemed by some to be an extension of quasi in rem jurisdiction at the time, it is paradoxically an "extension" that is likely to survive the curtailments of the

Shaffer case. It relies on a soundly based contacts analysis of the very kind to which Shaffer leaves the door open.

Another instance in which a kind of quasi in rem jurisdiction will be allowed under the Shaffer case notwithstanding a want of claim-defendant-state nexus appears to be where D has all of his property in, or has moved all of his property to, State X, thus making it the only place where a judgment can be enforced. But that will apparently support proceedings in State X only for enforcement purposes after a judgment has been duly rendered in the more appropriate forum, or to support an attachment for security purposes while the judgment is being sought in that other forum; it will probably not authorize the adjudication of the claim in the forum of the property if that forum otherwise lacks contacts.

A third category in which Shaffer leaves the door open to quasi in rem jurisdiction is where there is no other, presumably more appropriate, forum in which the claim can be heard, which is not a common situation. Wartime or political upheaval might fall under this category, as might also a case in which the more appropriate forum is far away and all parties have left it.

Some states have sequestration, garnishment, attachment, or like devices to enable a spouse or child in a matrimonial or family dispute to seize and even sell the locally available property of the parent or other spouse for support purposes while the action is pending. If in personam jurisdiction of that spouse or parent is lacking, it can be argued that Shaffer would bar the property seizure because it is an exercise of quasi in rem jurisdiction that seeks any property to enforce a money claim. If the action is for divorce, however, and jurisdiction for that purpose rests on the local presence of the "marital res" spelled out through the domicile of the plaintiff spouse (§ 43), perhaps that can be deemed an additional "contact" sufficient to ground the quasi in rem seizure needed to carry out the monetary demand in the divorce action, thereby satisfying the Shaffer standards. But assume an ordinary support proceeding brought by a wife and/or child now present in the forum, against a husband or father who is absent, or, indeed, who never had any connection with the forum. Would Shaffer bar quasi in rem jurisdiction for the support purpose if the husband or father should happen to have property in the forum? Perhaps the local presence of his family, with or without his consent, can be deemed to supply the contacts needed to satisfy the claim-defendant-forum nexus demanded by Shaffer for the limited but important purpose of support and maintenance.

New York in 1966 raised quasi in rem jurisdiction to a greater height than even the Harris case (USSC 1905) had reached. In Seider v. Roth, the New York Court of Appeals gave quasi in rem jurisdiction to a New York plaintiff injured in an accident occurring outside the state and involving a nondomiciliary tortfeasor. The court held that if the tortfeasor was insured with a carrier that also happened to maintain a New York office (in Seider it did), the insurance policy would be deemed to have a New York "situs", could be attached in New York, would support quasi in rem jurisdiction of a tort suit in New York, and would thus enable any New Yorker injured anywhere in the world to sue at home merely because of the New York presence of the carrier.

This "Seider-based" theory of jurisdiction raised many issues as well as eyebrows, was rejected by almost every other state that was asked to follow it (e.g., Javorek, Cal.1976), and was ultimately overruled by the U.S. Supreme Court in Rush v. Savchuk in 1980 on due process grounds. (Seider's bizarre history is summarized in Siegel, New York Practice 4th Ed. § 105.) The Rush case was from Minnesota, the only other state to embrace (or try to embrace) the doctrine in full. Before that, New Hampshire made what we may call a "retaliatory" adoption of the doctrine, permitting attachment only of an insurance policy covering a New York tortfeasor (Forbes, NH 1973). Savchuk stops all of it.

Seider depended on the forum state being the "situs" of the intangible obligations arising out of the insurance policy. The situs of intangibles has been a frequent problem in conflict of laws and is a separate subject in the next section.

We can't take leave of this subject without saying a word in defense of Harris v. Balk. One periodically heard criticism of it at various times since its 1905 rendition. It must be in remembered that Harris labored in the jurisdictional darkness cast in 1878 by the Pennoyer case, which barred in personam jurisdiction unless the defendant were served locally. Harris was an endeavor to broaden jurisdiction at a time when the International Shoe case (USSC 1945), the monarch of jurisdiction broadeners, was still 40 years away. So Harris turned to in rem jurisdiction as a way station. If Shaffer (USSC) in 1977 found Harris to be unnecessary because of what International Shoe and its progeny afterwards accomplished, gentlefolk would say not that Harris was bad law and deserves oblivion, but that Harris did yeoman's service during hard times and has been retired with honor to judicial archives.

§ 45. "Situs" of Property; Documents

Criticism leveled at Harris (USSC 1905) over the years sometimes centered on the situs it ascribed to the "debt" involved in that case. G owed the debt to D, and both were North Carolinians. Nevertheless, G was deemed to have carried the "debt" with him to Maryland (where it was attached by one of D's creditors in the Harris case). This presumably meant that a debt is present wherever the debtor is. The Seider case (NY 1966; § 44) said the same of the intangible obligations arising out of a liability insurance policy: the obligations to defend the insured in a tort suit and to indemnify the insured should it go to judgment. Those obligations, said Seider, are present wherever the insurance company is, so that the insurance policy would be present everywhere—and subject to seizure anywhere through appropriate process, the theory goes—if the insurer is present everywhere.

These phenomena are only the tip of the iceberg. Since every category of "in rem" jurisdiction depends on the local presence of the "res", it is indispensable that hands be laid on the res, literally or constructively, or no in rem jurisdiction of any class can proceed. There is little difficulty in the case of tangible property. Land is easy because it doesn't move. Its situs is always fixed, although California has been known to take a few steps from time to time. Tangible personal property, although movable, is also comparatively easy. Its local presence, even if transient, may support an actual or constructive seizure through judicial process and thus support local in rem jurisdiction. Even there, however, a difficult issue will sometimes crop up. A chattel "in the course of transit in interstate or foreign commerce", for example, is said to be insulated from in rem jurisdictional use, and a chattel brought into the state through fraudulent representations and the like may be similarly insulated (Rst.2d §§ 60, 82).

Problems magnify when the property interest is an intangible one, such as a debt owed to or a cause of action owned by the defendant. Harris theorized that the debt is present where the debtor is, but that will work, if it works at all, only when the debtor concedes the debt, as he did in Harris. Should the debtor (the debtor of the would-be defendant) dispute that he owes it, the alleged creditor (the defendant) could not be adjudicated out of it except by a court with in personam jurisdiction of him. In other words, the alleged debtor can't enter a state wanting in jurisdiction of the creditor and obtain an adjudication that the debt is not owed or that it is less than the creditor claims (New York Life, USSC 1916).

The situs of intangibles, said Judge Cardozo (Severnoe, NY 1931), is a legal fiction,

> but there are times when justice or convenience requires that a legal situs be ascribed to them. The locality selected is for some purposes, the domicile of the creditor; for others, the domicile or place of business of the debtor, the place, that is to say, where the obligation was created or was meant to be discharged; for others, any place the debtor can be found. At the root of the selection is generally a common sense appraisal of the requirements of justice and convenience in particular conditions.

It is therefore incumbent on the lawyer to find out precisely how an intangible is to be treated in a given case, and this can require some research into the laws of several places. The Restatement has several sections addressing cases in which the property involved, tangible and intangible both, is represented by a document, such as a promissory note, warehouse receipt, bill of lading, or the like. Does the property have its situs where the document is? where the property represented by the document is? where the owner of the document is? where the owner of the property is? These are the questions to ask, and the answers—if answers have been formulated—may have to be sought in the law of several places (Rst.2d §§ 62, 63). Perhaps the prime question to ask in these document cases is whether the document itself is deemed the "property". If it is, then pursuit should be of the paper and the person holding it; if it is not, the property itself and the person having custody or possession of it will probably have to be pursued. The methods of pursuit may vary from state to state.

Here an additional question of occasional difficulty will appear: whose law governs the question of whether the document is to be deemed the property? This can become important when shares in a corporation are the subject, for example. It will have bearing in other instances as well. Whether the written certificates representing the shares are to be deemed the property, enabling seizure of the certificates to do in rem service, or the shares are to be deemed intangible and thus to require that a seizure be effected through the corporation itself, is usually governed by the law of the state of incorporation (Baker, USSC 1917; Rst.2d § 64).

The U.S. Supreme Court has indicated that money documents, such as a certificate of deposit, have a situs of their own and that a state having jurisdiction of neither the document nor its holder can't reach the represented money even though it is the state of the deposit (Bank of Jasper, USSC 1922). This principle is of special importance when the document is negotiable. A different general rule would create undue risks for the person owing the money represented by the instrument.

Special problems may arise in escheat cases involving unclaimed money. The Supreme Court set forth guideposts in Texas v. New Jersey (USSC 1965), in which a number of small debts were owed by a large company incorporated in State C but with its main office in State M. Most of the debts arose outside both states. The Supreme Court, rejecting a "significant contacts" approach (see § 78) as unworkable, held that escheat should be to the state of each creditor's domicile according to the creditor's address as last appearing on the corporate books, and to the debtor's corporate domicile (the state of incorporation) for debts owed to those having no record addresses. A modest extension of this principle occurred in Delaware v. New York (USSC 1993), a case that held that unclaimed securities distributions go first to the state of the creditor's last known address but, in the event that this is unknown, to the state of the place of incorporation of the securities intermediary, not its principal place of business. Of course, the state adversaries in this case were not chosen randomly as New York is the principal place of business of many such firms, while many of them are incorporated in Delaware.

On this occasion, it was Delaware's position that carried the day.

The position of the debtor must be considered. Neither in an escheat nor any other case should a state compel a debtor to pay a sum of money or deliver property to one person if the judgment will not bind others who have conflicting claims. It exposes the debtor to multiple liability. He would be "deprived of due process of law if he is compelled to relinquish [the property or pay the debt] without assurance that he will not be held liable again in another jurisdiction or in a suit brought by a claimant who is not bound by the first judgment" (Western Union, USSC 1961).

In a multistate business transaction the Uniform Commercial Code may of course be applicable, and prove especially helpful. Section 7–602 of the Code, for example, addresses the attachment of goods covered by a negotiable document, and in essence treats the document as the property. This is done primarily to protect the one who has possession of the property and who would face a dilemma if compelled to surrender it to one person when another has the document and can be expected to claim the property with it. Article 9 of the Code, dealing with secured transactions, is also a fertile research ground when the property involved has been subjected to some kind of security interest (lien, mortgage, conditional sales agreement, etc.); or, indeed, when the security interest is itself the property sought and its owner is the defendant against whom the plaintiff has a claim. In dictating where papers reflecting security interests have to be filed, for example (e.g., UCC § 9–401), the Code is in effect addressing and trying to resolve situs problems connected both with the security interest and with the property upon which the security interest is affixed.

The 2001 revision of Article 9 (§§ 9–301 through 9–307) now generally gives the chattel on which the security rests a situs at the debtor's "location", defined usually as an individual's residence or a corporation's state of incorporation. The switch to a "debtor-location" nexus was probably undertaken on the theory that debtors move less often than does their secured property. If a debtor changes "locations," the Code gives the creditor four months to refile in the state of the new "location," lest the security interest become "unperfected" and thus unenforcible against third parties who take the property for value.

Another way a state may indirectly affix a situs to an intangible obligation is by designating a particular person as a proper "garnishee". A garnishee under the usual definition is a person who has possession of property belonging to a defendant, who owes the defendant a debt, or against whom the defendant has some claim. If a state statute should say, for example, that, with respect to an interest the defendant may have in a decedent's estate, it is the estate's personal representative who is the garnishee, the plaintiff should pursue that interest through appropriate papers (attachment, execution, garnishment, sequestration, or whatever other description the state bestows) served on that garnishee. Such an indication is a way of saying that the interest is present where the garnishee is.

A final note on this subject is that Harris, and for that matter all cases that endeavor to affix a situs to an intangible, are not necessarily overruled by the Shaffer case (§ 44) in this "situs" respect. Shaffer, remember, is concerned only with the attempted use of quasi in rem jurisdiction as a way to enable a forum to adjudicate an unrelated claim. If that claim is adjudicated by an appropriate forum, and with full jurisdiction, but the judgment needs enforcement elsewhere for want of sufficient property of the defendant in the original forum, the plaintiff is going to take that judgment to a place where the defendant has property and seek enforcement there. If the "property" is intangible, where is "there"? While cases (like Harris) that affix a situs to an intangible property interest may have done so in the now-discredited context of an action based on quasi in rem jurisdiction, in which the property was sought before judgment as the basis on which to obtain the judgment, those cases will still be relevant to determine an intangible's situs when, valid judgment already in hand, a creditor is pursuing the property only for enforcement purposes.

G. FEDERAL BASES

§ 46. Jurisdictional Bases in Federal Courts

Because the federal courts are created by Congress, their summonses and processes could be served nationwide at Congress' pleasure, at least as long as no unreasonable burden is placed on the defendant by forcing him to defend in a truly inconvenient forum. (Republic of Panama, CA 11 1997). But Congress has permitted such service in only certain instances, such as under the federal statutory interpleader provision (28 U.S.C.A. § 2361; see 4A Wright & Miller, Fed.Pr. & Proc.: Civil §§ 1118, 1125, for others).

The general rule under Federal Rule of Civil Procedure 4(k)(1)(A) is that a federal court has personal jurisdiction over a defendant "who could be subjected to the jurisdiction of a court of general jurisdiction in the state in which the district court is located." Thus, a federal court ordinarily must apply the longarm statute of its home state and the attendant constitutional limits, namely, the requirement of minimum contacts with the forum state. (Congress has made some important exceptions to this, recognized in Rule 4(k)(1)(C and D), which allow a broad reach for federal process.)

Rule 4(k)(1)(B) is a quaint old provision known as the "100–mile bulge" rule. In the case of parties who are impleaded under Rule 14, or are necessary to the disposition of the action under Rule 19, the rule allows them to be served anywhere within 100 miles (as the crow flies) of the federal courthouse, even if that 100–mile bulge extends into a state where there wouldn't otherwise be jurisdiction. For courthouses close to state lines this can be a significant jurisdictional extension. Most courts, however, require that the Rule 14 or 19 defendant have minimum contacts with the "bulge area" so as to protect an otherwise unconnected party who happens to wander too close to a federal court building. (Quinones, CA10 1986).

Finally there is an exception contained in Rule 4(k)(2) added in 1993 that allows jurisdiction to the maximum extent permitted by the Constitution for "claims arising under federal law ... over the person of any defendant who is not subject to the courts of general jurisdiction of any state." The theory here is that defendants who manage to spread their contacts out among many different states ought not be able to evade civil enforcement of federal law if their contacts in the aggregate with the U.S. are enough to make jurisdiction fair.

H. NOTICE

§ 47. Notice Requirement

In all actions there must be reasonable steps taken to afford the defendant notice of the plaintiff's claim and an opportunity to meet it. This is a federal due process requirement, and hence the U.S. Supreme Court is again the custodian of the last word. All this has to do with process service.

Each state is free to devise methods of service. The Supreme Court "has not committed itself to any formula", but insists only that the notice method settled on by the particular state be "reasonably calculated, under all the circumstances, to apprise interested parties of the pendency of the action and afford them an opportunity to present their objections" (Mullane, USSC 1950).

Personal delivery of the summons is the "classic" form and "always adequate" (Mullane, id.), but not indispensable. Mere mail to an appropriate address will do, or delivery to a person of suitable age at such address. The Supreme Court leaves the states on their own as to method, and, indeed, this "notice" aspect of the due process requirement generates less case law than the "basis" aspect. (The Supreme Court's internal preferences for process service in the federal system are embodied in Rule 4 of the Federal Rules of Civil Procedure—the Supreme Court being the promulgator of the Federal Rules subject to Congressional veto, 28 U.S.C.A. §§ 2072, 2074.)

The method of service that has generated periodic trouble, and Supreme Court rejection, is service by publication. It was the method rejected in the Mullane case, which involved a proceeding to settle a trustee's accounts with a number of beneficiaries. Notwithstanding their number, due process required that a better effort than publication in a newspaper be used to give them notice. "[W]hen notice is a person's due", wrote Justice Jackson for the Supreme Court in Mullane, "process which is a mere gesture is not due process". Publication is in effect just a gesture when all else more reasonable proves unavailable. In yet another case, Schroeder (USSC 1962), the Supreme Court unanimously reversed a state court's sustaining of publication service. In this instance a public taking of land under the eminent domain power was involved. The state statute directed that service on the affected owners be made both by publication and by posting notices on local trees. The latter may have been acceptable to the tree-reading public, but it was unacceptable to due process. Publication in local papers was also held insufficient. A mere letter to each owner, said the court in offering a gratuitous example, would have done the job.

When the defendant is not a competent, adult, natural person, the plaintiff should inquire into the persons who may be served in behalf of such a defendant. This is usually just a matter of consulting the appropriate lists in local statutes and rules. If the defendant is an adjudicated incompetent, for example, and has a conservator or committee, local law is likely to require service on that person, or on that person and the incompetent both. If the defendant is an infant, there is likely to be a local provision listing the persons (parent, guardian, next friend, etc.) servable in the infant's behalf. Corporations, partnerships, estates, trusts, municipalities (counties, cities, towns, villages, etc.), school districts, and other governmental authorities, commissions, boards, and the like, are also likely to be the subject of attention in a local statute or rule prescribing service and proper servees. Service on a foreign nation and its political subdivisions, when sovereign immunity has been lifted as a barrier (28 U.S.C.A. § 1605), is centrally prescribed by federal law (28 U.S.C.A. § 1608) applicable in federal and state courts alike. Such a uniform prescription is rare. Most provisions on whom to serve in behalf of a given category of defendant derive from local preference, and, because they have usually been devised to fall within the broad tolerance of due process, they dominate the scene and must be checked out carefully. Since a defect here can void jurisdiction, a relatively minor oversight can carry disproportionate consequences.

Service of process in the federal courts is facilitated by a rule (Rule 4 of the Federal Rules of Civil Procedure) that offers its own prescriptions for service and also, for most categories of defendant, permits service according to forum state law as an alternative.

Notice of a reasonable kind is necessary in in rem actions as well as in in personam actions (Griffin, USSC 1946). There is no truth to the rumor that a defendant is always presumed to have notice of what is happening to her property.

Since due process requirements govern everywhere in the country, a want of adequate notice will invalidate jurisdiction against a domiciliary as well as against a nondomiciliary and will make a default judgment just as void within the forum as without (McDonald, USSC 1917), although it may take additional court proceedings, such as a motion to vacate the judgment, to establish its voidness.

I. MECHANICS

§ 48. Contesting Jurisdiction

In § 39 there was discussion about who has the final say about jurisdiction, addressing whether F–2 is bound by F–1's finding of its own jurisdiction. It was pointed out that if the defendant appeared in the F–1 proceedings and raised an objection to jurisdiction, he thereby submitted it to F–1 and bound himself (and F–2) by whatever F–1 held on it. Later (§ 124) it will also be seen that an appearing defendant who does not raise the objection is deemed to concede jurisdiction, and that the concession binds F–2.

All of this manifests how important it is, when the defendant has and wishes to inject and preserve a jurisdictional objection, to follow the forum's procedural instructions for doing so. A "special" appearance, which is an appearance made for the sole purpose of contesting jurisdiction (§ 38), may be required in the particular forum. If it is, the defendant had best be sure to fulfill its demands. If it is of a strict variety, it may forbid the defendant from simultaneously raising any other (than jurisdictional) issues when he first appears, under penalty of forfeiting the jurisdictional objection. (Other issues can be raised later, under such a practice, if and when the jurisdictional objection fails.)

Whether calling it a "special appearance" or anything else, state practice will usually enable the defendant to raise a jurisdictional objection expeditiously, without fear that the very step into court to put the objection will somehow slip him into the court's clutches permanently (i.e., constitute what is known as a "general" appearance). (Hall, Tenn. 1950.) If the objection succeeds, the defendant should grab his hat and run. If it fails, however, the state may now exact a "general" appearance of the defendant as the price for being allowed to defend on the merits. This merely means that the defendant may not, should he lose on the merits, raise the jurisdictional point again, as part of an appeal. Other states may preserve that appellate right even should the defendant proceed on the merits. In New York there is not only a right to appeal an adverse jurisdictional ruling; the appeal may be taken immediately, without awaiting an outcome on the merits (NY Civ.Prac.L. & Rules 5701). The right to an immediate appeal does not obtain in federal practice (or in most other state practices), which discourages piecemeal appeal of nonfinal ("interlocutory") orders unless the trial-level judge herself sets the stage for such an appeal by certifying the jurisdictional order (28 U.S.C.A. § 1292[b]). The jurisdictional point should in any event be disposed of at trial level before the defendant is required to address the merits at all. (Halverson, So.Dak.1945.)

Influential in the decline of the rigid special appearance in the United States is its omission from the Federal Rules of Civil Procedure. The Federal

Rules govern in fact in the federal courts and in effect in the practices of many states that have adopted them. Under the Federal Rules, the defendant has the option of raising a jurisdictional objection either by a pre-answer motion to dismiss or as a defense in the answer, the defendant's responsive pleading. So provides Federal Rule 12(b). But there is also this trap: If the defendant makes any pre-answer dismissal motion at all under Rule 12, such as for defective venue or failure to state a claim or on any other ground, without including such objection to personal jurisdiction as the defendant may have, the omission, even if inadvertent, will forfeit the objection. This means that if the moved-on ground fails, and the defendant must now serve an answer, the jurisdictional objection may not be included in it (as it could have been had the defendant made no Rule 12 motion at all). This is the consequence of subdivisions (g) and (h) of Rule 12, designed to facilitate early judicial address to objections of personal jurisdiction. Only if the defendant makes no Rule 12 motion at all may he safely use the defense-in-the-answer method for raising the jurisdictional objection.

J. RESTRICTIONS ON JURISDICTION

§ 49. Curbs on Jurisdiction: Ousters; Immunities; Enticements

Even when jurisdiction may appear to be present in respect of basis, notice, and opportunity to be heard—the due process trio—it may be cut back by other factors. Perhaps chief among them is the doctrine of forum non conveniens, separately treated in § 53. There is a handful of considerations that we can review briefly here and in the several sections following.

Sometimes a contract between the parties may stipulate to confer jurisdiction on a given court. Indeed, that may itself be the "basis" for the jurisdiction of the stipulated court (§ 30). But at this point consider the negative implications of such a conferral, especially when the contract provides that the stipulated court shall have "exclusive" jurisdiction, or uses words to that effect. Such a contract purports to oust all other possible courts of jurisdiction, for which reason the clause purporting to do this has come to be known popularly as an "ouster" clause. For a long time courts would not deem themselves so summarily divested of their jurisdiction, flatly refusing to recognize such clauses. This view eased, most notably in Bremen (USSC 1972), which held that such a clause would thenceforth be honored in the federal courts if it is demonstrably reasonable and the contract containing it is an arms-length one between self-sufficient parties who knew what they were doing. In Bremen they did. While neither party was English, nor was England the situs of any of the events, the subject matter was admiralty and the stipulation to English jurisdiction was designed to obtain a neutral forum with maritime-experienced judges. Hence the ouster would be upheld, said the U.S. Supreme Court, and federal jurisdiction otherwise competent would be rejected unless the plaintiff could demonstrate that the choice of an English court was "so manifestly and gravely inconvenient" that he would be "deprived of a meaningful day in court".

The Supreme Court moved still further in that direction in Carnival Cruise Lines, Inc. v. Shute (USSC 1991), in which it sustained a clause in an ordinary passenger ticket requiring that all disputes be resolved only in Florida courts. As the dissent pointed out, the passenger didn't even get to see the ticket until it was bought, at which point the passenger could cancel the purchase only by forfeiting the fare. Nevertheless, the clause was upheld.

State courts in non-federal matters—Bremen and Carnival were both admiralty cases and federal law governed the enforcement of the forum-selection clause—are of course free to determine the validity of ouster agreements for themselves, and may not be as receptive to them as the U.S. Supreme Court has come to be. While some states may still prefer to refuse the ouster any effect, there has been some trend towards upholding it "unless it is unfair or unreasonable" (Rst.2d § 80). Perhaps the ouster clause is best treated as just one of the elements relevant to a forum non conveniens (§ 53) disposition (e.g., Export, NY App.Div.1966).

Ironically, given its 1991 view in the Carnival case enforcing ouster clauses in actions governed by federal law, the U.S. Supreme Court had earlier held in Stewart (1988), a diversity case, that when state law governs and presumes to make an ouster clause binding, it will not bind in a federal court, where, at best, it will be treated as just one of the factors to be considered in determining whether to transfer the case under 28 U.S.C.A. § 1404(a), the federal equivalent of the conveniens doctrine. (In view of Carnival, is this aspect of the Stewart case still valid? If Stewart remains viable, is it because it governs in diversity cases while Carnival is designed to govern in admiralty, which is in some respects a "federal question" category?)

A corporate plaintiff may be barred by a local statute from suing in the state courts as a penalty for doing business in the state without duly licensing itself. Such a statute, in effect a curb on jurisdiction, has been held to bar even a federal action in that state if the federal jurisdictional basis is diversity of citizenship (Woods, USSC 1949; § 105).

There are several so-called "immunity" doctrines that may act as restrictions on jurisdiction. Diplomatic immunity insulates ambassadors and their staffs from local jurisdiction. Sovereign immunity insulates the foreign states proper, a troublesome area now addressed by statutes (28 U.S.C.A. §§ 1602–1611) applicable in both federal and state courts. One of the federal statutes (28 U.S.C.A. § 1605) denies the immunity when the subject matter of the suit concerns a commercial rather than governmental activity or property situated in the United States.

To encourage nonresidents to enter the state voluntarily to testify in judicial and like proceedings, a doctrine has arisen that voids summons service made on a person here on such a benevolent mission. (Rst.2d § 83.) The scope of some of these immunity doctrines will vary and local preferences must be ascertained.

Analogous to the immunity doctrines is an often found rule that bars fraud or enticement from luring an unsuspecting person, otherwise beyond local jurisdiction, into it. Hence, if a false representation or other piece of misleading conduct causes the defendant to enter the jurisdiction, service made on her during her unintended sojourn will be set aside. A classic ruse was employed in Terlizzi v. Brodie (NY App 1972) in which a New Jersey couple was told that they had won free theater tickets to a New York show. After enjoying the performance they were distressed to learn that the man seated behind them was no ordinary patron, but the plaintiff's process server, who gleefully handed them the summons for a New York civil action. While the service processor must be given high marks for creativity, the service was quashed with the curt observation that service effected on a "lured" defendant is ineffective to establish jurisdiction.

§ 50. Violation of Forum's "Public Policy"

When choice of law is reached in Chapter IV, we will have occasion to discuss at more length the famous "public policy" rule one finds bruited about in the conflicts area (§ 57), especially in older cases. Its gist is that a state court will not undertake to enforce any foreign claim obnoxious to the forum's "public policy". This is a Pandora's Box, since its application requires us to say precisely what the forum's "public policy" is. The subject is delved into at that later point, but we mention "public policy" briefly here because its application may result, not necessarily in an unfavorable judgment on the merits through the application of some other law after rejection of the one that violates forum policy, but rather in a flat refusal by the forum to entertain the action at all. When that happens, the dismissal is in effect a jurisdictional one, enabling the plaintiff to sue afresh in some other forum that has jurisdiction of the defendant and doesn't have a similar policy objection on the merits.

Such public policy dismissals are not frequent today in the United States, for the reason, elaborated in § 57, that seldom is one state's sensitivities so violated by another's law as to result in rejecting the case altogether.

§ 51. "Penal Law" Prosecutions

A state will not lend its courts to the prosecution of crimes committed elsewhere and governed by the penal laws of the other state. If the culprit has sought refuge locally, the state in which the crime was committed should, if intent on prosecution, pursue the extradition route. The rule is simple to state and easy to apply in the obvious case of a district attorney from State A who comes into State F and tries to conduct a prosecution under State A's penal statutes. He will be sent from the State F courthouse with the gratitude of the judge and staff for a good laugh.

But there are, to be sure, a variety of situations in ordinary civil actions in which the claim asserted involves what our language denominates a "penalty" of some kind, and in which the defendant, intent on getting out of jurisdiction in any way he can, becomes the etymologist of the moment and calls the court's attention to the relationship between "penal" and "penalty". If there is a penalty of any kind involved in the case, he contends, the "penal laws" exclusion is invoked and the case must be dismissed. Today the court usually thanks the defendant for the lesson, and rejects his motion to dismiss. The reason is that it is really only the out-and-out criminal prosecution that this rule was designed to oust, not a civil action involving (for example) a monetary sanction that can be perceived as having some element of penalty. Even in civil actions, the plaintiff is after the defendant for some kind of wrongdoing, as innocent, perhaps, as a breach of contract, and it would not take much to describe the damages that the breach gives rise to as a kind of "penalty".

Since a criminal prosecution brought (or rather, attempted) in State F based on the penal laws of State A does result in a dismissal, the "penal laws" theme necessarily bears on the subject of jurisdiction and has been touched on here. Its appearance is more frequent in the choice of law context, however, where the defendant may be seeking to steer the court away from the application of an unfavorable rule of substantive law by contending that it is penal in nature. A nice question is whether the objection, should it succeed, will result in a jurisdictional dismissal, which presumably entitles the plaintiff to sue again elsewhere unfettered by the res judicata doctrine, or bring about a judgment on the merits, perhaps by applying forum law after rejecting the foreign "penal" law. (A merits judgment will invoke the res judicata doctrine.) It is presumably a matter of what the forum intends the result to be. Because the "penal laws" objection rarely succeeds, rare is the occasion to reach these issues.

The facts of the Loucks case (NY 1918) illustrate how a defendant can try to inject the "penal laws" objection into a civil case. The action, brought in a New York court, was based on a wrongful death in Massachusetts, whose statute, a generator of much case law, set both upper and lower limits on the amount of recovery it would allow on a wrongful death claim. If the defendant was found to be at fault, the award of damages could not at the time be less than $500, even though the actual damages may not have been that much. Since this minimum aspect of the statute was not compensatory in its nature, the defendant said it was "penal" and that the action should therefore be dismissed by New York under the "penal laws" rule. Analogizing to forum rules authorizing punitive damages in civil cases and noting that the Massachusetts statute's purpose is not "atonement for a crime" but rather "solace to the individual who has suffered a private wrong", the court rejected the penal laws characterization and entertained the claim. (The Loucks case is also a major pronouncement on when the "public policy" objection can be cited by the forum in rejection of a foreign claim. Treatment of that aspect of the case and Judge Cardozo's often quoted statement on the point are in § 57.)

The success of the penal laws objection "depends upon the question whether its purpose is to punish an offence against the public justice of the State, or to afford a private remedy to a person injured by the wrongful act" (Huntington, USSC 1892). Only the former invokes the objection.

Conflicts among the states' penal laws are occasionally seen when a defendant just convicted of a felony in State F is up for sentence. The prosecutor says that the defendant is a second-felony offender under State F's definition of that term and must thus be given the higher sentence that State F applies to such offenders. The difficulty is that the earlier conviction, sought to be used as a prior felony conviction for the present sentencing purpose, was in State X for conduct that took place there. If State F invokes the higher penalty only when the earlier offense was also a felony, and State F and State X differ on the criminal classifications of given conduct, what shall State F do? Probably the soundest approach is that taken in People v. Olah (NY 1949). Since State F is invoking the multiple-offender rule, whether the earlier conduct and conviction in State X qualifies as an earlier offense under the State F statute must be governed by State F law. The State X indictment and conviction and all surrounding circumstances must be analyzed and a determination made as to whether, had the same conduct and conviction occurred in State F, it would have qualified as a prior conviction under State F's statute. So held Olah.

The Olah case is really an occupant of the choice of law scene. It illustrates, however, that when a true "penal" issue is at hand, the forum will not ordinarily invoke a law-choosing process. It will apply its own law, even translating relevant foreign events into terms of its own law for the purpose. Just as the State X prosecutor could not have brought her earlier prosecution in a State F court, so the impact of the prosecution that she brings in State X, to the extent relevant in a later State F case, may be measured by State F law.

§ 52. Tax Claims

At an earlier time it was assumed that a forum would refuse to entertain a claim by another state's tax official to collect the latter's taxes from a person found in the forum. Some cases so held (e.g., Colorado, NY 1921), but there is really no reason for such trepidation, at least within the United States where the federal constitution oversees all state and federal laws to assure minimal fairness. The refusal has therefore been criticized as encouraging "willful, dishonest tax evasion" (Oklahoma ex rel. Oklahoma Tax Comm'n, Ark.1955). Perhaps it is this supervisory function of the constitution that has led to today's more receptive attitude among the states of the United States. Tax claims have often been entertained in sister-state courts (e.g., J.A. Holshouser Co., No.Car.1905; City of Detroit, Ill.1957). Some states have reciprocity statutes in the tax area. These direct local courts to entertain the tax claims of only those states that do likewise (e.g., NY Tax L. § 902).

The U.S. Supreme Court, in holding that a *judgment* for taxes must be given full faith and credit (Milwaukee, USSC 1935), left open the question of whether the constitution requires a state to entertain a direct claim (i.e., one not yet reduced to judgment) for taxes by a sister state or one of its taxing units. Of course, the fact that recognition becomes mandatory when the tax claim is reduced to judgment teaches the taxing unit to bring the tax suit at home, invoking a longarm statute against the taxpayer if necessary (longarm jurisdiction is available for tax claims, see US v. Montreal Trust, CA2 cert.den. 1966). Since the judgment secures mandatory recognition and as simple a phenomenon as a longarm statute can secure that judgment at home, the taxing unit pursuing the taxpayer outside the state should do so with a judgment, which insists on recognition, instead of the underlying tax claim itself, whose call on recognition is less certain.

This so-called "revenue rule" has seen modern application in cases in which foreign governments have made claims under a federal statute known as

RICO (the Racketeer Influenced and Corrupt Organizations Act) for lost tax revenues due to alleged cigarette smuggling through their countries and into the United States. The federal courts, however, have refused to adjudicate these claims, holding that the venerable status of the revenue rule requires that it be clearly abrogated by Congress. Because Congress has not said that it wishes the federal courts to become the collection agents for foreign taxes due, those governments have thus far been left to proceed in their own courts. (Attorney Gen. of Canada, CA 2 cert. den. 2002).

§ 53. Forum Non Conveniens

Assume a case in which D is served with the summons by personal delivery in the forum, in a money action brought in a forum court of general jurisdiction. The court clearly has subject matter jurisdiction as well as jurisdiction of the defendant's person. But assume further that D is a nondomiciliary who just happened to be passing through the state, or is a company with only a minor office in the state; that P is also a nondomiciliary; and that the claim arose elsewhere and has no connection with the state. Although the court has jurisdiction of every kind, it is obvious that it should not have to entertain a case having no connection whatever with the forum. Indeed, to allow such cases to impose on the local judicial machinery would reduce its availability to local domiciliaries who through their taxes sustain it and to domestic claims that have the primary right to use it.

The doctrine of "forum non conveniens", or inconvenient forum, was devised to meet this problem. It protects the local courts from being imposed on by a case in which there is jurisdiction but which for want of a reasonable local relationship should be brought elsewhere.

Each state is on its own in devising forum non conveniens rules. A given state may have statutes addressed to the matter, or a body of decisional law setting up the principles, or a combination of both. Indeed, a given state may reject the doctrine altogether, electing to entertain every case that fits itself into jurisdiction.

The doctrine becomes relevant in a case entirely between nonresidents on a claim arising elsewhere, but under a given state's practice a conveniens dismissal may be allowed even when one of the parties is a local resident, as long as some other forum is the obviously more appropriate one. This last element is the touchstone. The position of the Restatement is that a conveniens dismissal will not be made unless "a more appropriate forum is available to the plaintiff" (Rst.2d § 84).

A number of factors to be considered in applying the conveniens doctrine were enumerated by the U.S. Supreme Court in Gulf (1947). They include

relative ease of access to sources of proof; availability of compulsory process for attendance of unwilling ... witnesses; possibility of view of premises ...; and all other practical problems that make trial of a case easy, expeditious and inexpensive. There may also be questions as to the enforceability of a judgment.... The court will weigh relative advantages and obstacles to fair trial.

Also acknowledged as a conveniens element in the Gulf case is "the private interest of the litigant". Convenience is considered from the vantage points of parties and court both.

The Gulf case of 1947 pronounced the doctrine as it would apply in the federal courts, but the very next year it was in some measure superseded in the federal courts by the enactment of § 1404(a) of Title 28 of the U.S. Code. While in most courts the application of the conveniens doctrine will result in a dismissal of the case—especially in state courts, which have no power to transfer their actions to other states—in the federal courts under § 1404(a) the doctrine results in a transfer of the action to the more convenient federal district, crossing state lines and even a continent for the purpose. The Gulf case, however, remains an important source of guidance for the elements to be considered in determining whether to make a § 1404(a) transfer, and it has been a beacon to state courts in the application of their internal conveniens principles.

There can still be a conveniens dismissal of a federal action, moreover, rather than a mere transfer, as where the more appropriate forum is a court in a foreign country. This is so even if the substantive law that would be applied there is less favorable to the plaintiff than the law the chosen forum would apply (Piper, USSC 1981). One also sees federal dismissals in deference to state-court jurisdiction, where they may be exercises of what are known in federal practice as the "abstention" doctrines (Wright, Fed.Cts. 6th ed. § 52).

Several situations sometimes discussed in terms of "jurisdiction" are more accurately treated as conveniens matters. One hears, for instance, of a rule that a court does not have jurisdiction of a case involving the internal affairs of a foreign corporation, but this is not a rule of jurisdiction; it is one of mere convenience. If the forum, while not the incorporating jurisdiction, is nonetheless a connected one in (for example) a corporate derivative action or an action designed to compel the declaration of a dividend or in some other way affect internal corporate management, and the forum has all needed jurisdiction over corporate directors and other interested persons, it can indeed entertain the case. If it chooses not to, it will be acting not under the rigid barrier of jurisdiction, but under the flexible doctrine of forum non conveniens (Rst.2d § 84, Comment d).

The same is true of an action that seeks to affect real property located elsewhere. Elsewhere is where the action usually belongs. Hence a court is likely to refuse on convenience grounds even so simple an action as one for the specific performance of a real property sale if the land is in another state, and will even more likely refuse the action when it is more complex, such as one to foreclose a mortgage on foreign land (Beach, Iowa 1933). But in special circumstances the action may be entertained, as where the subject property, covered by a blanket mortgage, is situated in several states. As soon as the word "may" appears, it ipso facto establishes that the question is not one of jurisdiction. Jurisdiction has no room for "may".

The court can effect a conveniens dismissal conditionally, and it's the technical presence of "jurisdiction" that enables a court to impose the condition. The imposing of a condition requires the exercise of power, and the existence of jurisdiction furnishes it. Thus a court dismissing an action under the conveniens doctrine may require the defendant to stipulate to accept process in a designated other place, or waive the statute of limitations that might otherwise bar an action in that place, or agree to the use there of the fruits of disclosure proceedings (e.g., depositions) already taken in the initial forum.

If a state's conveniens rules are reasonable, rejecting only cases wanting in legitimate forum contacts, they may even be applied to dismiss federal claims sued on in a state court (Missouri, USSC 1950). This is not an excuse for refusing to entertain a claim merely because it arises under federal law, however. Federal law is the supreme law of the land (Const. Art. VI [the "supremacy" clause]), and unless jurisdiction of a federal claim has been conferred on the federal courts exclusively by an Act of Congress, the jurisdiction is concurrent and the state court, when the plaintiff opts for it, can't reject the claim on the sole ground that it's a federal one. It amounts to unconstitutional discrimination (McKnett, USSC 1934).

The 11th Amendment may of course permit a state to insulate itself from federal jurisdiction, but the U.S. Supreme Court has held that even when it does, it does so only for the state and its arms—entities that have "traditionally enjoyed" 11th Amendment immunity; that the immunity does not extend to "municipalities, counties, and school districts" and the like; that an attempt so to extend it raises the suspicion that the state "may be evading federal law and discriminating against federal causes of action" (Howlett USSC 1990).

The Missouri and McKnett cases cited above involved the Federal Employers' Liability Act (FELA), which has generated a substantial body of case law, including some cases that address an endeavor by one court to stop an action in another, a subject taken up in § 54.

Another objection analogous to forum non conveniens is that the entertainment of the action will constitute an undue interference with the defendant's interstate commerce. This objection comes from the commerce clause of the federal constitution and becomes relevant when a court without reasonable contacts presumes to entertain a case against a commercially active defendant. The contacts to be examined in resolving the "commerce" objection are similar to if not the same as those obtaining under conveniens principles (Davis,

USSC 1923), and the major word from the U.S. Supreme Court on the subject is that the action need not be dismissed merely because it is a "burden" on the defendant's interstate activities. Every law suit is a burden. The burden will earn a dismissal only when it is found in context to be "oppressive and unreasonable" (International Milling, USSC 1934). The Davis case cited above resulted in a "commerce" dismissal because the forum lacked contacts with the transaction and claim and had insufficient contacts with the parties. By further analogy, this suggests that the presence of jurisdiction under a longarm statute, since it turns on contacts of that kind, would also tend to insulate the case from a commerce dismissal.

§ 54. Barring Actions Elsewhere

Related to the forum non conveniens doctrine, with which a court can dismiss one of its own actions, is an endeavor by a court in one state to stop an action in another. This is a mixed bag.

On several occasions, the U.S. Supreme Court has held that a court cannot enjoin a person from prosecuting an FELA claim in a court (federal or state) elsewhere, at least where the latter has reasonable contacts with the case (Baltimore, USSC 1941; Miles, USSC 1942). FELA is a federal law. When a state claim is involved, there has yet to be a definitive ruling about how far the state can go in enjoining prosecution of the claim elsewhere. The absence of guideposts accounts for some ugly situations.

One spectacular case is James (Ill.1958), in which courts in both Michigan and Illinois were issuing injunctions designed to stop proceedings in the other. A wrongful death occurred in Michigan through the alleged fault of a railroad. The widow, of Michigan (as was the deceased), was appointed administratrix there but elected to bring the wrongful death action in Illinois, where the railroad was also amenable to jurisdiction. The railroad then obtained a Michigan injunction to bar the widow's prosecution of the Illinois action, whereupon the Illinois court granted the widow a "counter-injunction" to bar the railroad from enforcing its Michigan injunction. One wonders whether the railroad did not then seek a "counter-counter-injunction" in Michigan so as to enjoin the widow from enforcing her Illinois counter-injunction for fear that she would then become a triple-counter-injunction threat with a further Illinois effort. Indeed, if proceedings like these are to be countenanced, revolving doors will have to be installed in all courthouses.

Probably the best place to draw the line is at the threshold, barring all such injunctions. If State X has and is willing to exercise jurisdiction, it is in almost every case a bad idea for State Y to try to stop it. Such an injunction will not be directed against the court or judge of the other state, of course, but rather against the party in State X who is the plaintiff in State Y, with the threat of a contempt sanction standing by. However that be, the court that starts such an injunction battle is asking for trouble. If it deems itself the better forum it should proceed to the merits expeditiously and anticipate full faith and credit for its judgment. If the other court, with all requisite jurisdiction, gets to judgment (and full faith and credit) first, the answer is that that's the way the cookie crumbles in a federal society.

The federal courts can enjoin state proceedings in some, but only a few, instances, tightly limited by 28 U.S.C.A. § 2283, the so-called "anti-injunction" statute. When such an instance is at hand, however (see Mitchum, USSC 1972, for a list of instances), the injunction can if need be run against the judge of the offending state court, and result in a federal contempt citation against him, a rare but possible event.

Trepidation in this sphere is healthy, recognizing the friction generated by inter-court injunction fights.

When a state injunction against a proceeding in another state's court does issue, the latter often ignores it and just gets on with the merits. The U.S. Supreme Court has yet to say that such an injunction is entitled to full faith and credit, but strongly hinted in Baker v. GM (USSC 1998) that it would not. In that case, the Supreme Court held that a Missouri court need not give effect to a Michigan injunction purporting to bar a former employee of the defendant from testifying against it in a products suit because to honor the injunction would allow the Michigan court to unreasonably interfere in the Missouri proceedings. If such an injunction constitutes unreasonable interference, it's hard to see how an injunction purporting to stop litigation in its tracks in another state court can survive. If the purpose at hand is to avoid duplicate actions, the party intent on avoiding them should ask one of the courts to dismiss or at least stay its own proceeding in deference to the other's. That may not work but should at least be tried.

A state may try to prevent another state's court from hearing a given claim by making a law purporting to retain exclusive jurisdiction at home, thereby trying with a law to accomplish what its courts were trying to do with injunctions in the prior examples. But when a state creates a right, it can't insist that the right be asserted only in its own courts. If a court elsewhere has jurisdiction and is willing to entertain the claim, it can ignore that part of the creating-state's law that purports to limit jurisdiction or venue to local courts only. A major case so holding is Tennessee Coal (USSC 1914), which allowed a Georgia court to entertain a personal injury claim arising in Alabama and governed by Alabama law despite a provision in the Alabama statute creating the claim to the effect that only in Alabama courts would the claim lie.

The court in Tennessee Coal said that the case might be different if "right and remedy are so united" that only a special tribunal set up by the creating state could hear it, but there was later a change of heart even on that score. In Crider (USSC 1965), an Alabama court was allowed to entertain a claim for workers' compensation arising in Georgia in the teeth of a Georgia statute that purported to confer exclusive jurisdiction on its own compensation board. (There appears to be some kind of tradition forming that all case law on this subject is to arise at the Alabama–Georgia border.)

If a court (F–1) has rendered a judgment with adequate jurisdiction, the judgment can't be refused recognition on the basis that F–2, where recognition is sought, feels that F–1 was not an appropriate forum. This is so even when F–1 has taken a radical step. In Buttron (Texas Ct.Civ.App.1906), for example, New Mexico (then a territory) had a peculiar statute that permitted an alleged tortfeasor to sue the locally injured person—reversing the usual lineup of a tort action—in the hope of forcing adjudication of the claim (and obtaining a judgment of no liability) in New Mexico. The injured person was duly served in New Mexico in such an action, but defaulted. The resulting judgment was nevertheless held entitled to recognition. New Mexico had carried out all jurisdictional requirements and there was nothing in the federal constitution to prevent New Mexico from putting the cart before the horse. Its judgment constituted a good defense to the injured person's later suit against the railroad (the plaintiff in the New Mexico action) in Texas.

CHAPTER IV

CHOICE OF LAW

A. PRELIMINARIES

§ 55. Choice of Law, Introductory

The second of the three major conflicts topics, in the chronological order in which they are usually met in litigation, is choice of law, but if the progression were in the order of challenge and difficulty, choice of law would come first.

The uncomplicated exemplar of a choice of law situation is a case in which jurisdiction is clearly present but both the forum (State F) and another state (State X) have had substantial contacts with the transaction and the parties. Assume that P is from State F and that D is from State X. D was driving his car and P, his friend, was a passenger. There was an accident and P was hurt. A key issue has arisen: whether P has a cause of action against D. There is no more fundamental issue in the law. Even assume that D was negligent. The problem is that one of the states has what is known in tort law as a "guest-host" statute, which bars a claim by a guest-passenger against a host-driver. The other state has no such barrier and would sustain P's claim. The only question is, whose law governs? But what a question! For P's claim, it is literally a question of life or death. How shall it be answered? Should State F apply its own law automatically? May it? Is there anything in the federal constitution that stops it, or requires it to apply the other state's law? Does the full faith and credit clause require that? Is it even relevant? Is anything else in the constitution relevant? If the constitution is no barrier and the choice is up to State F, what elements should State F consider in making its choice? These are some of the questions that can arise in a choice of law situation, and on even as simple a set of facts as the one in our example.

And if the lawyers and the judge have noted all of the issues, which is no small accomplishment in itself, and have properly decided what sources to look to for their resolution, which is also no mean accomplishment in itself, and have gone to those sources, they had all better hope that the sources consulted will supply the answers needed.

Choice of law considerations are seldom taken into consideration by a legislature. Legislators are almost always preoccupied with substantive rights and issues, so that when they enact a law, even after much debate and deliberation, the new law is likely to contain no treatment of how it fits into a situation in which some other state also has an interest. No wonder, then, that most "choice of law" rules come from case law. Few statutes address the subject, although there are some important exceptions, to be met in due course (e.g., §§ 71, 72, 92).

"Choice of law" is untidy. Elements of it can sometimes overlap even the subject of jurisdiction, posing fascinating issues. If, for example, State F–1 purports to exploit a certain jurisdictional basis— say, a stipulation in a contract agreeing to F–1 jurisdiction—and in an action based on such a stipulation the defendant defaults and the default judgment seeks recognition in F–2, which does not recognize a contract as a source of jurisdiction, the very question of whether State F–1 had jurisdiction will turn on whether it was permissible for F–1 to choose its own law to determine the issue.

Suppose, for another example, that the parties are all domiciliaries of F–2, where the contract was made and to be performed. F–1's only "contact" was that the parties agreed in the contract to F–1's jurisdiction. Did that agreement by itself supply F–1 with a sufficient nexus in the constitutional sense so that F–1, willing enough to entertain jurisdiction, got it? The issue turns on whether a contract is by itself a sufficient basis for jurisdiction. F–1 says it is; F–2 says it is not. It would seem to be a simple question of choice of law, and yet the very issue of jurisdiction depends on the choice.

If F–1, as the initial forum, has the initial choice, who can prevent F–1 from choosing as it will? Certainly F–2 cannot dictate F–1's choices. True enough, but has the federal constitution, to which F–1 and F–2 are both subject, nothing to say here? Is F–1 unfettered in its choices? Can F–1, if it wishes, assume jurisdiction in a case with which it has no connection at all, and over parties with whom it has no connection at all, except for a contract containing a statement void by the law of the only jurisdiction having any connection with the contract? It would probably be unconstitutional.

Before examining into the diverse choice of law rules one sees applied in a variety of substantive contexts, it is well to examine the scope given by the federal constitution to the states in their adoption of choice of law rules. The states are not free to choose whatever they wish. There are indeed constitutional restrictions, but the impact of the lot of them will be found in most cases merely to set outer limits on state options, permitting the states broad scope within those outer limits and thus building a choice of law arena with many rings and an endless progression of absorbing performances.

In the ensuing treatment, constitutional elements will start things off, after which choice of law rules themselves will be pursued. They lie at the nucleus of a big cell, which is best penetrated gradually. The statute of limitations will be an early subject. It will act as an appropriate introduction to other matters sometimes said to concern mere "procedure"— which the forum takes from its own law without going through a law-choosing process—but which often defy the "procedure" category in conflicts context and require treatment as if substantive. When treated as substantive they set in motion the law-choosing process that is supposedly restricted to only substantive issues. Some issues of burden of proof and evidence also end up in that seemingly procedural but actually substantive category.

There is also the threshold question, when foreign law is relevant, of how a party gets the court to apply it. And there is the important "public policy" matter, which, carelessly applied, could easily become an excuse for a forum to refuse to apply any foreign law at all. That has not come to pass, and only judicial reins on this wild "public policy" creature account for that.

Choice of law rules will be treated in their substantive law contexts—contract, tort, compensation, succession, property, divorce, and the like—because it is always in context that the lawyer meets them in practice.

§ 56. Constitutional   Considerations   in Choice of Law

Several provisions of the federal constitution are relevant to the choice of law process, but the U.S. Supreme Court has not always been consistent about which of them shall be allowed a role, or the extent of it. It is not hard to find seeds of relevancy in the full faith and credit, due process, privileges and immunities, equal protection, supremacy, and contracts clauses, and perhaps even others, but only a few have been allowed to germinate. Because the dozen or so key cases from the Supreme Court reflect on several clauses and show an interplay among them, they are best treated together. That's the effort that will be made in this section, a strenuous one that makes the section the longest in the book. An attempt to break it into smaller pieces, perhaps giving each constitutional clause its own section, would not work as well.

The case at the top of the constitutional heap is Home Insurance Co. v. Dick (USSC 1930), and it manifests that the potent overseer of choice of law is the due process clause (Amendments 5 and 14) of the federal constitution.

The full faith and credit clause of course embraces judgments ("judicial proceedings"), and for that reason plays a dominant role in the recognition and enforcement of judgments, the third major conflicts subject, studied in Chapter VI in this book. But the clause also speaks of the "public acts" of the states, language that could easily lend itself to a judicial construction that would give full faith and credit a prime role on the choice of law scene. It has not been given that construction, however. The principal reason is that if it were, every forum hearing a case also having contacts with a sister state would have to defer its own law to the sister state's, thereby creating the paradox whereby application of the law of one state could be obtained only by suit in the other. Such a rigid application of the full faith and credit clause would be "absurd", said the Supreme Court (Alaska, 1935), and retired the clause from such service in all but a few cases (to be met in due course).

Hence today, if two states have interests in the case, and even strong policies underlying the different rules of law they would apply to an issue, and one will have to give way, the decision of which one that will be is the forum's, unhindered by the full faith and credit clause (Pacific, USSC 1939).

That leaves due process to act as superintendent, and it has become a watchful but lenient parent. A state can devise whatever choice of law rules it wishes, to apply in whatever situations it designates, provided only that the law chosen be that of a place having a reasonable connection to the transaction or occurrence involved. A party cannot be expected to anticipate that his rights will be governed by the law of a place lacking such a connection. It would not be fair, and due process is just a synonym for fairness. But if each of several states has "a sufficiently substantial contact with the activity" involved in the case (Richards, USSC 1962), the forum can choose the law of any of them to govern the consequences of the activity.

Home Ins. Co. v. Dick involved a Texas action on a fire insurance policy. The policy was issued to a Mexican in Mexico for coverage of a vessel only in Mexican waters. It required that suit be brought within a year after a loss. Plaintiff, a Texas domiciliary to whom the policy had been assigned, brought the action in a Texas court (in rem jurisdiction was the basis but need not concern us here) after the year had expired. Under Mexican law the one-year contract limitation was valid; under Texas law it was not. The U.S. Supreme Court held that Texas was too lacking in contacts to permit it to apply its own law and preserve the case: the Texas attempt "to impose a greater obligation than that agreed upon and to seize property in payment of the imposed obligation violates the guaranty against deprivation of property without due process of law". An endeavor to classify the issue as involving mere "remedy" (i.e., "procedure") instead of "substance" was rejected in the Dick case. The court said that the issue "deals with the powers and capacities of persons" and cannot be obscured with a label.

Today, when a court writes about whether a given choice is constitutionally available, the Dick case usually leads the citations.

When the competition is between only two states, and a want of contacts on the part of one of them eliminates its law under the due process clause, the other becomes the winner by default. Some cases attribute that result to the full faith and credit clause, but congratulations are unwarranted. In John Hancock (USSC 1936), for instance, New York had all of the contacts with a life insurance policy, and only after the insured died did his spouse move to Georgia and sue on the policy. A defense was interposed, good under New York law but invalid under Georgia law. The U.S. Supreme Court held that Georgia's sustaining of the claim by applying its own law to bar the defense denied full faith and credit to New York law. The court stressed that there were no Georgia contacts that could serve as a basis for the application of Georgia law.

Had there been such Georgia contacts in John Hancock, it would have been no less a denial of "credit" to New York law for Georgia to have applied its own, but now the denial would have been a permissible one. Confused semantics is a by-product of injecting full faith and credit into this test. Due process does the job better, and it can be argued that it has in fact won out in Supreme Court favor in later cases. Even on the John Hancock facts it is conceptually more comfortable to say, not that Georgia was denying full faith and credit to New York law, but rather that Georgia was denying due process to the defendant by applying Georgia law. The operative constraint was not the affirmative one of full faith and credit pointing to New York law, but rather the negative one of due process barring Georgia law—and thus leaving New York, as the only state with contacts, the winner by a process of elimination.

Perhaps the reason for the lingering appearance of the full faith and credit clause on the choice of law scene is the treatment it got in Hughes v. Fetter (USSC) in 1951. But Hughes is not a typical choice of law case at all. It is an unusual situation that arose when Wisconsin backed itself into a corner. One of its residents was killed in an Illinois accident involving another Wisconsin resident, and the decedent's personal representative, also of Wisconsin, brought a wrongful death action in Wisconsin. Wrongful death actions, as creatures of statute, were at the time held applicable only to deaths resulting from injuries within the state, and here the injury occurred in Illinois. This was a rigid view and is relaxed in some quarters today (see § 76). It was not a restriction imposed by the constitution, but Wisconsin subscribed to it as a matter of internal preference. Wisconsin had its own wrongful death statute, however, which it could have chosen to apply to the case (its residential contacts with the parties were sufficient for that), but it refused to. It held that its statute could apply only to deaths caused in Wisconsin, and, moreover, that this evinced a policy against entertaining an action brought under another state's wrongful death statute. The result was Wisconsin's dismissal of an action entirely between Wisconsin residents because, said Wisconsin, the Wisconsin statute is inapplicable and the Illinois statute, though applicable, will not be entertained in a Wisconsin court. This was a losing combination for Wisconsin in the Hughes case. The U.S. Supreme Court, reversing, held that Wisconsin could not refuse the parties a forum by citing as a reason that Wisconsin would not apply Illinois law.

Forum non conveniens principles could not have supported the dismissal because of the Wisconsin residence of the parties. Indeed, noted the court, problems of jurisdiction might have made Wisconsin the only available forum. As a result, Wisconsin discriminated (irrationally, it would seem) between decedents lucky enough to die in Wisconsin and those killed elsewhere. And public policy could not be cited because the fact that Wisconsin had its own wrongful death statute meant that Wisconsin had "no real feeling of antagonism against wrongful death suits in general".

Having no legitimate basis on which to deny the parties a forum, Wisconsin's basing its denial on a refusal to apply the Illinois wrongful death statute amounted to denying Illinois law full faith and credit. The Hughes case is best relied on to establish a state's obligation to supply a forum under circumstances similar to those in Hughes. It is hardly a straightforward choice of law lesson. Full faith and credit was not telling Wisconsin that it had to choose Illinois law for the case. It was only telling Wisconsin that if it wished by its own lights to withdraw its own law from the competition, leaving only Illinois law in the picture, it could not then reject the Illinois law. It is only that unusual combination of factors that invoked the full faith and credit clause in Hughes, and the combination is rare enough to suggest that Hughes gives the clause slim pickings in the choice of law vineyard.

An aggravating element in Hughes was the fact—at least the court assumed it was a fact—that Wisconsin was the only available forum. It was afterwards held (First National, USSC 1952) that full faith and credit would be equally offended in such circumstances even if it did appear that another forum was available. A statute that excludes local jurisdiction for the sole reason that the claim arises under sister state law is a denial of full faith and credit whether the foreign place would be able the hear the case or not.

There have been instances in the past when the full faith and credit clause was applied by the

Supreme Court to require a state to make a particular choice despite what appeared to be contacts with two states such that due process would admit an application of the law of either, but with a backtracking to the due process position afterwards. Juxtaposing such cases strengthens the governing position of the due process clause. In Bradford (USSC 1932), for example, the Vermont workers' compensation act declared itself the exclusive remedy in a given situation and barred an ordinary tort action. When Vermont was the state of the employment contract in such a situation, New Hampshire, the state where the injury occurred during the employment, was held bound by full faith and credit to apply Vermont law and bar the tort claim, deferring its own law, which would have permitted it. Bradford was sent into history when on indistinguishable facts the Supreme Court held (Carroll, USSC 1955) that full faith and credit did not bar the state of the injury (Arkansas) from allowing a tort claim despite the law of the place of the employment contract (Missouri) purporting to make compensation benefits the exclusive remedy. The court in Carroll said that "Arkansas ... is not adopting any policy of hostility to the public Acts of Missouri. It is choosing to apply its own rule of law to ... an action arising within its borders."

One can translate this to say that full faith and credit is simply not in issue when two concerned states have different laws and a choice must be made; that due process reigns, and permits the forum to choose either. This is of course the simple, classic fact pattern of choice of law. When the facts vary, and the issues are similar but not the same (as in the Hughes case), so that the sailing is not all that clear for due process and a little navigational aid from another nearby vessel, though not indispensable, is helpful, perhaps that's where full faith and credit is allowed the feeling of participation. Or, as long as we keep in mind the variability of the fact situations and the expressed Supreme Court preferences in each of them, perhaps we can say that the two clauses travel nearly parallel courses: due process watchful that the state does right by the individual litigant and full faith and credit attentive to the states' obligations among their sovereign selves.

The position that when two states have contacts the forum can apply the law of either appears to have become the due process beacon-in-chief. The Supreme Court has retreated to it from other, more arbitrary, positions it took earlier even on the due process clause itself. In Hartford (USSC 1934), for example, an employee fidelity bond issued in Tennessee to cover employees in several places, including Mississippi, was held to require a Mississippi court to defer to Tennessee law, which sustained an abbreviated limitation period in the contract and barred an action as untimely under it. Mississippi would have held such a provision void, but was precluded from choosing its own law despite the fact that Mississippi was the scene of the defalcation and the domicile of the defalcating employee.

Due process was the ground cited, and there was some talk about the obligations of contracts.

The obligations of contracts were also involved in the cases in which the Supreme Court in effect took back its Hartford conclusions. In Watson (USSC 1946), a Louisiana woman was injured in Louisiana by a hair product she bought there. Louisiana allowed a direct action against the foreign insurer of the foreign manufacturer of this nationally-sold product, but such a direct action was barred by the insurance policy itself. It had a prohibitory clause that was valid under the laws of the states where the insurance contract was negotiated and delivered (Massachusetts and Illinois). No matter, said the Supreme Court, sustaining the direct action: Louisiana has a "legitimate interest in safeguarding the rights of persons injured there", and this interest permits it to choose its own law despite the additional involvement and interest of other states. The Hartford case can hardly breathe in that new air.

Clay (USSC 1964) also involved insurance, and can also be cited as hostile to the Hartford result, although Clay by its distinguishing language purports to be at peace with it. In Clay, a personal property loss was sustained in Florida. It was insured by a policy issued to the policy holder in Illinois, where he was domiciled at the time of issuance, only afterwards moving to Florida. Again the policy had an abbreviated period which had expired by the time the Florida suit was brought. The time curtailment was valid under Illinois but not Florida law. The Supreme Court held it permissible for Florida to apply its own rule, invalidate the time restriction, and sustain the suit. The contract was "ambulatory", said the court, effective wherever the loss was sustained and putting the insurer on notice that it could be subjected to the laws of other states that might become legitimately involved, like Florida at bar.

It is interesting to note that the issue in many of these key constitutional cases was the validity of a contract clause purporting to limit the time within which an action under the contract might be brought. The Home Insurance, Hartford, and Clay cases had it. The Hartford position, mandating that the validity of such a provision be judged only by the law of the place of contracting, is largely abandoned today. The Clay rule, that a second state having reasonable contacts with the case may refuse to apply the clause (and may thus sustain an action brought after the stipulated period) is the one now applied. It is compatible with the rule of the Home Insurance case, that when the clause is valid by the law of the only state having contacts, and the forum state itself lacks them, the forum may not refuse to apply the clause (and must therefore dismiss the action as untimely).

In effect, this is the same as saying that a forum can't apply its own statute of limitations to keep alive a claim already barred by the law of the place with which the transaction had its sole contacts. Yet that's not the rule when the statute of limitations is involved before the court directly rather than through a contract. There, the court is free to apply its own local statute of limitations even though the forum has had no significant contacts with the case at all. (Ferens, USSC 1990; see § 61.)

In holding that neither full faith and credit nor due process is offended when a forum with reasonable contacts applies its own law rather than that of another connected state to an issue concerning an insurance company, the Clay case distinguishes cases affecting the fraternal benefit society. The society is a category of insurer with an "indivisible unity" and "unique", says the Supreme Court, and all matters of its operation must therefore be resolved under the law of its incorporating state (Order of United, USSC 1947). The court does not find such a result necessary in the case of an ordinary insurance company, however, and the case of the fraternal society is an exceedingly rare example of where the Supreme Court has adopted or countenanced a rigid choice of law rule.

Unlike the full faith and credit clause of Article IV of the constitution, whose primary if not sole mission is in what is broadly known as the conflict of laws area, the other constitutional precepts one meets in conflicts do their main work elsewhere. This is so of the due process clause, already much discussed, and it is notably the case with the other 14th Amendment entries: the privileges and immunities and the equal protection clauses. Neither aims exclusively at a multi-state situation. Either can become operative to restrict a state's activities with respect to its own people when no outsiders are involved at all, and probably for that reason these clauses are not regarded in law school curricula as the exclusive possession of the conflicts course. A case nevertheless becomes a conflict of laws entry, by an overlap if nothing else, whenever the state action complained of is designed to differentiate a local domiciliary or resident from an out-of-stater, and especially when the design contains a disadvantage for the outsider, as it usually does. So, for example, when an estate is insolvent and lacks sufficient assets to pay off all its creditors, state action that seeks to favor local over foreign creditors may be stricken down as a privileges and immunities violation, as it was in C.G. Blake Co. (USSC 1898). And in a case of this kind today the equal protection clause would probably be just as relevant and effective.

Of course, the role of the supremacy clause (Article VI of the federal constitution) must be remembered. It requires state courts to apply all federal law relevant to cases before them, an instruction so obvious that one may forget to classify it as a choice of law lesson. A state court can't refuse to entertain an action merely because it involves federal law, for example. It can, however, if it does so even-handedly, apply something like a forum non conveniens rule and dismiss the claim on that ground. (Should the claim then be brought in a federal court, however, the state court's determination is not binding and the federal court can apply its own conveniens standards to it. [Parsons, USSC 1963; § 105.])

In a sense, though, all of this is prologue, because the Supreme Court eventually merged the due process and full faith and credit tests in Allstate Ins. Co. v. Hague (USSC 1981). In that case, the plaintiff's husband, a lifelong Wisconsite, died in a motorcycle accident in his home state. Minnesota insurance law, however, was more favorable, so his widow brought the suit in the Minnesota state court, hoping it would apply Minnesota insurance law, and it did. The contacts with Minnesota were slight. The decedent had actually worked in Minnesota (he had lived right across the border), Allstate (as its name would suggest) did (and still does) business in all states including Minnesota, and the decedent's widow had relocated to Minnesota for apparently unrelated reasons after the lawsuit had begun. Not much, but good enough for the court to find that the Minnesota courts did not violate the constitution in applying their own law. The court ruled that courts may apply their own law as long as they "have a significant contact or significant aggregation of contacts, creating state interests, such that choice of its law is neither arbitrary nor fundamentally unfair".

In light of Allstate, many concluded that just about any choice of law would survive constitutional scrutiny. Close, but not quite. In Phillips Petrol. v. Shutts (USSC, 1985) the court decided that Kansas's decision to apply its own law to disputes involving royalty payments on gas wells in other states was unconstitutional. At least as to the disputes involving wells in other states, owned by residents living in other states, there was literally nothing to connect the cases to Kansas, other than that its courts provided the forum.

But later the court made clear that it would only rarely upset a court's choice of law. In Franchise Tax Board v. Hyatt (USSC, 2003) the Supreme Court allowed Nevada to override California's sovereign immunity. In that case a Nevada citizen complained that the California tax authorities were being overly aggressive in attempting to collect taxes from him. In their efforts, of course, those agents of California contacted the Nevada would-be taxpayer, disturbing his blissful existence at home. California would have immunized the defendants, but Nevada law allowed some of the claims to proceed, and they could do so constitutionally, said the Supreme Court. "Significant" contacts doesn't necessarily mean "most of" the contacts, and Nevada had significant contacts in Hyatt.

§ 57. Rejecting Foreign Law on "Public Policy" Grounds

At an earlier juncture there was some discussion of "public policy" as a barrier to the maintenance of a court action (§ 50). It was treated there because it affected jurisdiction in the sense that the forum might close its judicial doors altogether if the foreign right was found to offend the forum's "public policy". An alternative possibility is that the court will entertain the action but refuse to apply the foreign law, and in that event a judgment on the merits can be the result. The latter possibility makes the "public policy" issue germane here, but on the American scene, where the federal constitution imposes minimum standards of fairness on all of the states, uncommon is the appearance of a law so offensive to a forum's "public policy" that the forum will refuse to apply it.

It is impossible to define a state's "public policy". Presumably it is the entirety of the state's law, whether embodied in statutes, rules, decisions, ordinances, or any other equivalent compilation. If that is its definition, then it could be argued that any foreign claim or rule of law not having a precise counterpart in forum law would violate forum "policy", and that would mean in turn that a state would "never enforce different laws of another state" (Curtis, CA3 1935). That is of course not the case.

A foreign law need not be shown to have a local counterpart before it is recognized and applied. Before a foreign claim or law is rejected on the ground that it violates forum "public policy", the forum feeling about the matter must be shown to be a deep one, to touch on something the forum deems to involve moral values rather than just a different way of doing things. The classic formulation of the standard is this often quoted language of Judge Cardozo in the Loucks case (NY 1918), whose facts are reviewed in § 51:

The courts are not free to refuse to enforce a foreign right at the pleasure of the judges, to suit the individual notion of expediency or fairness. They do not close their doors unless help would violate some fundamental principle of justice, some prevalent conception of good morals, some deep-rooted tradition of the common weal.

A good illustration is what occurred in New York in respect of gambling transactions in Intercontinental Hotels (NY 1964). New York does not allow private betting, and for a time this was held to be a moral issue so deep that New York would also refuse to entertain a claim on a foreign gambling transaction valid where incurred. Then New York in Intercontinental took into account that New York did recognize betting at the racetrack, and that off-track betting was on its way in as well. Hence, although the state might still not permit private betting as an internal matter, a bet could not be deemed so immoral as to require the New York courts to reject it even if the state of its making upheld it. However one might describe the difference between a bet at a racetrack window and one made at some other place, it would be difficult to cast the difference in terms of morality. Hence New York undertook to enforce the foreign gambling claim; it did not violate "public policy" in the conflict of laws sense.

Curiously, it was another New York case (Mertz, NY 1936) that has earned some questionable distinction as an example of a "public policy" violation that did result in the rejection of foreign law. H's negligent driving in Connecticut resulted in an injury to his wife, W. Both were New Yorkers. New York at the time barred tort actions between spouses; Connecticut did not. New York refused to entertain the action on the ground that the suit would offend New York's public policy. The assumption was that Connecticut law would ordinarily govern, based on the then-applicable rule that all issues in tort cases are governed by the law of the place of the tort (§ 65). Today, a "public policy" issue of this kind might not arise in such a case at all because the inter-spouse suit issue would likely be governed directly by the law of the marital domicile rather than the situs of the tort. That would avoid the two-step process whereby in Mertz (1) the situs of the accident rule was assumed to govern the issue but (2) it was refused implementation because it was found to violate the forum's public policy.

In the few instances in which the public policy objection is seen, it is usually the plaintiff's claim that is accused of the violation. But it may happen that a defense is alleged to violate the policy. That is what lay tacitly at the root of Holzer (NY 1938), an action for wrongful discharge. Plaintiff was a German Jew dismissed by the defendant corporation whose defense was that it was forced to the dismissal under the pressure of the Nazi regime. The court recognized that Nazi law, whatever the rest of the world might think of it, was supreme in Germany (see § 98). It sidestepped the issue by refusing to dismiss the action at the pleading stage and deferring a final resolution to the trial.

One may ask how much room there is today for an American court to refuse a sister-state claim on the ground that it offends forum public policy. The answer is: little. And what little there is exists only if the claim is sued on directly. If it has been sued on in another state's court, and a judgment has been duly rendered on it, and it is the judgment that is seeking recognition, there is probably no room at all today for a refusal of recognition. Here the issue is no longer the entertainment of a sister-state claim, but rather the recognition of a sister-state judgment, which is virtually an absolute obligation (Milwaukee, USSC 1935; § 112).

Claim-rejecting phenomena akin to "public policy" are the rules about a forum not undertaking to enforce another state's penal laws or tax laws. Those subjects were treated in §§ 51 and 52.

B. STATUTE OF LIMITATIONS

§ 58. Statute of Limitations

Nothing is more deadly to a plaintiff than an effective visit from the statute of limitations. This is as true of conflict of laws as it is of a state's internal law. It is quite an experience to bring an action in time only to learn that it has been measured by the wrong yardstick and is not timely at all. The lawyer happy with the statute of limitations is one who represents only defendants. For the defendant it will usually put an end to the case as finally as a victory on the merits, and without the inconvenience of a trial. Hence the plaintiff who plays loose with the time elements of a case is courting trouble. Mark Twain put it better when he observed that a person who picks a bull up by the tail is about to get a world of information.

If there are several possible forums in a case having multistate contacts, the plaintiff's lawyer about to make a choice must inquire into a number of things (§ 86), foremost among them being the statute of limitations. That inquiry must address not only the internal limitation period applicable to the claim under the law of each of the states involved in the case (along with its respective "tolling" provisions—provisions that operate to stop, extend, or otherwise influence the running of the period on stated contingencies)—but also the question of what limitations period each forum would apply to a case having foreign elements. Will the forum apply its own limitations period to domestic and foreign claims alike? Will it apply only the foreign one to a foreign claim? If there are several other states involved, which one's period will be looked to? Will there be any kind of "mixing" of elements, so that (for example) the choice of the local or foreign period may depend on whether the plaintiff is a forum resident? Each of these potentially conflicting questions, with yet other variations, can probably find an affirmative answer in one state or another.

If the client has come to the lawyer late in the game, and careful research considering all (including choice of law) elements reveals that there is only one possible forum in which the claim would be deemed alive, there will be little need to treat any further choice of forum considerations. Keeton (USSC 1984; § 61) is a striking illustration of that. The lawyer may hope that the open forum is his own. If it is some other, the lawyer's duty is to retain counsel for suit there.

As elaborated in § 61, addressing constitutional factors in choosing a period of limitation in a conflicts setting, full faith and credit does not require a state, when it entertains a foreign claim, to apply the foreign period of limitations to it (Wells, USSC 1953). This leaves the matter largely to forum preference, and each forum determines for itself whether to apply to a foreign claim the forum or the foreign law in respect of a time limitation, or some combination of both (Rst.2d § 142). A number of states have "borrowing statutes", by which is meant a statute that directs the court to apply the foreign period to a foreign claim in designated situations, usually only if its effect will be to bar the action. The typical approach of these statutes is to hold the claim barred if barred by either the forum or foreign period, in effect insisting that a foreign claim be alive under both before imposing on the forum (Girth, Mo.1966). Some of these borrowing statutes may apply only the forum period if the claim, although foreign, accrued to a forum resident. If the forum period is alive and the foreign one dead at the moment of suit, a statute of that genre has the effect of preserving the claim only for the local plaintiff, a discrimination against nonresidents that the U.S. Supreme Court has held permissible because not "fundamental" enough to breach the privileges and immunities clause (Art. IV, § 2) of the federal constitution (Canadian, USSC 1920; § 61).

If there are only two states involved, the forum and the one in which the operative facts of the claim took place, there will be little trouble in determining whose statute to "borrow" under a borrowing statute. But if several foreign states have had some involvement, and the forum's borrowing statute speaks (for example) only of the state in which the claim "arose", there may be difficulty in singling out which of the foreign states that may be. An analysis of the policies underlying the given forum's borrowing statute may be necessary, and may even lead to the application of the limitations period not of the place where the claim technically "arose", but of some other state having different but even more compelling contacts. In George (CA2, cert. den. 1964), for example, New York was the forum of a tort claim involving a breach of warranty, Florida was the place of the airplane crash, and California the place of the plane's manufacture. The court held, under the New York borrowing statute, that California was the place where the claim "arose".

Some courts have decided that the question of whose period of limitations applies to a foreign claim should be resolved by applying the same choice of law principles applicable to the substantive issues in the case (e.g., Central, Wis.1974), or simply held that the foreign period of limitations should be adopted when the foreign substantive law is being chosen (e.g., Henry, CA3 1975, applying New Jersey choice of law). Others say that the policy purposes differ and reject that approach (e.g., Sack, CA2 1973, ostensibly applying New York choice of law).

If a lawyer were off-handedly asked to niche the statute of limitations under a "substantive" or "procedural" label, the response would almost always be "procedural". This merits some attention. We have noted that nothing in the law disposes of a case more conveniently than a valid timeliness objection. The case is ordinarily as dead as if a jury had rendered a merits verdict for the defendant. And yet many lawyers persist in treating or at least calling a timeliness issue one of mere "procedure". If a client's case is dead, and his lawyer informs him that it is only the result of a rule of "procedure", the client is not likely to celebrate.

We may call the statute of limitations what we will, but we must treat it with no less respect than we would reserve for the guillotine. The reason that it is often niched as a "procedural" matter is that in our jurisprudence an objection of untimeliness is generally treated as an affirmative defense for the defendant to plead and prove. This means that a plaintiff can plead his claim with no reference whatever to its time elements, because a late claim is nonetheless a valid one and will in fact survive unless the defendant properly raises the timeliness objection. A wise plaintiff would best assume that she is up against a wise defendant, and that the statute of limitations will, if relevant, be used.

The theory underlying this rule is that the passing of the period does not bar the right; it merely suspends the remedy. Try explaining that one to a client. Death is notably wanting in gradations.

When the cause of action is one created by statute rather than through the decisional processes of the common law, and the creating statute has also affixed a limitations period to the new claim, the theory underlying the time period may be treated differently. Many states hold this kind of limitations period to be "substantive" in the sense that right and remedy are intertwined to such a degree that the passing of the period destroys the claim substantively (Bournias, CA2 1955). Here timeliness may be deemed a substantive element (a "condition precedent") of the claim, which removes it from the "defense" category and makes it the plaintiff's burden both of pleading and of proof. Things cannot be taken for granted here either, however. The classic illustration of a claim that would meet this criterion is the wrongful death action, a statute-created claim unknown to the common law and usually enacted with an accompanying period of limitation. Some states may elect, however, to treat the period as an ordinary suspend-the-remedy kind (e.g., Sharrow,

NY 1915), and a defendant who neglects to plead the time barrier as a defense on the theory that it is the plaintiff's burden to address it may find the timeliness objection untimely.

When the parties seek to provide a limitation (usually a short one) in a contract, the validity of the period selected will likely turn on choice of law principles applicable in the contract area. The forum will have some freedom of choice here, too, however, provided that the law ultimately chosen is that of a reasonably related state. It was a forum endeavor to apply its own law in this context, when it lacked adequate contacts, that generated the leading constitutional case on choice of law. That was the Home Insurance case (USSC 1930; § 56), in which Texas was precluded, for want of a reasonable relationship to the activities at issue, from applying its own law to invalidate an abbreviated time period valid under the law of Mexico, which had all of the significant contacts with the case.

§ 59. Laches

Related to the statute of limitations is the doctrine of laches. Laches is an equitable doctrine usually applied only to those claims that evolved through the English court of chancery (e.g., claims for an injunction, specific performance of a contract, reformation, formal rescission, and the like). The statute of limitations is an arbitrary time period, while laches is a doctrine applied sui generis. Laches bars the claim if on the facts of the particular case the plaintiff has waited an unreasonable time to sue and the defendant is prejudiced by the delay (loss of witnesses and evidence, changes in value of property involved, etc.). The Restatement's position is that "the local law of the forum determines whether an action is barred by laches" (Rst.2d § 142, Comment b).

§ 60. Statute of Limitations in Federal Actions

The plaintiff must be particularly sensitive to the statute of limitations in federal actions, and mindful of the basis on which federal subject matter jurisdiction (§ 22) depends, because it figures in determining the applicable limitation. If diversity of citizenship is the federal jurisdictional basis, state law will govern limitations questions under the Erie doctrine (USSC 1938; § 101). But if subject matter jurisdiction rests on some other basis, such as that the claim arises under federal law (often called "federal question" but more accurately described as "arising under" jurisdiction), seeking out the applicable period of limitations is more involved.

If the federal statute that creates the claim is enacted with an accompanying limitations period, it will of course apply. But if it is not, state law enters the picture again, but in different ways, depending on whether the claim sounds at law or in equity. If the federal claim is a law claim, the forum state's statute of limitations will be applied, and numerous are the federal cases seeking out the most closely analogous state claim so as to appropriate its limitations period. It's a messy situation that often makes unpredictable even the fundamental determination of what statute of limitations applies to the claim. (Different judges may find different analogies in state law.) This borrowing will often include the state's tolling provisions as well, that is, state rules that suspend the running of the period on different contingencies. (E.g., Board of Regents, USSC 1980.) In recent years, the U.S. Supreme Court has taken to borrowing the statute of limitations applicable to analogous federal claims, when available, instead of state law. (DelCostello, USSC 1983.)

To meet this unfortunate situation, a uniform four-year statute of limitations for federal claims was enacted by Congress in 1990 (28 U.S.C.A. § 1658), but it applies only to causes of action or claims created by Congress after December 1, 1990. The myriad of claims already recognized in federal law, accruing to the plaintiff before or after that date, continue to be governed by the above rules, which means that it will be decades or generations before § 1658 begins to solve the very problem it was designed to meet. (See Commentary on 28 U.S.C.A. § 1658.)

If the federal claim is an equitable claim, the more flexible doctrine of laches will apply, but with a not-binding look-see into the period of limitation that the forum state would apply, just to get some feeling for what the neighborhood deems a reasonable time on the particular facts.

A notice of claim requirement, such as is often a condition precedent to the maintenance of a tort

action against a governmental unit, like a munici-
pality, should be distinguished from the statute of
limitations. Its application may be prohibited in a
federal action even though the statute of limitations
itself may come from state law. That was held to be
the case with civil rights actions under 42 U.S.C.A.
§ 1983, for example. (Felder, USSC 1988.)

§ 61. Statute of Limitations; Constitutional Considerations

Of the key Supreme Court cases reflecting on
choice of law in general (§ 56), several turn on
whether a forum may or must apply a time restriction contained in a contract between the parties.
Home Insurance, Hartford and Clay, all treated in
§ 56, are prime examples and influential cases on
choice of law. But they involve contractual time
periods and do not necessarily prescribe what statute of limitations a forum is obliged to apply to a
foreign cause of action brought before it when there
is no contract provision addressed to the matter.

A forum entertaining a foreign cause of action is
free to apply its own statute of limitations even
though it would bar the action and the foreign
period would preserve it. So holds Wells (USSC
1953), saying that the full faith and credit clause is
not offended as long as the forum applies to the
foreign claim at least as long a period as it would
apply to a counterpart claim arising locally. Thus a
claim alive under the law of the state that created it
can be barred by the shorter period applicable under the law of the place where the plaintiff has

brought suit. The lesson to such a plaintiff, at least in this modern age of longarm jurisdiction, is to sue in the first state if he wants the longer period, or, if he would prefer some other forum, to check into its time limitation promptly and arrange for suit within whatever shorter period it offers.

Wells stresses that the forum in that case did not discriminate against the foreign claim: it and the equivalent domestic claim got the same period under forum law. But the Supreme Court has countenanced a kind of discrimination against a foreign claimant. If, when suit is brought in the forum, the claim is alive by forum law but dead by the law of the state where the claim arose, the forum is free to sustain the claim if the claimant is a forum resident and yet bar it if she is not. This is the holding of Canadian (USSC 1920), in which the constitutional provision involved was the federal privileges and immunities clause (Art. IV, § 2), which bars discrimination based on citizenship. The court in Canadian held that the clause is satisfied as long as the outsider is given at least a reasonable time for forum suit on the foreign claim; that giving more time to the local claimant on such a claim is a discrimination not "fundamental" enough to offend the constitution. That proposition can stand some reexamination.

Sometimes the commerce clause has been applied to restrain an over-zealous state. In Bendix, for example (USSC 1988), a forum (Ohio) law purported to keep a claim against a foreign corporation alive during the corporation's absence from the state even if the forum could have entertained jurisdiction against the corporation during its absence (as with a longarm statute), unless the corporation designated a local person as an agent for service. Designating such an agent, on the other hand, would have subjected the corporation to forum jurisdiction on all claims, related or not to the forum. The law was struck down as an unreasonable interference with interstate commerce.

In a spectacular case on the marvels of the choice of forum, a plaintiff libeled by Hustler magazine waited until she was too late for suit anywhere in the country except New Hampshire. She therefore had only New Hampshire for suit, where contacts were minimal—but still enough for jurisdiction, held the Supreme Court. (Keeton, USSC 1984; § 36.) Now, with jurisdiction in tow, New Hampshire was happy to offer the plaintiff its long statute of limitations. (Thorny issues remained to be decided, particularly about whether New Hampshire would use its tenuous jurisdictional hold on the case, and its generous statute of limitations, as a base on which to award damages suffered by the plaintiff outside as well as inside New Hampshire. (See Keeton, CA1 1987; Keeton, NH 1988.)

The root of the problem, manifest graphically in Keeton, is laxness in the application of the due process clause to restrict statute of limitations' choices in multi-state cases. Each state is allowed to apply its own statute of limitations to a claim before it no matter how light or altogether nonexistent the forum's contacts may be with the claim. (Sun Oil, USSC 1988; § 62.) This is premised on the continuing assumption that the statute of limitations is merely a matter of "procedure", not substantive law, and hence always fair for a forum to take from its own law. An in-depth analysis, however, made of the statute of limitations in the Erie realm (see § 101), involving federal versus state law, prompted the abandonment of this facile "procedural" characterization. It seems to abide, however, when the statute of limitations competition is between states and the federal court is a mere bystander, as it is in diversity cases. (See Ferens [USSC 1990], discussed in § 105.)

There is a contradiction here. When there's no contract in the picture, a forum is free to apply its own statute of limitations and preserve a claim dead by the law of the other and more related state, but is impeded from such doing when there is a contract present and the time restriction comes from the contract. If the contract nexus is with a place that validates the time limit, the forum is not free to disregard it. (Home Insurance, USSC 1930; § 56.) Why does due process require the forum to honor the contract and bar the claim, even if the forum's disposition is to disregard the contract limit and preserve the claim, while when no contract is present the forum can do what it likes? This seems to require the forum to show more respect for a contract between the parties than for the law of a sister state.

A state statute of limitations that seemed to discriminate based on the claim instead of the status of the parties was sustained in Watkins (USSC 1966), but only because of a peculiar twist that enabled the claimant to "revive" the claim where it arose. The case involved a Georgia suit on a Florida judgment. Georgia allowed a shorter time for suit on a foreign judgment than on one of its own judgments, and applied the shorter to bar the suit. (Suit in a domestic court on a domestic judgment is not as idle as it sounds; it is a kind of renewal procedure and may serve to perpetuate a lien, or restart a statute of limitations, or the like.) But it appeared that the judgment creditor could go back to Florida and renew the judgment there (there was still time for that under Florida law), in which event, if she then came back to Georgia with a Florida "renewal" judgment, Georgia could still apply its shorter time period to the Florida judgment but would have to measure it from the date of renewal in Florida, thus keeping the cause alive and avoiding a constitutional issue. (If reviving the judgment at home in F–1 makes it the equivalent of a new one, the new one is all F–2 can work with, and this is so even if F–2 has no internal renewal procedures of its own [Union National, USSC 1949].)

C. "PROCEDURE" LABEL

§ 62. "Substance" Versus "Procedure"

The statute of limitations just treated is among the best examples of how misleading it can be to try to resolve an issue by affixing a label to it—what the conflict of laws calls "characterization". A simple-minded version of this labeling phenomenon is to conclude quickly that the statute of limitations is "procedural" and that a forum will therefore apply its own statute of limitations automatically, to foreign and domestic claims alike. Since the choice of law process is devised for "substantive" issues, goes this notion, the process would be avoided by simply affixing a "procedural" label to an issue. Only a brain in a total state of rest would trust such reasoning.

Nor does this imply that a given rule ceases to be "procedural" merely because it is important. Even rules of an undeniably "procedural" nature need to be backed up with meaningful sanctions or there would be no way to enforce them. (See § 102.) It merely says that if the purpose of a given rule, otherwise safely treatable as one of "procedure", is not one of bookkeeping or mechanics but rather one whose very design is to decide between life and death, its application in a conflicts setting needs thinking, not labeling.

Many other things in the law are "substantive" for conflicts purposes—which merely means that they are of sufficient substantive impact to invoke choice of law policies and hence the rules that implement them—even though they may be deemed "procedural" for other purposes.

On the statute of limitations, nevertheless, the label continues to be the thing. In the Sun Oil case (USSC 1988), the Supreme Court reaffirmed that a forum can apply its statute of limitations to a claim even though the forum may be obliged, for lack of appropriate contacts, to apply the law of some other state to the "substantive" issues on that claim. This broad permission enabled New Hampshire to apply its six-year statute of limitations to a libel that had little impact in New Hampshire, and much more impact in other states in all of which the statute of limitations had long since run. (See Keeton, USSC 1984.)

A major purpose of choice of law rules is to prevent a choice of forum from dictating the result on the merits. (It may still do so in some instances. See § 86.) A choice of forum would come unnecessarily close to a choice of law if the "procedure" label were too freely used.

The labeling process, moreover, can often be manipulated into doing service on any side at all. There are reported cases that can be paired off to show how different labels can be made to serve similar purposes in different settings. One such set is Lams (Del.1935) and Emery (Mass.1895) (§ 69). Their significance at this point is that both involved the statute of frauds, and to implement a similar policy—that of assuring the application of the forum's statute of frauds to cases having their predominant contacts with the forum—one treated the statute of frauds as procedural and the other treated it as substantive.

The only rules that can qualify as so wholly procedural as to avoid the law-choosing process entirely, and thus be taken from forum law for domestic and foreign claims indifferently, are those that are really concerned with only method and mechanics. The manner of summons service is governed by forum law (Rst.2d § 126), for example, as is pleading, "the conduct of proceedings in court", the mode of trial (whether by court or jury), and the methods of enforcing the orders and judgments of the court (Rst.2d §§ 127–131). Not even a sister state judgment can dictate a forum's enforcement methods (Baker, USSC 1998, Lynde, USSC 1901).

The manipulatability of labels can also be seen in the "direct action" cases. The more common rule in personal injury actions in the United States is that suit must be brought against the tortfeasor only, with the tortfeasor's liability insurer supplying a lawyer and conducting the defense without being named or identified in the action. But some states allow a "direct action" against the insurer. Is such a rule substantive or procedural? In a leading case, Oltarsh (NY 1965), it was held substantive enough to warrant a law choosing. New York, which did not permit a direct action, applied Puerto Rican law, which did, because the claim arose in Puerto Rico and the right to sue the insurer directly was found to be more than a mere "procedural shortcut". But on similar facts in Noe (Mo.1966), the issue was deemed procedural and a direct action was held barred for want of a forum rule permitting it.

There have even been cases in which a plaintiff's claim was kept alive only by brewing mixed ingredients of the two categories. These are treated in § 84.

§ 63. Evidence

Most rules of evidence are merely housekeeping devices designed to direct the court along the best route to the truth. If states differ on what the best route is, the matter would not seem to be of such import as to require one forum to defer to another's views, and hence most rules of evidence are strictly procedural and come from forum law alone (Rst.2d §§ 137, 138). But even some of these presumably "housekeeping" rules can take a turn for the substantive. When they do, a choice of law examination may be appropriate. Presumptions, for example, are usually governed by forum law when they are rebuttable. That they are rebuttable makes them the equivalent of rules affecting the burden of proof, and the burden of proof is also governed by forum law as a general rule. As long as both sides can put in proof on an issue, the allotment of the initial burden of proof and the creation of a rebuttable presumption are just temporary shifts during the battle. But when a presumption is a conclusive one, it does indeed dictate the outcome of an issue and as such should be treated as a substantive item and go through a law-choosing process (Rst.2d § 134, Comment a).

Other burden of proof issues periodically become embroiled in the procedure-substance dispute. In Levy v. Steiger (Mass.1919), for example, the issue was whether the plaintiff or the defendant had the burden of proof on an issue of the plaintiff's contributory negligence. Massachusetts held that this is a procedural matter and applied its own rule, which placed the burden on the defendant. Yet, if there is no one alive who can testify on the issue, such as where all witnesses are dead and the suit is being prosecuted through the parties' estates, the party who carries the burden of proof on a key issue can lose the case, and that is hardly a "procedural" outcome. If the burden has such a potential, it should be put through a law-choosing process, which is what Fitzpatrick (NY 1929) held. There the state of the accident had adopted the comparative negligence rule, under which a negligent plaintiff can recover in a tort action but with his damages reduced by the percentage of his own contributory fault, while the forum retained the contributory negligence rule, under which any contributory fault on a plaintiff's part destroys the claim entirely. The forum rejected the notion that the difference between the two things is merely procedural, put the issue through a law choosing process, and chose the other state's comparative negligence rule.

Hence, whenever an issue of which "burden of proof" is part appears to do more than merely shift the trial initiative from one side to the other, the lawyer—certainly the lawyer for the side that would be benefitted—should consider urging the court to apply foreign rather than forum law.

One usually hears the "burden" described as one of "pleading and proof", as if the two are inseparable. They need not and sometimes should not be. While it would be easy enough to describe the "pleading" burden as procedural—just a matter of saying a few words on a piece of paper—the burden of "proof" more often merits treatment as a matter of substance sufficient to invoke choice of law principles. It was so treated in Palmer (USSC 1943), for the purpose of requiring a federal diversity court to look to state law under the Erie doctrine (§ 102).

Up to now the assumption has been that evidence rules are only truth-seeking devices designed to prescribe courtroom conduct. Rules of privileged communications (e.g., lawyer-client, doctor-patient, clergyman-penitent, husband-wife, etc.), although associated with the subject of evidence, are exceptions. Their concern is to insulate certain communications and sanctify certain relationships outside the courtroom, and to accomplish that end the legislature that enacts a rule of privilege is willing to impede the truth-finding purpose by making some evidence—and perhaps some very important evidence—unavailable. The policies underlying these rules of privilege give them an aura of substance sufficient to take them out of the "mere procedure" realm and involve them in the law-choosing process. It was in respect of privileges, in fact, that the initial drafts of the Federal Rules of Evidence faltered, Congress rejecting an effort to supersede state law in this regard and directing that at least in diversity cases the federal courts continue to look to state law (Fed.R.Evid. Rule 501).

The Restatement's position is that if evidence is privileged under forum law but not under the law of the state with the "most significant relationship with the communication", the forum will let it in unless the forum has a "strong public policy" against it (Rst.2d § 139[1]). Since a rule of privilege can without much difficulty be found to involve a "strong public policy", the rationale here is apparently that the forum's policy is not on the line when it is the other state with the predominant contacts. Conversely, says the Restatement, if it is the other state that confers the privilege, while the forum does not, the forum will admit the evidence unless there is some "special reason" for deferring to the foreign law. If forum contacts are few, deference is more likely (Rst.2d § 139, Comment on Subsection [2]).

The taking of a deposition in one state for use in another poses an interesting problem if an issue of privilege arises and only one state recognizes the privilege. In that situation, if the state of the deposition is the one that upholds the privilege, it is not likely to violate it just to serve another forum. If the latter is the one with the privilege, it is not likely to admit into evidence that portion of a deposition that violates it. A contrary rule might find the proponent snooping around in an "unprivileged" state to see if the deposition can be taken there (Cepeda, SDNY 1964). This suggests that the objectionable evidence is not likely to get into the courtroom even if it managed to get into the deposition.

D. INJECTING FOREIGN LAW

§ 64. Getting the Foreign Law Into the Case

There have been a number of cases on how foreign law is injected into a case. It was at first considered an issue of fact and had to be proved as such (Hanley, USSC 1885), but many states have adopted judicial notice statutes of one kind or another. Even these statutes may require some initiative of the party relying on the foreign law, however, especially if it is the law of a foreign country, such as by making it incumbent on the relier to supply copies of the foreign law, with a translation if need be, or to make a formal request that the court take notice of it and advise the other side of reliance on it.

In the federal courts, FRCP Rule 44.1 applies, requiring the party relying on foreign law to give reasonable notice of it (this is usually done in the pleading) and permitting the court to consider "any relevant material or source" reflecting on it. The matter is treated as one of law rather than of fact, and is thus determined by the court rather than a jury.

In the absence of statutory instruction on how to treat foreign law, there are several presumptions that a forum may turn to. These are reviewed in Leary (NJ 1951). One is that the common law prevails in the foreign place, which would not be a suitable presumption if the foreign place is plainly not a common law jurisdiction (which was so of France, the place involved in Leary). A second is that the foreign law is the same as the forum's. A third is that certain fundamental principles exist in all civilized nations (which would be relevant only if the principle involved in the case is fundamental rather than subtle). A fourth is that the parties have agreed to forum law by failing to address foreign law. This last was the approach taken in Leary. The plaintiff was lucky. Another possibility, which occurred in Walton (CA2 1956), is simply to dismiss the action for want of proof of the foreign law.

The main reason accounting for case law on what to do when foreign law is relevant but not adequately raised before the court is that somebody's lawyer was remiss. If foreign law is at all relevant, every lawyer in the case, on no matter what side, should research it closely. It may have good news for the client. And if it has bad news, it is best to be prepared to meet it. If the foreign law is favorable, the lawyer should not depend on presumptions or anything else; he should obtain and submit a copy of the foreign law in writing, with a translation, and perhaps even have an expert in the foreign law standing by to do service at the trial.

E. OLD RULES

§ 65. Old and Arbitrary Choice of Law Rules

Most of the efforts of the past several decades have been to escape from the old choice of law rules, formulated when the world was bigger, transportation more expensive and cumbersome, and the movement of people and things much slower and less frequent. Those circumstances did not make the old rules, many of which we consider archaic today, ideal even for their own time, but there were fewer cases around to test them in diverse situations that later showed them up as unfair as well as arbitrary.

The traditional choice of law rule in tort cases was that all substantive issues must be governed by the law of the place of the wrong, the "lex loci delicti". This was usually understood to mean the place where the injury was suffered, which served well enough because the wrongful act and the resulting injury usually occurred in the same state. In the average case, that state also had the predominant if not the sole interest by other measures as well. That is probably still true of most tort cases, but today their numbers are so great that even if the ratio of cases departing from the average is small, their numbers are high.

Rigidly applied, the lex loci rule got demerits whenever the facts deviated from the old-world norm that found all of the elements centered in one place. In Alabama Great Southern R.R. (Ala.1892), for example, the plaintiff was a railroad brakeman injured in Mississippi by the negligence of his fellow servants in failing to carry out certain inspections in Alabama. All parties were Alabamians, and while both Alabama and Mississippi barred common law actions against the railroad when the wrong was that of a fellow servant, Alabama had adopted an employer's liability act that would have given the plaintiff at least some recovery. The plaintiff got no recovery, however, because the injury occurred in Mississippi, whose law therefore had to govern, and Mississippi had no such liability act. On a set of facts like that today, the plaintiff would likely recover.

Several new choice of law approaches, as we shall see, vie for judicial attention today, and while none is perfect, most are more flexible than the lex loci rule. Many of these new choice of law techniques have been applied in tort cases in which the issue was whether a guest injured in a car driven by his host would be barred because of a guest-host barrier statute in the state of the accident. Old law barred the action by applying such an accident-situs statute almost automatically (e.g., Pando, Colo. 1956). New approaches often avoided a guest-host statute in multistate tort cases (e.g., Babcock, NY 1963). Interesting interim steps on the road to the new rules appeared.

In torts, the lex loci rule is the agent of the so-called "vested rights" theory that reached its zenith in the First Restatement under the influence of Professor Beale. This theory singles out what it supposes to be the key element in an occurrence or transaction and holds that the law applicable to that case—the whole case—is the law of the state to which that element relates, and in tort that state is the one in which the injury is sustained. On the Alabama facts, for example, the injury was sustained in Mississippi, which, affording no claim, had nothing to "vest", while the other, more interested state, Alabama, with much to vest, was arbitrarily excluded from participation because it wasn't the state in which the injury was sustained.

The old choice of law rules that do the bidding of the vested rights theory in the contracts realm also have the potential for arbitrary results. They can be more complicated. Ironically, their convolutions sometimes enabled a court (and still do where they are followed) to obtain what we would today consider an appropriate result, but for the wrong reason.

The traditional choice of law rules in contract cases are that issues relating to performance, such as whether the contract has been breached and what the remedy shall be, are governed by the law of the place of performance, but that issues of basic validity (formalities of execution, capacity to contract, and the like) are governed by the law of the place where the contract is made. This could prove arbitrary even if the place of making were clear, as where the contract was executed on a train or plane in a state having nothing to do with the parties or the contract. But what should the court do when the two (or more) states involved differ on the very issue of where a contract is deemed made? In Linn (Pa.1958), for example, a statute of frauds issue was involved, New York law barring the particular oral contract but Pennsylvania law accepting it. Whose law to apply turned on where the contract was made. P in New York telephoned to D in Pennsylvania to accept an offer and the issue was whether the acceptance would be deemed to take place in New York, where the words of acceptance were spoken, or in Pennsylvania, where they were heard. The say in these matters always belongs to the forum, which was Pennsylvania in this case; it held that the place of speaking is the place of making. Suppose New York's rule was that the place of hearing is the place of making? A rule that lays all bets on where a contract is "made" is opening the door to issues like that: a big bunch of problems just to determine the place of making. More modern contract rules (§ 68) reduce, if they don't avoid, those prospects.

Another well-known example of this rule about where the contract is made is Milliken (Mass.1878). D was a Massachusetts domiciliary whose husband wanted credit from P of Maine. P would extend it only if D would guarantee it. Under Massachusetts law, D at the time lacked the capacity to guarantee (a sexual discrimination that would be unconstitutional today), but she had it under Maine law. The court held that the contract was made in Maine; that the making occurred when P acted on it (by advancing credit) there. P won. If Maine rather than Massachusetts law was properly chosen, a better reason should have been found than that the technical "making" of the contract occurred in Maine.

Difficulties can become absurdities when State F, the forum, in a flourish of cosmopolitan fervor, decides that a contract is made in State X and then, instead of just taking State X's law about validity, applies X's rule as to where the contract is made, only to find that State X says it was made in State F, so that State F internal law is found to govern validity after all (University of Chicago, Mich.1936).

Also among the older rules in contract cases is one that would have the place of performance govern issues of validity as well as performance (e.g., Denison, Okla.1922).

Increasing quantities of choice of law cases with expanding contacts and variables undermined the narrow base supporting these old rules. There had been too long a calm acceptance of them. A new variation on an ancient adage appeared: if you can keep your head when all those around you are losing theirs, then perhaps you have overlooked something. Much had been overlooked. The pressure for change, at first building gradually, became intense from about the 1950's to the 1970's, the era that brought about the most dramatic choice of law developments. Although the old rules had been long decaying, only now had note been taken, recalling the response of William S. Gilbert when an insufferable patroness approached him during his 1880 visit to the United States, volunteered that "Baytch" was her favorite composer, and inquired whether

"Baytch" was still composing. "Madam," he answered, " 'Baytch' is at the present time by way of decomposing".

We will visit the older rules from time to time as we discuss the new ones.

F. CHOICE OF LAW FACTORS

§ 66. Elements for Consideration in Choosing Law

Modern thinking in choice of law has formulated lists of elements for courts to consider in making a choice. Assume that two or more states are concerned with an issue and the laws of the two differ. There may be some reasons for applying the law of one state, other and different reasons for applying the law of the other state. The only thing the court knows for sure is that a choice must be made. If the legislature has addressed the situation at hand and offered a solution, the court would be bound by the legislative direction and probably delighted to have it. More often than not the legislature has not spoken. The result is a field day for the common law: most choice of law rules are judge-made, the product of experience.

The Second Restatement adopts the "most significant relationship" test for choice of law problems (e.g., Rst.2d §§ 145 [wrongs], 188 [contracts]). In each case with a multistate involvement the issues are separated and to each issue is applied the law of the state having the most significant relationship to the issue. While that standard is self-evidently appealing, it sometimes results in different choices being made by different judges in the same case; they simply disagree on which state has the "most" significant relationship.

The Restatement lists (Rst.2d § 6) factors that the court should consider in making a choice:

(a) the needs of the interstate and international systems,

(b) the relevant policies of the forum,

(c) the relevant policies of other interested states and the relative interests of those states in the determination of the particular issue,

(d) the protection of justified expectations,

(e) the basic policies underlying the particular field of law,

(f) certainty, predictability, and uniformity of result, and

(g) ease in the determination and application of the law to be applied.

With a few variations and some different stress, the list is modeled on that prescribed in Choice of the Applicable Law (52 Col.L.Rev. 959 [1952]), co-authored by Professors Cheatham and Reese, the latter the Second Restatement's reporter. The Restatement, like the article, makes clear that no single factor is decisive, and that the standing of any one of them can vary, sometimes dramatically, from case to case. All should be weighed. Some will have little significance in one realm, great significance in another. Predictability of result, for example, is important in contracts, less so in torts.

Professor Robert A. Leflar has formulated a list of five "choice-influencing considerations ... as a practical working basis for choice of law decisions" (Leflar, Amer.Confl.Law 4th Ed., § 95). It has influenced many judges. The list is

(a) predictability of result,

(b) maintenance of interstate and international order,

(c) simplification of the judicial task,

(d) advancement of the forum's governmental interests, and

(e) application of the better rule of law.

Note the overlap of some of these elements with those on the Restatement's list. Note also the uniqueness of Professor Leflar's last item: looking for the "better rule of law". The sound of it grates harshly on the ear, introducing almost an issue of personal taste. But as we shall see with examples later, it is not as arbitrary as it sounds. It gives the court a flexible weapon in an arsenal still looking for the right set of tools for choosing law.

There are yet other formulations of factors, elements, considerations, principles, ingredients, etc., devised to guide the choice of law process. It is of course possible to take each item on each list and discuss it individually and abstractly. Possible, but for the most part idle. Concrete examples are better instructors, balancing one factor against another in different contexts and showing how an element that looms large in one case can become insignificant in another.

There are various progressions in which the new choice of law approaches may be studied, and probably as much disagreement about the sequence of study as about the approaches themselves. We will proceed by substantive subject matter, beginning with contracts. The most detailed and probing study of the new rules will be reached in the tort cases, which because of their predominant numbers were the main channels through which the new rules evolved.

G. CONTRACT AND BUSINESS CASES

§ 67. Contracts; Stipulating the Choice

A contract having contacts with several states can stipulate whose law is to apply to issues connected with the contract. If the parties so stipulate, the courts will generally honor their choice. So says the Restatement, noting also an exception when the law chosen would violate a "fundamental policy" of a state with a "materially greater interest than the chosen state". (Rst.2d § 187.) This has the effect, among other accomplishments, of preventing one party in a superior bargaining position (such as an insurer) from exacting from the weaker party (such as an insured) a stipulation selecting the law of a state that would benefit the stronger party in a situation in which the law of another state, with a "materially greater interest", would benefit the weaker one.

The rule authorizing the stipulation presumably applies to issues of validity as well as to issues of performance. The courts do not have much difficulty on the performance side. To the extent that the parties could have spelled out in terms what the requirements of performance and the consequences of breach were to be, their stipulating to have the law of a given place determine these things is just a short-hand substitute for the spelling-out. But that is not the case with issues of basic validity, such as whether the contract has to be in writing (statute of frauds requirements), or have certain formalities of execution, or whether a given party, such as an infant (and who determines what infancy is?), has the capacity to contract.

On matters like these, there is a theoretical dilemma in allowing the parties to stipulate to the law that will govern. Since it is only the contract that gives life to the stipulation, how can the stipulation, unborn until a contract validates it, itself choose the law that will do the validating? It is like the traffic statute Ripley once reported in his "Believe It or Not" column. It provided that when two cars approach an intersection, both shall stop and neither shall proceed until the other has passed.

It was said in E. Gerli & Co. (CA2 1931) that "[s]ome law must impose the obligation"—that is, recognize that an agreement is a binding contract—and that "the parties have nothing whatever to do with that". The Restatement acknowledges that if only one state has contacts with the parties and with the contract, and invalidates it, the parties will not secure validity for it by trying to stipulate to have the issue governed by the law of some other place. Usually, however, adds the Restatement (Rst.2d § 187, Comment d on Subsection 2), the local law of the state chosen by the parties will be applied even to matters of validity in a multistate situation. Perhaps a fair compromise on this point, and surely a sound lesson to the parties, is the Siegelman case (CA2 1955). It says that if the parties want to be able to choose the law that is to govern validity, they had best choose a place related to the contract. If the contract is invalid by the laws of all related jurisdictions, in other words, it will not buy validity by reaching for the validating law of a wholly unrelated state.

If the state chosen has any significant relationship, on the other hand, the courts are likely to be receptive to the choice. Indeed, even when there is no express stipulation, the court may find a "presumed" one to pick a validating law. In Pritchard (USSC 1882), the Supreme Court said that the parties "cannot be presumed to have contemplated a law which would defeat their engagements", and applied the law of the place of performance to sustain a contract that would have been invalid under the law of the place where it was made (which usually governs validity under traditional rules).

The lesson to the lawyer is to include in the client's contract, if the contract touches more than one state in any way, a stipulation as to governing law with respect to all issues or at least to whatever issues the parties turn their minds to and agree on. If the lawyer's purpose is only to assure that the law of but one place need be consulted should a dispute arise, the place chosen may be of secondary importance. In that case, a stipulation to the law of her own or her client's state, if she can arrange that, may be satisfactory. If the lawyer is familiar with the kinds of issues that are likely to arise under the contract, and with the different resolutions the laws of the several connected states may come up with, she should of course stipulate to the law of the state whose resolutions most favor her client—and hope that the other lawyer will not see through the ploy and balk. This becomes a matter for negotiation.

While the stipulation will usually be honored, it will not always be. The court may find, as the Restatement (Rst.2d § 187) anticipates, that the interests of a given state override the stipulation. In Desantis (Tex, cert. den. 1991), the court concluded that the parties' choice of Florida law had to give way to a Texas policy restricting non-competition agreements.

§ 68. Contracts; Choice of Law in Absence of Stipulation

The Restatement's position is that if there is no stipulation in the contract as to governing law, the law of the state with the "most significant relationship" should be applied. (Rst.2d § 188[1].) The earlier "grouping of contacts" or "center of gravity" descriptions (e.g., Auten, NY 1954) were sires if not synonyms of this approach, and "interest analysis" or "governmental interest analysis", such as first seen exemplified in key California cases (e.g., Bernkrant, Cal.1961), are other names by which it goes. All of these captions intend to describe a method whereby each issue in the case is resolved by applying the law of the state deemed to have the predominant "interest" or "contacts" or "relationship" with the issue. Quality of contacts and interests rather than quantity determines, and it is appropriate to note that the results achieved are often the same as would have obtained under the older rules, to which some courts may still wish to adhere, about the place of "making" and the place of "performance".

As far as basic validity of the contract is concerned, even the older cases often found ways to sustain an agreement in multistate cases. If, of the several states involved, the law of one would sustain, its law was likely to be the one chosen. Thus, where only one of two states involved in a surety case recognized an antecedent obligation as furnishing an adequate contract consideration, its law was chosen and the contract upheld. This was the Pritchard case (USSC 1882), mentioned in § 67, in which the court said that the parties "can not be presumed to have contemplated a law which would defeat their engagements".

Prominent cases can be found using the more modern formulations to sustain agreements. The Bernkrant case (Cal.1961) applied Nevada law to uphold an oral agreement to make a will forgiving the unpaid balance of a mortgage on Nevada land. Applying an interests test, the court found Nevada's interest in upholding the reasonable expectations of the parties to a Nevada agreement respecting Nevada property to outweigh California's policy requiring that certain agreements be written.

The "most significant relationship" test worked a similar result in Downs (NY 1964). New Yorkers H and W made an agreement in New York whereby husband H assigned half his wages to wife W. New York allowed such assignments. Massachusetts, to which H later moved, did not. New York, as the domicile of the wife and children for whose benefit the agreement was made, was held to have the predominant relationship with the validity issue, and H's employer, when sued for the half share of H's wages, was not allowed to use Massachusetts law as a defense. The "relationship" and "contacts" of which New York spoke in Downs have the same function as the "interest" that California used in Bernkrant.

A "rule of validation" approach, under which the law that validates an agreement will be chosen from between two laws if the other would invalidate, is often found in consensual transaction cases and can also account for these results, but if the state with the predominant interest rejects the transaction its law will be applied, and the transaction rejected, notwithstanding the parties' wish to validate implicit in the very fact of the contract. So, for example, in Wood (Colo.1979), adopting the "relationship" approach for contract actions, a claim based on construction in New Mexico was rejected because the contractor did not obtain a license there. New Mexico, which voided claims under such circumstances, was held to have the predominant interest, despite the fact that all of the parties' states would have sustained the claim.

The "better rule of law", a member of Professor Leflar's list of choice-influencing considerations, has entered the contracts arena. In Haines (Wis.1970), wife W was injured in husband H's car in Wisconsin. An exclusion clause in H's insurance policy denied coverage to W. The exclusion was void (so that coverage existed) under Wisconsin law, where the accident occurred, H worked, and the policy was issued, but valid (so that there would be no coverage) under Minnesota law, where both H and W were domiciled. Wisconsin applied its own law and held that the policy did cover W. One of its bases was that a rule that allows an injured person to recover from the insurer is better than a rule that does not. Had a Minnesota court had the case, it could have held the other way, applying its own law as the better rule and insulating the insurer on these facts.

While flexible choice of law rules will frequently lead to a choice of law against an insurer, as in

Haines, they will not invariably do so, despite canons of construction in other parts of the insurance realm that resolve ambiguities in favor of the insured. In Lowe's (CA4 1963), for example, a choice could constitutionally have gone either way, but the court, on a "most significant relationships" test, applied Pennsylvania law, which did not recognize an insured's claim for an insurer's alleged delay in processing a policy, instead of North Carolina's law, which did.

The Haines case is a better lesson about how to choose a forum than it is about better rules of law. To a plaintiff, the best rule of all is one that supports a recovery. The plaintiff's lawyer in Haines chose well. It is always important for the lawyer to choose the forum carefully. A separate section is devoted to this later (§ 86), but the point is such a key one in choice of law that it should not be by-passed no matter when it appears. If there is a genuine conflict of laws between two states on a key issue, and an investigation does not assure that their choice of law rules would both agree on which is to govern, the whole ball game may turn on choice of forum.

Consider Lilienthal (Oreg.1964). D of Oregon was adjudicated a spendthrift in that state, which disabled him from making contracts. D borrowed money from P in California for a business venture, and out of that loan arose the notes on which P now sued D in Oregon. P lost. A divided Oregon court held that Oregon's interest in protecting the spendthrift's family outweighed all other interests, including those of California in seeing to it that California agreements are carried out. Had California's courts had the case, P would likely have recovered. The lesson to one in P's position is to sue in California, which should not be hard to do today with California's generous longarm statute.

The newer approaches to choice of law in the contracts area do not stress, as earlier rules did, differences between issues of validity and issues of performance, even assuming differences are always sharply definable, which they aren't. Auten, a pioneer New York case (1954), involved a question of whether certain conduct was a breach of the contract, a separation agreement. An English couple made the agreement in New York, to which the husband had moved after leaving the wife in England. After making the agreement in New York, the wife returned to England and brought suit there when the husband did not fulfill his contractual commitment. The suit was not fruitful and in this later New York action by the wife to recover under the agreement, the husband contended that the suit in England was a repudiation of the agreement, freeing him of his obligations under it. The court, sustaining the wife's action, held that the issue was governed by the law of England, which was found to have "the greatest concern ... in securing ... essential support" to the wife and children.

Predictability of result, especially desirable in contracts cases, is more difficult when the parties do not stipulate to governing law. But assuming the absence of a stipulation in a given case, the new choice of law approaches do not compromise predictability appreciably more than the older and more rigid rules did. The older ones put premiums on place of "making" and place of "performance", and, as previously seen (§ 65), predictability would sometimes become a casualty while the judges argued, for example, about the technical place and moment of a contract's execution. Arguments under the newer rules are also inevitable, but the subjects will be worthier. Which state has a stronger "interest in" or "relationship to" or "contacts with" a given issue is more deserving of attention than where two parties set pen to paper, mailed a letter, or vocalized an acceptance.

§ 69. Statute of Frauds

If two states are involved in a contract case, and State X has a statute of frauds requiring the particular kind of contract to be written while State Y has not and will recognize an oral one, whose law governs? The resolution follows the usual course of contract choice of law, as set forth in § 68, but is assigned this separate section because the issue arises so often.

The Bernkrant case discussed in § 68 applied an interest analysis approach to a statute of frauds issue, applying Nevada's law to recognize an oral contract that California would have rejected. Nevada was found to have the predominant interest in the issue. New York applied the same approach in Intercontinental Planning (NY 1969), where New York was held to have the dominant contacts with the issue and the New York statute of frauds, rejecting the contract, was applied instead of New Jersey law, which found the oral contract acceptable. The case involved a finder's fee.

The court in Intercontinental Planning discussed and rejected the old approach that would niche the statute of frauds under a "procedural" or "substantive" heading and choose law accordingly: usually the law of the place of the contract's making if the particular court deemed the matter "substantive" but the forum's own law if the court considered the matter "procedural". Such an archaic approach lingers, but can seldom do decent law work. One can find cases pronouncing common goals and then using different characterizations of the issue to reach them. In both Lams (Del.1935) and Emery (Mass.1895), for example, it was plain that the court's purpose was to insulate local domiciliaries from certain oral agreements. Lams on its fact pattern implemented the purpose by treating the statute of frauds as substantive; Emery did by treating it as procedural. Emery was a decision by Justice Holmes, and to his credit, as usual, one finds in the case elements of a contacts-type analysis suggesting that the "procedural" stamp was called on for service only after it was found to support a result warranted by the substantive policies underlying Massachusetts' law.

It was on a statute of frauds matter that characterization reached one of its most bizarre results. In Marie (NY Sup'r.Ct.1883), New York and Missouri were the states involved and both had statutes barring the type of oral contract before the court. The thinking of lawyer and layperson alike would probably have been satisfied to hear the court recite that fact and reject the contract. The court did something quite different. It said that Missouri had the main contacts with the case but that its statute of frauds was a "procedural" one and would apply only to a case sued in a Missouri court. This case was brought in New York and hence Missouri's statute could not apply, held the court. The New York statute, on the other hand, was found through an analysis of its language to be of the "substantive" variety and hence not applicable to this predominantly Missouri transaction. The result was the enforcement of a contract that all of the related states condemned. The plaintiff had much to celebrate in the Marie case. He is one of the few litigants on record who won a contest between two sovereigns by offending both of them.

A case with an oral contract is usually one in which a party did not consult a lawyer in advance of the transaction. If he did, the advice of a writing would probably have been the first offered. If the case has contacts with several states and the lawyer does not insist on a writing for his client, at least where he has the bargaining power to do so, he will be exposing the client to a high chance of litigation and the unpredictability of its results.

§ 70. Land Contract Cases

The choice of law rule in contracts involving the transfer of interests in land comes as close as any in conflicts to being a simple one. Because of land's immobility, the simple fact is that a land transaction that offends the situs is asking for trouble. Hence the general rule has evolved that the validity of a land contract and the duties of the parties to it are governed by the law of the land's situs. (Rst.2d §§ 189, 190.) This leaves little room for the operation of the "interest", "relationship", and "contacts" tests that would at least leave open the possibility of applying other than situs law in real property cases. Of course, even in old cases the situs rule was not absolute. Where, for example, all of the elements in the case were connected with a different state than the situs, situs law was not applied in Selover (USSC 1912, involving Minn. law).

A lawyer whose client participates in any contract affecting land should see to it that the law of its situs is satisfied in all particulars, from the incidentals of the contract's physical execution to the core of its substantive elements, whoever else's law may also be satisfied in the bargain. And this applies not only to transfers of title to the land, but also to transactions that merely lien it. The validity of a mortgage of State L land, for example, although the mortgage and its underlying loan transaction are executed in State M, will be determined by the law of State L (Swank, Ind.1887).

§ 71. UCC Cases, Generally

The Uniform Commercial Code has specific choice of law instructions, an example of that uncommon but increasing phenomenon in conflict of laws: statutory direction. Section 1–105(1) of the Code provides:

> ... when a transaction bears a reasonable relation to this state and also to another state or nation the parties may agree that the law either of this state or of such other state or nation shall govern their rights and duties. Failing such agreement this Act applies to transactions bearing an appropriate relation to this state.

This provision governs (among other things) sales transactions under Article 2 of the UCC. (Its application in secured transactions is discussed in § 72.) Its first lesson is that the contract itself can direct as to choice of law and that the choice will be honored as long as the state whose law is chosen has a significant relationship to the case. This is essentially the same as the rule prevailing in the contracts realm generally (§ 67).

If the contract contains no law-choosing clause, the second sentence of UCC § 1–105(1) applies, but, for all its fine intentions, it is ambiguous. Instead of clearly pointing a way, it just seems to spin in place. It says, addressing now the judge of the forum court who is reading it, that "this Act applies to transactions bearing an appropriate relation to this state". This apparently means the forum's own UCC is to apply as long as the forum has an "appropriate" relation to the transaction. (The word "appropriate" is not defined; arguably, it means "reasonable", implying a forum connection at least adequate enough to permit the choice of forum law under the due process principles discussed in § 56.) Such a reading has been made in many courts (e.g., Skinner, Mass.1963) and is consistent with the official comments accompanying the UCC. Deeming itself a work of international scope and vision, the UCC seeks to get itself applied wherever possible, and if this instruction sends the court directly to the substantive law of the forum, which has the UCC, the chance of choosing the law of some other place, which may not have adopted the UCC, is avoided.

Nevertheless, UCC § 1–105(1) is so ambiguous that other courts—most courts—have read it as merely an invitation to apply the forum's usual choice of law rules rather than as a mandate to go directly to the substantive parts of the forum's UCC. (Golden, D.So.Dak. 1984.) Some courts have resorted to those choice of law rules on the premise that they offer the very uniformity that others find in the direct route to the forum's UCC. In Merritt (CA4 1988), for example, the court held that the "most significant relationship" test is the "appropriate" one to apply under UCC § 1–105(1) because it "best promotes the UCC's policies of uniformity and predictability". The judges then divided, 2–1, on which of the two states involved had the "most significant relationship". We may predict, uniformly, that the only thing uniform and predictable is that the judges will disagree about uniformity and predictability.

The first interpretation noted directs the court to forum UCC substantive law, the second to forum choice of law rules, which can lead to the substantive law of another place. The first puts a premium on choice of forum, because by suing in that forum the plaintiff is in effect forcing the court to choose forum law, which includes the UCC. The second, by having the court apply regular choice of law principles, at least enables the court to implement the purposes that underlie choice of law rules.

The reader's reaction may be that this is just a tempest in a teapot; that since the UCC has been adopted in almost every American jurisdiction, it makes no difference whose law is chosen because the choice will end up in somebody's UCC and the ultimate substantive law will therefore be the same. If that were so, the matter would indeed be academic and the occasions to choose law in UCC cases few. The number of cases belie that assumption, however, and the need to choose may exist for any of three reasons.

First and most obvious is that one of the jurisdictions involved (a foreign nation, for example) may not have adopted the UCC.

Second, although both (or all) have adopted the UCC, one of them may have rejected or modified the substantive provision at issue. Many states did not swallow the UCC whole, rejecting or qualifying certain parts of it. Such a part may be the one involved in the action.

Third, and least obvious, may be the case in which both states involved have the UCC and even have identical versions of the provision in point, but their case-law interpretations of it differ. Section 2–318 of the UCC, for example, lists third persons who are to be deemed beneficiaries of a seller's warranty, but the official comment on the section acknowledges "the developing case law" expanding the list. If P is damaged by the breach of a seller's warranty and is not on the § 2–318 list, she may nevertheless be among those to whom State X has extended the warranty through case law. If State Y has not so extended it, the most fundamental of all substantive law issues—whether P has a cause of action—will turn on whether the law of State X or State Y is chosen.

Subdivision 1 of UCC § 1–105 applies to all of the UCC (not just the sales article that we have been principally addressing) except to the extent that subdivision 2 provides otherwise. Subdivision 2 does not provide otherwise as to Article 3, the article on commercial paper, thus leaving subdivision 1 in charge of that, but with not too much to do for the reason that the UCC has achieved much uniformity on commercial paper. Uniform rules avoid many of the differences about bills and notes met in earlier cases, sometimes on issues as fundamental as whether an instrument is negotiable (e.g., McCornick, Idaho 1928), but there remain occasions for conflict nevertheless. Indeed, even the Restatement retains several sections (Rst.2d §§ 214–217) directed to negotiable instruments.

Subdivision 2 of UCC § 1–105 refers to several other parts of the UCC. Among other things, it designates the UCC sections that are to control choice of law in the articles on bank deposits and collections, bulk transfers, and investment securities. It also directs that UCC § 2–402 is to govern "rights of creditors in goods sold", thus taking that subject out from under the choice of law instructions of subdivision 1. (Section 2–402 chooses the law of the place where goods are situated to determine whether their sale is fraudulent as against the seller's creditor.)

Section 1–105 is in the process of being replaced by a new provision, § 1–301. The new section makes a couple of changes. First, the new section allows parties to select in their contracts an applicable law, even if doesn't bear a "reasonable relationship" to the transaction. The theory here is that parties ought to have the freedom to pick their own rules. There is an exception, however, to protect consumers. Consumers cannot be subject to the choice of the law of a place that does not bear a reasonable relationship to the transaction; they must get the benefit of "mandatory" consumer protection rules of their home state or country.

New § 1–301 also drops the "appropriate relationship" language of § 1–105. In its stead, the new section says simply that without a choice of law clause courts should apply their ordinary choice of law principles. In effect, however, this is not likely to be much of a change, as this is usually what courts did anyway in trying to figure out what was an "appropriate" relationship to their state.

§ 72. UCC Cases; Secured Transactions

So-called "secured" transactions under the UCC are an important class of commercial transactions. Creditors wanting security for their loans seek a security interest in personal property of the debtor. The question is often whether that security interest is "perfected", meaning whether it can be enforced against a third party who buys the secured property. If the third party buys the secured property and the security interest is "unperfected", the creditor has a problem. The creditor is left to trying to get the debt back from the debtor, which may well prove difficult if she has no assets. If, however, the security interest is perfected, the creditor can take the secured property and sell it if necessary to satisfy the debt. In other words, now it's the third party's problem. Obviously, creditors would prefer the exalted status of "perfection" when it comes to their security interests.

Article 9 of the UCC (as revised effective 2001) provides for a system of public filing of security interests. That way, third parties inclined to buy property can check the public records to see if they're buying a debt along with the property. The question, though, is where (what state) to look? This is where choice of law comes into play. The 2001 revision of Article 9 provides that in general the financing statement (the evidence of the security interest) must be filed in the state in which the debtor is "located." Individual debtors are located in their state of residence. Non-individual (business) debtors with only one place of business are located at their place of business. Business debtors with multiple places of business are located at the "chief executive office." For "registered organizations" (most obviously corporations) the location is the state of registration (incorporation).

However, if any of these "locations" gives a non-U.S. location, then the UCC "location" can only be in a country that has a system of public filing. Why? Remember the basic philosophy here. We want third parties to know what they're buying, and they can't find out if it's not available somewhere publicly. If the "location" would be in a non-U.S. place that does not require public filing, then the Code gives the debtor a (wildly fictional) location in the District of Columbia. Again why? We want the filing in some place that it will be public, and if all else fails – check out D.C.

§ 73. Corporations

Many aspects of corporate formation and operation may touch on conflict of laws. Once a corporation, duly formed under the laws of a given state, seeks to do business in another, it may find itself immediately faced with the requirement that it file papers in the other, submitting to regulation and taxation there to the extent that its local activities make this constitutionally permissible. This is sometimes referred to as "licensing". By whatever name, the requirement may be imposed on any corporation doing an intrastate business in the state. (Eli Lilly, USSC 1961.) Local licensing may not be required, however, when the corporation's business is exclusively interstate. (Allenberg, USSC 1974.)

In the conduct of its regular business activities, a corporation as a general rule will qualify as just another person, subject to the same rules of substance, procedure, and choice of law as any other. But we must of course separate the corporation's business with others from matters of its internal organization and structure, as to which the law of the state of incorporation will almost invariably govern. There will be occasional exceptions, when the law of some state other than that of incorporation will have a predominant interest in some matter of internal corporate regulation, but those will be infrequent. The Restatement acknowledges them as exceptions as it sets up the several divisions of the general rule.

Chief among the internal matters to which the law of the state of incorporation is applicable are the rights and liabilities of shareholders among themselves and vis-à-vis the corporation (Rst.2d §§ 303–307), and the liabilities of directors and officers (Rst.2d § 309).

While formal dissolution of a corporation is governed by the law of the state of incorporation, other states may be able to eject the foreign corporation, at least insofar as intrastate business is concerned, for given conduct, such as the failure to file for a license as mentioned above.

The need for uniformity of result, and hence an unambiguous reference to the law of but one state to resolve internal corporate issues, is most apparent in the case of the giant multistate or multinational corporation. One buying shares in such a corporation should do so with the understanding that all intra-familial issues about benefits and burdens appended to those shares will be governed by the law of the state of incorporation, wherever the action that presents those issues may be brought.

The requirement to apply the law of the state of incorporation to intra-corporate relationships may even be perceived in terms of a full faith and credit obligation. In Broderick (USSC 1935), for example, a New York banking corporation was involved. New York's superintendent of banks assessed its shareholders for certain sums and among these shareholders were several hundred New Jersey residents, whom the superintendent then sued in New Jersey to recover the sums assessed. A New Jersey statute purported to bar its courts from entertaining such suits except in respect of New Jersey corporations. The statute was held unconstitutional and New Jersey was required to entertain the action. The court might simply have treated this as a recognition-of-judgments case, with the New York administrative determination (which is what the superintendent's assessment was) treated as if a judgment rendered by a court. (See § 120.) That would have been an even more obvious use of the full faith and credit principle, which had previously been applied to such a judgment (Converse, USSC 1912). But the court did not restrict itself to that. It said that "[t]he assessment is an incident of the incorporation. Thus the subject matter is peculiarly within the regulatory power of New York, as the State of incorporation." Hence New Jersey's refusal to entertain the case, even if couched in terms of a mere want of jurisdiction (see § 56 and the treatment of the Hughes case, USSC 1951), amounted in effect to a refusal of full faith and credit to New York's corporation law in respect of an internal matter of New York corporate business, and was unacceptable.

Today, longarm statutes in the state of incorporation will sometimes enable its officials to obtain home-state judgments against nonresident shareholders, directors, and officers for assessments and like obligations arising out of the corporate relationship. Since the full faith and credit obligation of a sister-state judgment is virtually unavoidable (§ 110), less frequently today will a state official (or the corporation itself, for that matter) have to go into the nonresident shareholder's state on the underlying claim itself.

Indeed, if the underlying claim is brought in a forum other than that of incorporation, it may confront the rule that one state will not undertake a suit that involves it in the internal affairs of a foreign corporation. This is a rule of forum non conveniens, however, rather than strictly one of jurisdiction (§ 53), so that a court in other than the incorporating state may occasionally entertain such a case. Indeed, it may have to, as it had to in Broderick. Whether it does so voluntarily or under federal compulsion, it had best have unusually strong contacts with the case before it applies its own law to the exclusion of the incorporating state's law on issues of internal corporate business.

§ 74. Usury Cases

A rule of validation generally applies to usury questions. If of several states involved in the lending transaction the law of any one of them would sustain the rate of interest, the courts tend to choose that one. Consistent with this, if all of the states involved deem the rate excessive but apply different penalties, the law of the smallest penalty governs. (Seeman, USSC 1927.) The theory is that the parties intended to be bound by their agreement and that if any of the related jurisdictions would uphold it, it should be upheld. If the agreement is invalid under the laws of all related jurisdictions, however, it will fall; it cannot derive validity from the law of an unrelated state, even if the parties should stipulate to that state's law in the agreement. (Rst.2d § 203, Comment.)

§ 75. Arbitrability

Arbitration as a means of dispute settlement, instead of the usual court litigation, ordinarily comes about by contract. It has been made mandatory in certain instances, especially in the areas of tort insurance and labor law, but these are special areas and it is only to the ordinary contract-stipulated, or consensual, arbitration that attention turns here.

Most American states have pro-arbitration attitudes today, and some of the more populous ones can even be described as enthusiastic about the arbitration process for what it spares the court system. A few states are still set against arbitration. When a contract involving states in each of those camps calls for arbitration, whose law governs it? The courts have had mixed feelings about that. The better view is that the matter is not merely procedural, calling for automatic reference to the attitudes of the forum, but substantive enough to invoke a law-choosing process. The Restatement's position (Rst.2d § 218) is that the parties may stipulate to the governing law in the agreement itself, which stipulation would presumably select the law of a pro-arbitration state, and that absent a stipulation the validity of the commitment to arbitrate should be gauged by the law of the state with the most significant relationship to the transaction (Rst.2d §§ 187, 188). Some cases hold the matter procedural, automatically applying forum law to the issue, or, if the forum is anti-arbitration, reject the arbitration commitment as violative of forum policy. New York adopted the latter posture (Meacham, NY 1914) before subsequent statutory changes made it a leading proponent instead of an enemy of arbitration. The change of heart was complete, New York afterwards even accepting agreements calling for arbitration in foreign nations and recognizing awards rendered there by default when a duly notified party would not honor the arbitration commitment

(Gilbert, NY 1931). (Today a treaty touches the point, a matter we will return to below.)

There are laws in some states that are still uncongenial to arbitration, but they are usually displaced by the Federal Arbitration Act. If the transaction falls into the maritime realm or involves interstate or foreign commerce, it is governed by the federal arbitration act, 9 U.S.C.A. §§ 1–16, which is distinct from the state acts. In Allied–Bruce Terminix (USSC 1995) an unlucky couple bought a termite-infested house in Alabama. They sued the pest control company which had contracted through its local office to fix the problem. The contract contained an arbitration clause, which Alabama law purported to make unenforcible. The Court held that Alabama law must give way. Despite the distinctly local flavor of the transaction, the Court held that its tangential connection to interstate commerce was enough to bring it within the reach of the federal act.

Involved and intertwined as these principles may be, they do not often present difficulty for the reason that most states have liberal arbitration acts and the federal act is a liberal one, too. Hence, more often than not when the federal act approves arbitration, so will the state act, leaving little to choose between them on the fundamental question of whether the dispute is arbitrable. (Many state court cases and even some federal cases applying state arbitration acts can probably be shown to have done so inadvertently, for the reason that an interstate commerce transaction was involved and the federal act was technically the applicable one.)

While the issue of whether a dispute is arbitrable is deemed substantive so that its resolution must come from the appropriate act—the federal act for maritime and interstate transactions, the state act for all others—no matter in which court the issue arises, the mechanics of raising the issue are procedural and each forum follows its own act. Hence a state court, for example, will entertain only the procedures of its own act to raise an arbitrability question, although it will answer the question by referring to the federal act in an interstate commerce or maritime case, while the federal court in any other kind of case will use the federal act and the federal rules to raise the issue procedurally but will resolve the issue on its merits by applying the appropriate state act.

The United States along with many other nations is a party to a treaty called the Convention on the Recognition and Enforcement of Foreign Arbitral Awards. Obligations to arbitrate (as well as awards in arbitrations already held) falling under the treaty, which is implemented in 9 U.S.C.A. §§ 201–208, must be recognized in both state and federal courts. The treaty applies only to commercial transactions (9 U.S.C.A. § 202) and governs principally when citizens of different signatory nations are involved.

H. TORTS—EVOLUTION OF MODERN TECHNIQUES

§ 76. Torts; Interim Steps From the Lex Loci

Of the several developments that began to expose the weaknesses of the lex loci rule, which chooses the law of the place of the wrong to govern everything substantive in a tort case, perhaps the most outstanding were technological advances in means of transportation and an expanding economy that put those means into the hands of vast numbers of people at diverse economic levels. The car became a common possession in most families. After World War II, it became common for suburban families to own two cars. One major American car manufacturer built an advertising campaign around a slogan of two-car ownership. Good times made money available. Young people hardly out of infancy, and many still in, bought cars, or were given them by their parents. These went faster and faster, and while they did, the airplane was gearing up and the jet age preparing to follow. Air travel contracts continents and shrinks worlds. And a booming economy put travel within the reach of millions. Commercial transactions as well as tortious events with multi-state elements began to proliferate. Choice of law rules could no longer meander on at leisure. Through the sheer numbers of the cases that tested them, their weaknesses became glaring. Forward movement could no longer be delayed.

The tort arena showed many harsh examples of the injustices to which rigid application of the old lex loci delicti rule could lead. If State X, which authorized a personal injury recovery in favor of P against D, was the domicile of both parties, the state of the subject vehicle's registration, and the place of issuance of the applicable insurance policy, most judges were ready to agree that it would be unsound to bar a recovery merely because the accident happened to occur in State Y, which happened to have some exclusionary rule, such as a guest-host statute (barring recovery by a passenger against a driver), or some restrictive rule (such as an arbitrary limit on the amount that could be awarded as a wrongful death recovery). In many instances it could easily be shown that State Y, although the situs of the accident, did not aim its exclusionary or restrictive rule against any but its own residents. And yet the law of the indifferent State Y was about to bar or limit a recovery between State X residents, to the undoing of the laws and policies of State X, the only truly interested state.

Fact patterns like these supplied the context for the major steps away from the old lex loci rule, but the steps were tentative and sometimes clumsy. While most of the judges might have been ready for a change, they were not ready to cut the umbilical cord; a stretching was the best they would tolerate. Hence we have some interim cases—precursors of the modern approaches that do seem to have cut the cord—that do the right thing by the lights of the future but describe their doing with the techniques and language of the past.

A major interim technique was to treat the tort issue as belonging to some other realm. In 1928, for example, Connecticut extruded a tort recovery through a "contract" treatment. P and D were both Connecticut residents. D had rented a car from a Connecticut rental agency in Connecticut. The accident occurred in Massachusetts while D was driving and P was a passenger. P wanted to recover against the agency. Connecticut law made the agency derivatively liable for the lessee's conduct; Massachusetts law did not. The court treated the issue as one of contract, holding that the liability-imposing Connecticut statute was part of the contract because the contract was made in Connecticut, and P was a beneficiary of the contract. Hence a "contract" caption enabled P to recover while a "tort" caption, by invoking the lex loci rule, would have resulted in a choice of Massachusetts law and barred recovery. (Levy, Conn.1928.)

In 1953, the California Supreme Court committed the villainy of calling an obviously substantive question "procedural" in order to justify a justifiable tort recovery. (Grant, Cal.1953.) All of the parties were Californians but the accident occurred in Arizona. The issue was whether a tort claim survives the death of the tortfeasor. California law said it does; Arizona, it does not. In order to apply California law, a result justifiable on such facts under just about all of the modern choice of law approaches, the court stamped the survival issue "procedural" and thus obtained the application of California (forum) law. Justice Traynor, who wrote for the court, would probably have liked to reach out then and there for one of today's rationales (he did so later, such as in the landmark Reich case, Cal.1967; § 79), but he apparently felt that the time was not yet ripe in 1953. He said as much in a later law review article (37 Texas L.Rev. 657 at 670, 1959). One winces to hear the description of "procedural" appended to the most substantive of all law issues: whether or not P has a cause of action. And yet this technique of "procedural" characterization, a heavy in most performances, could be trotted out as a hero on this interim stage in the development of choice of law rules. It says something about the mindlessness of the lex loci rule when rigidly applied. It would have denied a recovery in Grant by forcing the application of Arizona's rule of non-survival despite the obviously higher interests of California in the outcome of the case. It would have been California's burden, for example—should Arizona law have been applied to bar recovery—to supply the survivors with such sustenance as they might need.

This "procedure" characterization would sometimes be used along with another, and theoretically more acceptable, rationale to escape the lex loci. In Kilberg (NY 1961), for example, a New Yorker (among others) was killed in the Massachusetts crash of an airplane. The airplane company was a Massachusetts corporation, but the deceased bought his ticket, for a New York City to Massachusetts flight, in New York. In a wrongful death suit brought against the airline in New York, the issue was whether the $15,000 damages limit contained in the Massachusetts wrongful death statute would apply. New York had no such limit. The court called the matter "procedural" and applied New York law, but it also cited New York's "strong public policy" against such arbitrary money limitations. In this context, the "public policy" basis was the more palatable. New York had a sufficient connection with the case to apply its own law, especially as against an interstate airline that could be said to be on notice of its exposure to the laws of the diverse states of its passengers, and the court's reference to New York's "strong public policy" was just another way of saying that New York had the predominant interest in the resolution of the issue. Indeed, Judge Fuld in a concurrence said that he would have preferred to reach the result by applying an outright "contacts" approach (which the New York Court of Appeals got around to two years later in Babcock, 1963; § 78).

Kilberg was a piecemeal approach, taking only the damages issue from New York law but applying Massachusetts law to the issue of liability. (The constitutionality of this approach was upheld by an en banc Second Circuit in Pearson [CA2 1962].) It paid at least lip service to the rule that a wrongful death claim could be governed only by the law of the place of the accident that caused the death for the reason that wrongful death is a statutory cause of action (unknown to the common law) and hence viable only insofar as the place of the wrong recognizes it. This was just another arbitrary adjunct of the lex loci rule and also began a trip into history as choice of law development proceeded. Under modern approaches, the wrongful death claim is just as subject to a choice of law treatment as any other claim, in respect of liability as well as damages. (E.g., Farber, NY 1967.)

Another characterization technique was used to allow a tort recovery between spouses when their domicile permitted it but the place of the accident did not. In Haumschild (Wis.1959), W and H were a Wisconsin couple. She sued him in Wisconsin for injuries he caused her in a California accident. Wisconsin recognized interspouse suits; California did not. Under the lex loci rule, the recovery would have been barred. But lex loci applies to tort, said the court, while here the issue is not one of tort, but of family law. Hence the law of the family domicile should govern, and it did: Wisconsin law was applied to sustain a recovery.

This may on its face seem like a "characterization" case, but upon closer scrutiny it is not, at least not in the sense of merely adopting an ad hoc label to justify a particular result. Whether one spouse should be able to sue the other is more legitimately of interest to their domicile than to the place of the underlying event, and that was in essence what Wisconsin was saying in Haumschild.

A landmark Minnesota case (Schmidt, 1957) similarly separated issues in order to escape an application of the lex loci rule that did not appeal to the court's sense of justice on the facts. The Minnesota dram shop act was involved, imposing liability on a person who unlawfully sells liquor to one who afterwards, drunk, injures someone else in an accident. The sale took place in Minnesota but the accident occurred in Wisconsin. The court held that there were "two distinct wrongs" here, one the liquor-selling and the other the driving. It applied the Minnesota act to sustain the claim against the dram shop. (Illinois on like facts denied such a claim, giving its dram shop statute narrower scope [Graham, Ill.1969].)

As most of these cases manifest, the lex loci rule made trouble only when it threatened to apply to all issues in what tradition might broadly describe as a "tort" case. To some issues the law of the place of the wrong is usually the most appropriate to apply by all measures: whether the driver was obeying the rules of the road, stopping at lights, staying under the speed limit, and the like. Judges bridled at the lex loci only when urged to apply it to an issue in which the situs had little interest, some other place had much interest, and, of course, when the two places had very different substantive laws and accompanying policies. We thus see the new rules being adopted in cases involving not standards of care and traffic rules, but guest-host issues, wrongful-death limits, survival-of-claim questions, interspousal-suit barriers, and the like. In the choice of law sphere, these issues are not simple adjuncts of a tort action. They claim individual attention, which the lex loci rule does not give them. The new rules do.

§ 77. Torts; Modern Approaches

No simple "rule" can govern in choice of law. The elements are too varied. Hence the courts and commentators have settled on "techniques" or "approaches" by which they hope to reach acceptable results. Several scholars have been influential in developing these approaches.

Professor Brainerd Currie gets the major credit for developing the interest analysis, or governmental interest analysis, technique. (Professor Currie's writings are collected in Currie, Selected Essays on the Conflict of Laws [1963].) Interest analysis requires an examination into competing laws to determine their underlying policies and the strength of the relative interests the competing sovereigns have in the application of their respective laws in the particular situation. The facts will vary and the strength of the relevant policies will wax and wane accordingly. There are many examples of this in recent cases. California's Reich case (Cal.1967) will serve as an example in the interest analysis treatment (§ 79).

The "most significant relationship" test is used in the Restatement (Rst.2d § 145). This parses the issues in each case having multistate elements and applies to each issue the law of the state deemed to have the "most significant relationship" to the issue. "Grouping of contacts" or "center of gravity" were precursors if not merely verbal substitutes of this test, which is illustrated in New York's Babcock case (NY 1963; § 78). The "most significant relationship" test uses much the same technique as the interest analysis does, and for practical purposes it can probably be deemed the same. The elements to be considered under the "most significant relationship" test are set forth in Rst.2d §§ 6, 145(2) (§ 66 in this Nutshell).

Many judges have found helpful Professor Leflar's list of "choice influencing considerations", set forth in § 66. It contains an invitation that the judge consider, among other things, which of the competing laws is the "better rule of law". A tool as flexible as that is often what a judge is looking for when the other elements on the several available lists tend to result in a standoff between the competing rules. Clark (NH 1966) and Milkovich (Minn. 1973) apply these considerations (§ 80).

Professor Ehrenzweig, the author of A Treatise on the Conflict of Laws (West 1962), was also a well-known theoretician in the Conflict of Laws. His view pointed to forum law. He held that with certain exceptions a forum ought to apply its own law because the function of the forum court is to advance the forum's own policies. To the argument that such an approach would put too much emphasis on forum shopping, Professor Ehrenzweig countered that a reworked, tightened, and nationalized rule of forum non conveniens would be the answer, permitting a court to exercise jurisdiction only if the forum had adequate contacts with the case and in effect applying those same contacts to justify the forum's choice of its own law to govern the substantive issues.

These are of course simplifications. Cases illustrating application of these and yet other approaches will afford us opportunity to see how current choice of law techniques work out in practice, and how the divergent competing elements fall into place.

Note that torts furnish the subject matter in the ensuing treatments. This is not to suggest that the new approaches are designed exclusively for tort cases. It merely acknowledges that on the choice of law stage, the tort roles have offered the new approaches their major opportunities. Since we are to be the critics, we may as well spend our energies on live performances.

While being critical, we must always try to be flexible. While no single approach or technique has unanimous support, those with any measure of success at all have had some flexibility. Choice of law is no place for a perfectionist. (A perfectionist has been described as a person who takes great pains, and gives them to you.)

§ 78. Torts; "Most Significant Relationship"

The Second Restatement's "most significant relationship" analysis applies, to each issue in a case, the law of the state found to have the predominant relationship to the particular issue. An illustration is the Babcock case (NY 1963) in which this approach, applied earlier in contract cases in New

York (Auten, NY 1954; § 68), was extended to tort in replacement of the lex loci delicti. Babcock was a perfect case for this step. The contacts were one-sided and the place of the injury was only that; it had no other contacts.

P and D were friends living in Rochester, New York. They took a ride into Ontario, Canada, with D driving and P a passenger. The car went off the road in Ontario and P was injured. The trip started and was to end in New York, where the car was garaged and with reference to whose laws the insurance on the car was issued. There was not even a second car involved to complicate matters; it was a one-car accident. Ontario had a guest-host statute barring a recovery by guest P against host D; New York had no such barrier. Under the lex loci, Ontario law would automatically have been applied and barred recovery. The court, acknowledging Ontario's interest in how the car was being driven and whether the driver was obeying Ontario's rules of the road, pointed out that those matters were not at issue. The only question was whether Ontario's guest-host barrier should be applied when both guest and host were New Yorkers and the other New York contacts were so plain. The court, applying the relationship approach, chose New York law for the guest-host issue and held that it was no barrier to recovery.

The relationship approach does not merely count the contacts that the respective states have. The approach "is not merely to count contacts, but rather to consider which contacts are most significant and to determine where these contacts are found" (Johnson, Wash.1976). The test is not one of quantity and never was (Cipolla, Pa.1970). The quality, the significance, of the contacts must be analyzed. Not only must the facial instructions of the competing laws be considered. As Pennsylvania noted in overruling the lex loci standard, the new approach must analyze "the policies and interests underlying the particular issue before the court" (Griffith, Pa.1964).

In Babcock, the policy of the Ontario guest-host statute had to be investigated. The statute's purpose was found to be the protection of the insurer from the fraudulent claim of a plaintiff acting in collusion with the insured (driver or owner) when they are family or friends. Such a purpose, insofar as relevant to an Ontario statute, would be for the protection of Ontario defendants and their insurers, observed the court, so that it is no offense to Ontario if such a statute is not applied when the parties are New Yorkers and the insurance policy was issued pursuant to New York law on a New York-licensed car.

When the required analysis of underlying policies reveals that one state really has no interest in the outcome of an issue despite the seeming conflict between the on-the-face statements of its and the other state's law, the situation is sometimes denominated a "false conflict". "False conflicts" are discussed in § 81.

One of the advantages of the lex loci rule was predictability. Because the finger pointed always to the place of the wrong, the law that would be chosen could be readily predicted. Cases rejecting the lex loci rule acknowledge that predictability is a casualty, but also note that predictability plays little role in torts, in contrast with the important place it has in contracts. People about to take a car ride don't stop to discuss the subtleties of choice of law. To the extent that a lawyer should be approached by an unusually prescient client and asked how the client can protect herself from all tort liabilities, there is really only one ultimate advice: be insured to the hilt, or don't go. To a client who does a lot of traveling, the lawyer should recommend heavy liability insurance, which insulates the insured from unpredictable financial exposure to others, and substantial accident insurance as well, to cover the insured (for her own personal injuries) and her family (should she be killed in the accident). An accident policy is a regular, always-applicable policy covering not just an occasional trip, but all-year-round activities. The client will learn this for herself if she does some flying and wearies of frantic, last-minute treks to insurance stands at airports.

That predictability suffers under modern choice of law approaches is seen, ironically, in the first relevant case to arrive in the New York Court of Appeals after the state's adoption of the relationship test in Babcock. The case (Dym, NY 1965) involved a car accident in Colorado. P was a passenger suing D, the driver, and both were New Yorkers. A guest-host statute was again at issue, this one a Colorado version requiring a showing of wilful misconduct before P could recover from D. The competing New York law imposed no such requirement. Stressing among other things the involvement of a second car and non-New Yorkers as distinctions from Babcock, a majority of four judges applied Colorado law. A three-judge dissent chose New York law. All of the judges said they were applying the law of the state with the most significant relationship! Dym was apparently overruled in yet another New York case presenting a guest-host issue (Tooker, NY 1969).

The guest-host issue appeared so often in New York cases involving foreign law that the New York Court of Appeals, building on the experience of these cases, afterwards formulated a list with an instruction about whose law to apply to a given combination of contacts (Neumeier, NY 1972, treated on its facts in § 83).

In the Oregon case that extended the "most significant relationship" test to tort cases (Casey, Oreg.1967), a damages issue was presented. D's negligent maintenance of a road in Washington caused an injury to H, an Oregon resident. H's wife sought recovery for loss of consortium, a compensable element under Oregon but not Washington law. Stressing that the place of injury was not mere "happenstance" in this case (contrast the Babcock case), the court held that Oregon's interest in obtaining compensation for loss of consortium was outweighed by Washington's policy of assuring those working in Washington that their liabilities would be measured by Washington law. Loss of consortium was held not to be a compensable item of damages.

A damages issue more frequently met in multistate tort cases involves an arbitrary maximum on the damages awardable for wrongful death, one state having such a limit and the other not. That was the issue in California's Reich case, treated in the next section, and in Miller (NY 1968). In Miller, X and D were brothers who had a business relationship, X living in New York and D in Maine. X went to Maine and while there was killed in an accident involving a car D was driving. Maine limited wrongful death damages to $20,000; New York had no stated limit. On such a state of facts, presumably Maine law would be chosen even under the "relationship" test. Two things occurred after the accident, however, which influenced the decision to choose New York law and impose no limit: D moved to New York and Maine repealed its damages limitation. The majority gave some weight to these factors; the dissenters would not.

Post-accident changes of domicile are of course suspect when made on the plaintiff's side, the fear being that if the factor is considered it will encourage post-event forum shopping by the plaintiff, but, at least when no intent to forum-shop is shown, it has been given some weight (Allstate, USSC 1981, plurality opinion). In Miller, the post-event change of domicile was on the defendant's side, but the defendant and the decedent were related. However, in Schultz (NY 1985) the court ignored a defendant's post-injury corporate move even though the defendant had moved to a state whose legal climate was actually more favorable to the plaintiff. The possibility of forum-shopping to the detriment of the defendant's insurer of course exists in that situation and should be considered.

Dissents are frequent in these cases. The judges may subscribe to the approach but disagree on its application. Some may find the application unconstitutional in a given case, a violation of due process or even full faith and credit. Rosenthal (CA2 1973) is considered by many to be an extreme case of the application of the "relationship" approach. X went to Boston for medical treatment and died in a Massachusetts hospital. His wife brought a wrongful death action in New York against the Massachusetts hospital and physician. A divided Second Circuit held that under the relationship test, the New York law forbidding any arbitrary limit on damages should govern and the ceiling contained in the Massachusetts wrongful death statute should not. The majority stressed the national status of the defendants and the high proportion of out-of-state patients they treated; they were not just a local physician and hospital. They also stressed that the defendants' insurance was not limited to correspond to the wrongful death limit and that although wrongful death damages are limited by Massachusetts law, personal injury damages are not. Hence the policy amount stood ready to apply up to its own stated limit, without regard to the Massachusetts limitation. The dissenting judge was influenced by what the majority merely acknowledged: the wide difference in medical malpractice insurance premiums applicable at the relevant times in New York ($1139) and Massachusetts ($192) and the effect that an increase in malpractice exposure would have in Massachusetts.

Note that to make a choice of law in Rosenthal, the federal court applied the choice of law rule of the forum. The case was based on the federal court's diversity jurisdiction. The Erie doctrine (Chapter V) thus applied to require the federal court to refer to forum state law, which includes choice of law rules (§ 103).

The difficulties of the "relationship" approach in a case like Rosenthal occasionally breeds a yearning for a return to the "certainty" of the lex loci rule. In O'Connor (CA2 1978), for example, which was also a diversity case, Judge Henry Friendly, reflecting on the "relationship" approach adopted by the New York Court of Appeals in Babcock (NY 1963), said that "we ... might think that, in the light of fifteen years of experience under Babcock, the departure from the certainty of the lex loci delicti rule was not such a famous victory as it first appeared to be.... " Old orthodoxy has merit, posits this wistful view, and one should not fall victim to new temptations too easily.

This may not be entirely fair to the "relationship" test, which, because of its flexibility, accommodates the lex loci rule by applying it whenever a thoughtful balancing of competing elements points to it. The trouble with the lex loci rule is that it's never willing to return the favor.

§ 79. Torts; "Interest Analysis"

As far as theory is concerned, there is scant ground for treatment of "interest analysis" separate from the "most significant relationship" test done in the prior section. They involve the same ingredients, and, properly applied, they involve the same values and ought to reach the same results. But it is a way to break choice of law into negotiable segments. And under "interest analysis" we can treat the California cases that champion it. Most notable here is Justice Traynor's thoughtful opinion in Reich (Cal.1967).

Reich involved the collision of two cars in Missouri. In one was D, a Californian on his way to Illinois for a visit. In the other was an Ohio family including M, the mother, on their way to California, to which they were planning to move. Suit was brought in California for the wrongful death of M. The issue was damages. Missouri restricted wrongful death damages to a $25,000 maximum; neither California nor Ohio had a limitation. Analyzing the interests of the respective jurisdictions, the court held that there would be no limit. Missouri's interest here was directed to the conduct of the parties in that state and the damage limit had nothing to do with conduct. The court applied the Ohio law, which favored the plaintiff Ohio family with the no-limit rule, and said that D could not complain because he was being called on to pay no more than his own state (California) would hold him to account for.

From yet another vantage point one could simply apply a "relationship" test and say that California and Ohio had the predominant contacts with the damages issue, and that since both agreed that there should be no limit, the aggregate contacts of both states together pushed Missouri out of the competition.

Had Missourians been involved in the case, either as defendants (who would argue that they should be permitted to depend on the lighter damages imposed by Missouri as both their home state and the state of their conduct) or as co-plaintiffs (who might in a given situation argue that if the Missouri limit is not applied to the Ohioans there might be less insurance available to protect the Missourians), the inquiry would not have been so smooth. Indeed, the California Supreme Court later observed that its Reich case did not involve a genuine conflict (Bernhard, Cal.1976, treated below).

The court said the same thing of its decision in Hurtado (Cal.1974), a case often cited for interest analysis techniques. A Mexican was killed in a California accident involving California defendants. His family sued in California, as well they should have: the law of the Mexican state severely limited wrongful death damages while California had no limit. The purpose of the Mexican limitation was found to be the protection of Mexican defendants, and since Hurtado involved California defendants the Mexican interest was held to have evaporated. California, on the other hand, in barring arbitrary damage limits, was held to aim at least in some measure to assure fair compensation for all hurt on its avenues, and that would include nonresidents. Had the suit been brought in Mexico, even assuming the availability of jurisdiction there, its damage limits would likely have restricted the recovery. By suing in California, the plaintiff escaped the Mexican limitation.

Great is the power to choose a forum.

"Interest analysis" is the banner under which Hurtado goes, but the case, along with Reich, is later described by the same court in Bernhard (Cal. 1976) as involving "false conflicts", which means that although the competing laws may seem in conflict on their face, an analysis of their underlying policies reveals that they aim at different targets and that there is no competition and hence no conflict after all. (See § 81 on false conflicts.) In Bernhard, the court says that it is presented with a "true" conflict for the first time since adopting the interest analysis approach. Resolving this true conflict, the court decided on a "comparative impairment" test. This test, said the court:

> proceeds on the principle that true conflicts should be resolved by applying the law of the

state whose interest would be the more impaired if its law were not applied.... [I]t is very different from a weighing process. The court does not "weigh" the conflicting governmental interests in the sense of determining which conflicting law manifested the "better" or the "worthier" social policy on the specific issue.

So describing the test, the court in Bernhard holds a Nevada bar civilly liable to a California plaintiff injured in California by a Californian to whom the bar had fed too much drink in Nevada shortly before. Nevada law also prohibited such conduct but imposed only criminal sanctions for it; California added civil liability. The court held that California's policy would be more impaired than Nevada's were California law not chosen. Since Nevada forbade the conduct, the net result of a choice of California law would only be to add civil liability to the violation, an extension less painful to Nevada than the total denial of a civil recovery to the plaintiff would be to California.

In Bernhard the "comparative impairment" test resulted in an application of forum law. In Offshore (Cal.1978) it resulted in California's deference to the other state, which was Louisiana. A Louisiana accident was caused by D, a Delaware corporation with its principal office in New York but also doing business in California. The accident injured E, an employee of the plaintiff, a California corporation. California gave the employer a cause of action for injury to its employee, whose services the employer lost; Louisiana law did not. The court reviewed a number of elements before choosing Louisiana law. It said that the impairment test tries to determine the "relative commitment" of the states to the law involved and concluded that Louisiana had a higher commitment to its law denying such claims than California had to its law allowing them. The court found its own state's law "antique" in that today the employer protects itself against the loss of a key employee's services by carrying insurance, while the Louisiana policy of promoting investment without excessive risks for employers is, said the court, more "progressive".

The court reached that conclusion only after analyzing the policy and history of the competing substantive laws of the two states. Some would argue that the banner of "comparative impairment" under which the court proceeded is merely an extension of the "interest analysis" approach. Professor Leflar would suggest that the court was merely trying to determine which of the competing laws was the "better rule of law". That inquiry is an unabashed member of Leflar's list of five "choice influencing considerations", which several courts have adopted outright and to which we now turn.

§ 80. Torts; Leflar's "Choice–Influencing Considerations"

Professor Leflar's list of five elements the court should consider in determining choice of law has found favor in several courts. (The elements are set forth in § 66.) New Hampshire used the list in

Clark (NH 1966) in a case with facts similar to those of Babcock (NY 1963; § 78). In Clark an accident occurred in Vermont involving only New Hampshire parties. The trip began and was to end in New Hampshire. A guest-host problem was again the issue, Vermont requiring a showing of gross negligence while New Hampshire required only ordinary negligence when guest-host was the relationship. The first three elements on the Leflar list were found to be of little relevance in Clark, but items four (advancement of the forum's interest) and five (the better rule of law) were deemed key ones and resulted in the application of New Hampshire law. Number four counted in New Hampshire's favor because New Hampshire was the forum, all of the parties were its residents, and the issue involved a recovery between those residents. Vermont (as with Ontario in the Babcock case) could have little interest in making it harder for one party to recover from another when neither had roots in Vermont. Number five also weighed for New Hampshire when the court found Vermont's rule about the extra guest-host burden of proof less modern than New Hampshire's, which imposed no extra burden.

Leading cases applying the Leflar approach can be found in a number of states (e.g., Conklin, Wis. 1968; Mitchell, Miss.1968). Its use in Minnesota is manifest in Allstate (USSC 1981), in which the Supreme Court sustained as constitutional the choice of Minnesota law that it led to there.

In Allstate, the parties were from Wisconsin and the accident occurred there while X was riding on the back of a motorcycle. X was killed. The others involved in the accident had no insurance, but X himself had a policy covering three cars he owned. That policy had an indorsement covering X should he be hit by an uninsured motorist. Its coverage was $15,000. P, X's wife, sued in Minnesota to determine the amount of the insurer's liability. The insurer said it was only $15,000; the plaintiff claimed that it was $15,000 for each of the three cars covered by X's policy, and thus a total of $45,000. This is called "stacking" and Minnesota law allowed it; Wisconsin law did not and would have limited the insurer's exposure to $15,000. The Minnesota court chose Minnesota law, relying in some measure on the facts that X, though a Wisconsin domiciliary, was regularly employed in Minnesota and thus a member of its work force, and that the insurer did business in Minnesota and was on reasonable notice of Minnesota law, especially because the item insured was mobile and the insured lived near the Minnesota border and regularly commuted to Minnesota. With these contacts, Minnesota's choice of its own law passed the constitutionality test (barely, Allstate was a 5–3 decision and Justice Stevens, among the five, had no praise for Minnesota's choice as a matter of conflicts law). In its choice of law analysis, Minnesota included treatment of the "better rule of law" principle and found its own rule, allowing stacking, the better one. Stacking was found to be the trend and the anti-stacking rule of Wisconsin was found to be losing ground nationwide.

Guest-host statutes that impede recovery in a tort case have been met on the conflicts scene more frequently than stacking cases. Minnesota, having no guest-host statute, has used the better-rule-of-law standard to reject them (Milkovich, Minn.1973).

I. PROBLEM AREAS

§ 81. "False Conflicts"—Only One State's Policies Involved

Different users of this term may have different meanings for it, but its most common use is where two competing rules have different instructions, and literally applied would lead to different results, but where an analysis of the policies underlying the rules shows that one of them was not aimed at the particular situation despite its facial content. Not intended to apply, it is removed from the competition, leaving the other rule, whose underlying policies do call for implementation, to govern. Under this kind of analysis, there is no real conflict at all despite the ostensible clash initially indicated. An analysis of the scope of both of the presumably competing laws, in other words, has revealed that one of them, despite its content, did not have the present situation in mind at all.

The technique of determining whether a prima facie conflict is in fact just a "false conflict" is discussed by Professor Currie in his Selected Essays on the Conflict of Laws (p. 189) and by Professor Cavers in his Choice of Law Process (p. 89).

California's Reich case (Cal.1967; § 79) can illustrate; the court that decided it later described it as involving "false conflicts". (Bernhard, Cal.1976.) In Reich, several members of an Ohio family were killed or injured in a Missouri collision with a car owned and driven by a Californian. Neither Ohio nor California had any arbitrary limit on wrongful death damages, but Missouri, the place of the accident, had. The court in Reich applied Ohio law after an interests analysis. A "false conflicts" analysis would merely have said that the Missouri limitation, whatever its scope, was not aimed at a case involving no Missourians on any side. Hence the idea that Missouri law was in conflict with the laws of either Ohio or California posed a "false conflict". Interest-analysis phraseology would simply say that Missouri had no interest in the issue in this case, or an interest subordinate to the higher interests of Ohio, or of California and Ohio together.

By these standards, a "false conflict" involving a guest-host statute imposing an extra burden of proof also appears in Pfau (NJ 1970). P of Connecticut was a guest in a car owned and driven by New Jersey domiciliaries. The car collided in Iowa with an Iowa car, but the Iowans' claims were settled, leaving only the non-Iowans' interests to be looked after. Neither New Jersey nor Connecticut imposed any higher burden of proof in a guest-host situation than in any other, and since between them they had the sole interest in the resolution of the issue, the idea that Iowa law (which had the guest-host statute) was in conflict was a false one.

So with New York's Babcock case (NY 1963; § 78) as well. The one-car accident occurred in Ontario, which barred suit between guest and host, which plaintiff and defendant were, but both were New Yorkers and the car was licensed and insured in New York. A "false conflicts" technique would have analyzed the policy underlying the Ontario guest-host statute, found it irrelevant to a suit entirely between foreigners, and hence concluded that there was no conflict, leaving the field to New York law (which contained no guest-host barrier) exclusively.

Sometimes, in the interplay of contacts, a court may find that "neither state has a vital interest in the outcome" and that the forum is therefore free to apply its own law as it would in a non-conflicts setting. That happened in Erwin (Oreg.1973; § 83). P and her husband were Washington residents. He was injured in Washington in an accident involving Oregon defendants. Washington did not allow a recovery for loss of consortium, but the policy underlying this was found to be the protection of Washington defendants, which made it irrelevant here. Oregon did allow such a recovery, but with the aim of protecting Oregon spouses, and there were none involved here. The result was a finding of indifference on both sides, prompting the forum to apply its own law simply because it was the more convenient. This would mean, on Erwin's facts, that a Washington wife was going to recover in an Oregon court for a loss of consortium her own state would not compensate.

When an analysis of underlying policies does reveal that one or the other of the states is going to have all or part of its purpose frustrated by the application of the other's law, the conflict at hand is a "true" one and the balancing of the opposing interests at its most delicate. Offshore (Cal.1978; § 79) in the tort area and Lilienthal (Oreg.1964; § 68) in the contracts realm illustrate true conflicts in every sense.

§ 82. True Conflicts—Two States' Differing Policies Involved: The Battleground of the Competing Techniques

In several of the prior sections we sampled some of the choice of law methods currently used, and in an earlier section (§ 66) some of the major commentators and sources were cited. All choice of law methods meet their best test in the case of a "true" conflict, the case in which there is antagonism not only between the instructions of the competing laws, but also between the policies that underlie them. The treatment in preceding sections of the principal new approaches obviates repetition here, but a few observations about competing techniques can help, and will incidentally enable us to acknowledge a few other standards that can account for some goings-on in choice of law perhaps better than such respectable citizens as interest analysis, significant relationship, choice-influence, and other senior members of the conflicts bar. Into this less reputable category might fall the choose-forum-law approach, and in tort cases the "plaintiff's viewpoint" rule, skeletons in the conflicts closet or in any event craftsmen received coldly at the better clubs. But like good politicians everywhere, they often pull the strings behind the scenes and end up controlling the election in fact if not in name.

There is no clear consensus behind any single standard, approach, "rule", technique, or whatever else might describe a choice of law process. The stuff of choice of law will occupy courts and scholars forever, or at least for as long as there are different sovereigns with different rules, each sovereign capable of asserting power through its courts. Even the same high court in the same state may prefer different approaches as its judicial personnel change. One thing that can probably be said for all of the modern approaches is that they aim to do good, to escape from the rigidity of the lex loci rule in tort cases and the analogous and equally rigid old rules of choice of law in contract and other cases. That they may sometimes reach different results is, under the circumstances, forgivable. What would be unforgivable would be a failure to reach at all.

In many of these cases, including those that ultimately settle on one approach, mention is often made of the others, usually just to show how similar they are (e.g., Reyno, CA3 1980, rev'd USSC 1981), but sometimes to disagree. It could probably be shown that disagreement is the exception rather than the rule. Although the less flexible among the advocates of a given approach may insist that each method can produce different results and only theirs aims true, the same panel of judges applying one of the other approaches would, it is submitted, more often than not reach the same result on the same facts. When California chooses the law of State X instead of State Y for the reason that State X's policy would be more undone by choosing State Y law than vice-versa, which is an application of the "comparative impairment" test, it is only saying in effect—although some of the sayers may gainsay what we say here—that State X has the predominant "governmental interest" in the outcome of the case, or that State X has the "most significant relationship" to the issue at hand, or that, on balancing all of the choice-influencing considerations, State X law, whether X be the forum or some other state, ought to apply. This is a basic truth, in any event, to most lawyers who have served as judges, or as law clerks to judges, and who know how often a judge hears the arguments and reads the briefs and then decides how the case ought to go, and then sees that it goes that way. Such a judge will summon forth the appropriate rationale. In conflicts, the judge has a parade of rationales, each of them flexible enough to support the decision. The technique or approach trotted out in a given case will have another day in the sun and another chance at the competition, but little hope of permanent applause. It is something like the cross-eyed javelin thrower. He didn't win any medals, but for a moment he had the undivided attention of the spectators.

Perhaps the fact that the result the judge thinks ought in fairness to be reached will often dictate the rationale chosen to support it is the reason why that seemingly subjective item number five on Professor Leflar's list of elements—the "better rule of law"—has found favor with many judges. It merely recites in candor what the judges often do in fact. "[H]onesty is the best policy," says Professor Leflar, "even in judicial opinions." (Amer.Confl.Law [4th Ed.] p. 300.)

Standing at another vantage point is the pro-forum-law approach advocated in one measure or another by some of the commentators. It sounds awful at first hearing, the quintessence of parochialism, and it surely had less to commend it in the pre-longarm jurisdiction era when the only place P may have had for suit against D was D's home state regardless of the contacts other states may have had with the case. But now, with jurisdiction likely to be available in the states that have had substantive contacts with the case, the forum's choice of its own law in the case of a true conflict is felt by some to have as much philosophical base as any other rule or approach or technique. If there is no conflict, or if there is a "false conflict" (§ 81), the forum should of course apply the law of the only interested state whether that turns out to be the forum or not. But if there is a genuine conflict, and the sensibilities of one of the states will necessarily be offended when the other's law is chosen, and one of the interested states is the forum (as it usually is), the view that the forum should choose its own law is one that deserves respect if not applause. The view is premised on the principle that the forum's courts exist to serve the forum's interest and should therefore strive to advance the forum's policies. If this puts a premium on forum shopping, and puts the plaintiff, who has the choice of forum, in the driver's seat, an advocate of the forum-law approach, such as Professor Ehrenzweig, would argue that accountability belongs to a system that gives the plaintiff the choice of forum, and that tightening up on forum non conveniens rules (§ 53), especially when jurisdiction is available in a number of courts under longarm concepts, is the answer.

The choose-forum-law approach has a guiding principle. So have the other approaches, but not as firm a guidepost. The most significant relationship approach can have the judges disagreeing on which state has the most significant relationship; the interest analysis approach, on which state has the predominant interest. Judges can also disagree on what the "better rule of law" is. Forum-law advocates, on the other hand, always know what they are about, but they come across to some judges as fanatics. (Churchill described a fanatic as a person who can't change his mind and won't change the subject.)

The forum-law advocate can come back with yet another argument. If in a given case State F (the forum) and State X are the only two states involved, and their interests are so evenly balanced that the "interest analysis", "most significant relationship", "comparative impairment" and all other tests would be hard pressed to choose, and each state, under each test, can muster an equal number of thoughtful advocates to support the application of its law, then none of those tests has a monopoly on the right answer. In those circumstances a flipped coin can do the job, and do it faster; and in those circumstances—the forum-law advocate would interpose—the forum-law rule would do the job just as fast, but do it better: it would at least have a philosophical mission to carry out.

Another philosopher with a mission is the advocate of the pro-plaintiff approach in tort cases. Most of the choice of law cases in the tort sphere, whatever their stated rationales, have chosen the law of the state that offers the plaintiff the greatest benefit. The most obvious explanation for this is that the plaintiff, with the choice of forum, has done his homework well and chosen wisely. But another may be that many judges, responding sympathetically to the privations visited on a tort-stricken family and recognizing that insurance coverage exists in most cases and spreads the cost among the whole premium-paying public, reach out on a sui generis basis for the law most advantageous to the tort plaintiff. This is sometimes called a "plaintiff's viewpoint" rule, but while many of the landmark tort cases in choice of law can be accounted for under such a caption, few judges will admit that it is their touchstone. The cases charted on a tic-tac-toe board in § 84 are especially apt examples of results that a "plaintiff's viewpoint" rule can explain better than any other technique. Indeed, the Second Circuit has described New York's choice of law approach, which presumes to be the Second Restatement's "relationship" test, as in effect a plaintiff's viewpoint rule when the plaintiff is a New Yorker, seeing "no indication that ... New York has wavered in its determination to afford New York tort plaintiffs the benefit of New York law more favorable than the law of the lex loci delicti whenever there is a fair basis for doing so." (O'Connor, CA2 1978.)

Some profound thinking has gone into choice of law. The advocates of an approach will write convincingly, stimulating and even provoking the reader. But if the reader then turns to an opposing advocate immediately afterwards, the scholarship met will be just as deep, the critical technique just as probing, but now a little frustration will be blended in, and after another bout or two with yet other entrants in the scholarship sweepstakes a little vertigo may come on, and a feeling of going about in an endless circle:

> The researches of many antiquarians [said Mark Twain] have already thrown much darkness on the subject, and it is probable, if they continue, that we shall soon know nothing at all.

There is no evidence that Mark Twain had conflict of laws in mind, but in present context the antiquarians are the conflicts scholars. They have written tomes, and they are often at odds with one another. They will never agree on a rule of universal application because the realm does not lend itself to it, but their arguments have led the judges away from rigid old choice of law rules resting on archaic premises and pursuing irrelevant missions. In no other sphere of law have the commentators exerted so great an influence, or occasioned a more productive ferment. They draw up different menus but all whet the appetite. And, whatever the subtleties among them, each new morsel will usually be found more stimulating to the palate than the unimaginative old grub it had to replace.

§ 83. The "Neutral" Case—No State's Policy Involved

Interesting to juxtapose alongside the case in which the inconsistent policies of two (or more) states are involved (the "true" conflict), and the case in which the policy of only one state is involved (the "false" conflict), is the case in which neither state much cares. This is the "neutral" or, as Professor Currie termed it, the "unprovided-for" case. Some call these "no interest" cases. It appears when, despite a superficial conflict between two competing laws on their face, an analysis of their underlying policies reveals that on the facts of the particular case neither is threatened.

Two cases can illustrate. One is Oregon's Erwin case (Oreg.1973), already met in § 81. The issue was whether a wife's loss of her injured husband's consortium was a compensable damages element.

Washington, where the accident occurred, said it was not, aiming to spare Washington defendants the extra financial burden. But the defendants in Erwin were from Oregon and the Washington purpose was therefore not involved. Oregon, on the other hand, authorized such a recovery, with the purpose of assuring the protection of Oregon spouses, but the spouses in Erwin were Washingtonians, so that Oregon's purpose was also not an element. The court, following a forum-law approach, held that Oregon should apply its own law in such a case.

This is quite in contrast with the rule that New York adopted for the similarly neutral facts involved in Neumeier (NY 1972), mentioned in § 78. Devising a list of factual situations to determine whether a guest-host statute should be applied, the court first disposed of cases in which there was some policy involvement. It then arrived at the Neumeier facts, where none was involved. The defendant was a New Yorker driving in Ontario with the plaintiff, an Ontario resident, as his guest. Ontario had a guest-host statute; New York did not. The purpose of the statute was to protect Ontario defendants and/or insurers; none were present here. New York's rule, putting an injured guest on the same footing as any other, was aimed at protecting New York plaintiffs; this plaintiff was from Ontario. Hence both states were neutral. New York retained the lex loci delicti rule for such a case: the law of Ontario, where the accident occurred, was applied.

Into these vacuums New York injected the lex loci rule, Oregon the forum-law rule. P won in the Erwin case because Oregon chose forum law; had Oregon instead resorted to the lex loci rule, as New York did, P would have lost. The Erwin case encourages forum shopping. One of New York's aims in using the lex loci rule in Neumeier was to discourage it.

Thus, the "neutral" case is also a challenge. (See Korn, The Choice–of–Law Revolution, A Critique, 83 Col.L.Rev. 772.) Since a theoretical balancing of competing forces is possible only when there is a competition, a choice of law rule that can answer without a competition and ground it with a strong supporting philosophy deserves an audience. Oregon in Erwin adopted the forum-law rule; New York in Neumeier adhered to the law of the place of the accident. Which is the wiser philosopher?

§ 84.　Different Choices for Different Issues

It may of course happen that there will be several issues in a case with foreign elements, with a choice of law application resulting in different sovereigns governing different issues. (This is sometimes called "dépeçage", borrowing from the French.) In James (NY 1967), for example, that happened with damages issues. D had transferred Puerto Rican real property to avoid having it applied to a New York judgment, and P wanted damages for his doing so. It was held that Puerto Rico law had to govern issues of compensatory damages because Puerto Rico had the entire say as to whether a debtor's real property there is subject to levy by his creditors at all. But as to punitive damages, in which motive is paramount, the presence of a motive to frustrate the collection of a New York judgment was held to give New York the paramount interest and so its law was held to govern issues of punitive damages.

Perhaps a better technique would have been to recognize the transfer as valid, if that is what the situs would have done, but, treating the case as one in tort, to measure all personal remedies against the transferor by the law of New York, the state most involved in the wrongdoer's conduct, a point Judge Learned Hand made in Irving (CA2 1936). That approach would have measured both categories of damages by New York law, but even though it chose different laws for each damage category, the James case nevertheless recognized that the availability and quantum of damages are clearly substantive issues and treated them as such. Each category was independently addressed under a choice of law approach giving due consideration to the different policies underlying both.

When policies and purposes are not appropriately analyzed, bizarre results can follow, and this is especially true when an open-minded investigation is foreclosed by use of a "procedural" label. This can occur when there are several issues in a case, or only one. There was only one, for example, in Marie (NY Sup'r Ct. 1883; § 69): the statute of frauds. Both states involved, New York and Missouri, barred an oral claim of the kind sued on in Marie, but, through an ingenious combination of labels, the court, allowing oral proof of the claim, managed to frustrate the policies of both states. The oral agreement had been made in Missouri, but the court divined that the language of the Missouri statute of frauds made it a "procedural" statute and thus applicable only to an action brought in Missouri. This action was brought in New York. The New York statute of frauds, on the other hand, because of some different language, was then found to be "substantive" and hence applicable only to an agreement having substantive roots in New York, which this agreement lacked. Ergo, though New York and Missouri, the only states involved, both frowned on such oral agreements, a technical use of labels let the plaintiff accomplish with the combination what he could not have accomplished in either state had it alone had all the contacts.

Marie is unusual. A recovery-sustaining result like that is more likely to occur when there are two distinct issues, one deemed substantive and calling for the law of one place and the other deemed procedural and invoking forum law. Lillegraven (Alaska 1962) is such a case. An accident in British Columbia resulted in a tort suit against the car owner in Alaska. One issue was whether the driver's fault was imputed to the owner. The law of British Columbia said it was; Alaska law said it was not. The second issue was whether the action was timely. It was brought within the Alaska period, which was two years, but beyond the one year that British Columbia allowed. The court chose British

Columbia law for the imputation issue (substantive) and Alaska law for the limitations issue (procedural), the only one of four possible combinations that could have preserved the plaintiff's claim against the owner. A kind of tic-tac-toe set-up can illustrate this graphically:

	Brit.Col.Rule	*Alaska Rule*
Imputation of fault to owner?	Yes	No
Action timely?	No	Yes

The plaintiff needs two yeses to win this one. It is plain enough that if the action concerned only British Columbia, as both the place of occurrence and the forum, the defendant would have won. The same is true were Alaska both the forum and the site of the occurrence. Any vertical line gives the defendant the game, as does a diagonal going from top right to bottom left. Only the reverse diagonal, top left to bottom right, works the combination the plaintiff needs, and that's the combination the plaintiff got. One is reminded of the enterprising biologist who crossed a clairvoyant with a contortionist, producing a man who could foresee his own end.

A similar interplay gave the plaintiff the game in another tic tac toe match. This one, Nelson v. Eckert (Ark.1959), concerned Arkansas parties involved in a Texas accident. The tortfeasor was killed in the accident and under Arkansas law the cause of action does not survive; under Texas law it does. That was one issue. The other was once again the statute of limitations. When the suit was brought it was alive by an Arkansas measure but too late under the Texas period. The board looked like this:

	Texas Rule	*Arkansas Rule*
Does claim survive?	Yes	No
Is action timely?	No	Yes

Once again the plaintiff took three-to-one odds, and won. A northwest to southeast diagonal was the court's holding: Texas law was applied to enable the claim to survive while Arkansas law was applied to keep the claim timely.

The process of applying the law of different states to different issues is sometimes called "dépeçage". (See 73 Col.L.Rev. 58 [1973].) There was always a "dépeçage" prospect in multistate cases, if in no other sense than that while choice of law processes were being followed for substantive issues, the forum was always applying its own law to plainly procedural issues.

Today "dépeçage" has lost its novelty and is often applied to substantive issues as well. In many of the landmark cases adopting modern choice of law techniques, for example, only one issue was drawing judicial attention, obscuring the fact that other matters involved, not disputed in point of choice of law, were destined to face the law of a state different from that chosen for the disputed issue. In Babcock (NY 1963; § 78), for example, all attention was devoted to the guest-host issue, to which New York law was ultimately applied, but it was assumed throughout that on the matter of due care in driving, the law of Ontario, as the place of the accident, would govern. The same is true of Reich (Cal.1967; § 79), which applied Ohio law to dispense with a damages limitation on a wrongful death claim while assuming that the law of Missouri, as the place of the event, would govern standards of care and the like. Sometimes parties inflict dépeçage on themselves by drafting choice of law clauses that cover only some of the issues that arise between them. (Fieger, CA 2 2001) Quite often, in other words, when there is hot discussion of one issue, resulting in a choice of State X law, the assumption is implicit that State Y law will apply to everything else.

The diagrams used earlier are only to illustrate the results of some substantive-procedure applications, not necessarily to criticize them. If each such application had some well-considered theoretical purpose to implement, it might withstand critical scrutiny, such as where the forum has settled on a pro-plaintiff approach in tort cases (§ 82), which could explain such results philosophically. It would not fare as well, though, if it were only the result of a few handy tools used to close out a case without thinking about aims and purposes.

§ 85. Jurisdictional "Contacts" Versus Choice of Law "Contacts"

Can the aggregate of a state's "contacts" with a case be sufficient for its law to govern the substantive issues while being insufficient to support jurisdiction of the defendant? Can it be that the courts of the very state whose law will dispose of the case on the merits may not hear the case in the first place? This most ingenious paradox, to borrow Gilbert's phrase, apparently does exist in our law, mentioned by the U.S. Supreme Court but never discussed head-on.

A study of state "contacts" pervades both Chapter III, on jurisdiction, and the present Chapter IV, on choice of law, but only now, at this advanced point, have we an adequate base on which to juxtapose and compare these separate housings. In several cases the Supreme Court has hinted if not held that the "contacts" measures differ for the two purposes. One would think, if there is to be a difference, that more contacts would be needed for an application of substantive law than for the presumably lesser purpose of jurisdiction, but it is just the other way around. Justice Brennan, in the court's plurality opinion in Allstate (USSC 1981), cites the few cases in which the Supreme Court had touched on the matter up to that point. In chronological order, they are Hanson (1958, treated in § 32), Shaffer (1977, treated in § 44), and Kulko (1978, treated later in § 128). Hanson, it will be recalled, was a trusts and estates case, the court hinting that although Florida's contacts did not suffice for jurisdiction, the substantive issues involved in the case might be resolved by the application of Florida law by whatever court might get jurisdiction. Shaffer turned down Delaware jurisdiction of a corporate derivative action while acknowledging that the Delaware interest "may support the application of Delaware law". And Kulko, a child support proceeding, held that California could not entertain jurisdiction of the father even though California law might "arguably" apply to measure his support obligation.

This distinction implicitly maintains that laying hands on a person is more burdensome than laying law on him, and maybe it has its point. We only mention the matter here; the Supreme Court has yet to clarify it. But it is a hard one to explain, and it can arise in a variety of situations. Take the wife in the Kulko case, for example. She wanted support for her child and sued the father, her former husband, in California to get it. The U.S. Supreme Court held that there was no jurisdiction. Assume that after a dismissal she troubles to cross the continent to New York, which would apparently have had jurisdiction of the father on the Kulko facts. Now assume that her lawyer brings a New York action and after a trial the judge announces that he will apply California law to measure the father's obligation. The wife, babe in arms, is likely to ask her lawyer if she heard right. "Didn't we have to cross the country because California couldn't hear the case?" she'd declaim. "Oh, that's about jurisdiction," her lawyer would answer, "this is about choice of law." If she can resist striking her lawyer about the head and face with closed fists, she may offer up some responsive patter (Gilbert again):

We've quips and quibbles heard in flocks, But none to beat this paradox!

Afterwards came a graphic illustration of the converse of this phenomenon. In the context of a class action it was held that a state could entertain jurisdiction over non-resident members of the class even though it lacked contacts with them (§ 113), but could not then choose its own law to apply to the non-residents on the substantive issues (Phillips, USSC 1985).

§ 86. Choice of Forum to Obtain Favorable Choice of Law

As long as states have different choice of law rules, as they have, and these fit within the perimeters of the constitution, as for the most part they do, the choice of an appropriate forum will sometimes be the lawyer's most sensitive task. Lawyers prefer to sue at home; they're familiar with the home forum. Even if an attorney gives thoughtful consideration to the prospect of suit elsewhere, she knows that suit elsewhere will usually entail the retention of a lawyer there. Or, should she have the temerity to bring the suit in the other state herself—always a bad idea unless she knows the other state's procedures and idiosyncrasies intimately—she will have to apply for admission there, ad hoc if not permanently. However this may be, the lawyer owes it to the client to consider choice of forum carefully. More often than the lawyer realizes, the whole case may turn on the choice.

In fact, there are at least three separate investigations the lawyer must undertake after gathering up the facts. Most obvious is a research into the substantive laws of the several related states to see how their internal laws would resolve the issues presented. Second is a determination of the states in which jurisdiction of all necessary defendants can be had and in which relevant forum non conveniens rules would not throw the case out. Then comes the third and often the most difficult inquiry: an examination into the choice of law rules of each of the states in which jurisdiction is available to see which of them would choose the substantive law found during the first phase of the research to be the most favorable to the client on the disputed substantive issues. Item three often gets insufficient treatment.

We can use the fact pattern of the Intercontinental Planning case (NY 1969), previously treated under the statute of frauds (§ 69), to illustrate. The issue was whether an oral contract would be recognized. New Jersey law said that it would; New York law, that it would not. Jurisdiction was available in both states. Suit was brought in a New York court, which, applying its most-significant-relationship test to the issue, found New York to have the predominant relationship on the statute of frauds question. New York law was chosen and the plaintiff, precluded from putting in oral proof of the contract, lost. Perhaps the plaintiff could have made the case a winner by suing in New Jersey, which would have applied its own choice of law rules to the issue. Then, even if New Jersey had deemed the issue substantive and put it through a law-choosing process on an interest-analysis test (see Woll, NJ 1969), it might have found itself the more interested state. The simple fact of conflicts life—that a forum is more likely to apply its own law than another state's when both have contacts with an issue—would have made New Jersey the better bet. And if New Jersey deemed the statute of frauds issue procedural, then it would automatically have applied its own law. We cannot say with certainty that the plaintiff would have prevailed on the statute of frauds issue had he sued in New Jersey. We can only say that the odds favored New Jersey, and that the time to calculate the odds is when the betting is still open. Choice of forum betting closes early.

The Lilienthal case (Oreg.1964), discussed under contracts choice of law (§ 68), can also illustrate. D had been adjudicated a spendthrift in Oregon, disabling him from making contracts. Unaware of this, P in California lent D money. When D defaulted, P sued D in Oregon, which implemented its own spendthrift determination and held for D. It is likely that California, had suit been brought there, would have upheld the contract by applying its own law under its choice of law rules. If a longarm statute was not available in California with which to obtain jurisdiction over the now absent D, and assuming of course that the statute of limitations had not become an element, it might have been best for P just to wait until D came back into California, thus becoming amenable to suit by personal service.

Or, a stipulation in the contract of loan, submitting to California jurisdiction, might have helped. (National Equipment, USSC 1964; § 30.) It could not have hurt.

Now look at the advantage the plaintiff in Allstate (USSC 1981; § 80) earned with an astute choice of forum. The "stacking" of uninsured motorist insurance coverages was involved. Under Wisconsin law the plaintiff would have recovered only $15,000 from the insurer. Minnesota law was that because the policy covered three cars, coverage emanated from each and the plaintiff would be entitled to $45,000 (stacking). Jurisdiction was available in both states. Wisconsin would almost certainly have applied its own law and limited the recovery to $15,000 (rejecting stacking). While it was not certain that Minnesota, under its choice of law rules, would choose its own law—it could well have chosen Wisconsin law on a contacts basis—the one thing the plaintiff knew was that she wanted the Minnesota substantive law applied. There was at least a chance that Minnesota would apply its own law and almost no chance that Wisconsin would apply Minnesota law. Plaintiff played the chances, sued in Minnesota, and trebled her recovery by so doing.

Note that in each of the cases just treated the forum ended up applying its own law. This merely illustrates the general rule, manifest from experience, that the chances of having State F (the forum) apply its own law are better than the chances of having State X apply State F law. But the reverse is possible. Suppose, for example, that an accident occurs in State A but that State C has all of the other contacts with the case (domicile of the parties, place of registration and insurance of the car, place where the trip starts and ends, etc.). State A internal law has a guest-host statute that would bar a recovery; State C law has not and would allow a recovery. On the conflicts front, however, assume that State A has adopted the interest-analysis approach and would choose State C law for the guest-host issue, under which the plaintiff would prevail. State C, on the other hand, retains a rigid application of the lex loci rule and would apply State A law to all issues, in this case barring recovery. In order to get State C's internal law applied, as the plaintiff very much wants, he would have to sue in State A. Under their respective choice of law rules, each state would choose the internal law of the other.

Choice of forum is often just as important as choice of law, and may in fact dictate it. Implicit in this is the importance of finding jurisdiction in the state with the favorable choice of law rule—the one that will choose the desired internal law. How fortunate the plaintiff was in the Rosenthal case (CA2 1973; § 78) in obtaining jurisdiction in New York, which chose its own law of unlimited damages for the death of the plaintiff's husband in Massachusetts, while Massachusetts law had an arbitrary limit on the recovery and would almost certainly have chosen its own law had it been the forum. But it was not the forum; New York was. The Massachusetts doctor whose alleged malpractice was the cause of the husband's death was subjected to this New York law of unlimited damages only because the plaintiff was able to find a way to bring him within the jurisdiction of the New York court, and that happened only because of the tenuous New York Seider doctrine—since overruled by the U.S. Supreme Court (Rush 1980; § 44)—authorizing the New York attachment of the malpractice insurance policy covering the Massachusetts clinic the doctor worked at.

Conversely, it appears to be the very absence of California jurisdiction that proved the plaintiff's undoing in the Lilienthal case mentioned a few paragraphs back. Forced to sue in Oregon, the plaintiff lost on a contract claim under an Oregon spendthrift law that California would almost certainly have refused to apply. The plaintiff's misfortune in that case would be imputable to the absence of a choice of forum.

It will sometimes happen that a seemingly astute choice of forum will come to nought because the forum itself suddenly leaves a road that it had itself paved. Many argue that this is what happened in Schultz (NY 1985), in which New York applied New Jersey law and immunized two charitable organizations (the Boy Scouts and the Franciscan Brothers) from tort liability. They were charged with negligently employing a man who sexually abused two New Jersey boys on a New York outing. New York law lacked the charitable immunity rule that New Jersey retained, and the plaintiffs hoped that by suing in New York they could escape the New Jersey immunity. The conduct complained of was, after all, deliberate, and New York was its situs. Nevertheless, their hopes were dashed.

The plaintiffs were all New Jersey domiciliaries: the survivor of the two boys who went on the outing, the administrator of the other boy (claimed to have committed suicide as a result of the sexual abuse), and the boys' parents. After balancing the interests of New Jersey, which was also the domicile of the Boy Scouts at the time; of Ohio, the Franciscans' domicile; and of New York, where the alleged abuse occurred, the court chose the law of New Jersey as having the predominant interest in what it called this "loss-allocating" rule.

"Loss-allocating" rules concede wrongful conduct but for special reasons let the defendant off the damages hook: the defendant is a host, or a charity, or the absent owner of the tortfeasor car, etc. The court used the phrase to distinguish it from "conduct-regulating" rules, such as standards of care in driving, maximum limits on speed—restraints on an individual's lusts?—and the like, which invoke different considerations. But why did New York choose to implement a "loss-allocating" rather than "conduct-regulating" standard? By doing so it undermined its own policy of including eleemosynary institutions in the warning it issues to all employers: superintend your personnel closely before releasing them to indulge their propensities in New York.

Another example of a careful choice of forum failing in its mission, at least in part, is Bader (CA2 1988), in which a New York family's young daughter was bitten by a dog owned by their Canadian friends while the family was visiting in Ontario. The parents figured they'd fare better before a New York jury and sued in a federal court in New York. (There was apparently no problem about jurisdiction or forum non conveniens.) They didn't expect, however, to be impleaded for themselves contributing to their child's injury by failing to supervise her. New York law did not recognize such a "non-supervision" claim, but Ontario law did, and was found to apply to the issue. The parents were impleaded for contribution. While they apparently expected a higher verdict in New York, they didn't expect to pay part of it themselves.

Notwithstanding occasional disappointments like these—things would apparently have been no worse had the Bader suit been brought elsewhere—when the plaintiff does have a choice, and analyzes how it will affect all the issues in the case, she should recognize that since the choice of law belongs to the forum, the hand that picks the forum picks the law.

J. RENVOI ISSUES

§ 87. Renvoi in Choice of Tort Law?

When under any of the diverse techniques a choice of tort law is made, the choice is generally of the internal law (or "local law" as the Restatement calls it, Rst.2d § 145) of the chosen state and not of that state's choice of law rules. This avoids the so-called "renvoi", in which State F, the forum, refers to the choice of law rules of State X, only to find that those rules differ from the forum's own choice of law rules and would lead off in yet other directions. One of those other directions might be right back to the forum's choice of law rules that started the journey in the first place. That possibility, as discussed in the renvoi section earlier (§ 18), is avoided when the forum's choice leads right over to the internal law of the state chosen.

Suppose that State F chooses State X internal law in an instance in which it is shown that State X, if it were the forum, would not; that State X has different choice of law rules and would apply the internal law of State Y, or, indeed, of State F, which State F itself would not apply under its choice of law rules. Can State F's choice of State X internal law be justified in that instance? It can. Although the policy (if any) underlying the State X choice of law rule may be frustrated, the policy underlying State F's (the forum's) choice of law rule would be fulfilled. (Pfau, NJ 1970.) If the forum, in other words, thinks that State X law ought to govern, and applies X law, it does so whether X likes it or not. It is a kind of forum-knows-best approach, and in view of the trouble that a forum reference to the other state's choice of law rules can make, it is probably a sound approach.

There may be some occasions to refer to the other state's choice of law rules, such as where a statute in point points to the whole law of the place pointed to. Richards (USSC 1962) is an example. It applied the Federal Tort Claims Act, which tests the tort liability of the United States by deeming the United States the equivalent of a private person governed by "the law of the place where the act or omission occurred" (28 U.S.C.A. § 1346[b]). The court construed this to mean that the result should be the same as it would be in the courts of the state of the act or omission complained of, thus mandating a reference to the choice of law rules of that place. The court's motive was to reach for a reasonable law-choosing technique. It felt that such a technique was likely to be part of the choice of law rules of the state of the act or omission, and that an application of such rules would probably assure a sounder choice of law than a construction that automatically required resort to the internal law of a state simply because the tortious act or omission originated there. It was, in other words, a bit of praise for the incoming choice of law approaches and a rebuke to the arbitrary choice of law contained on the face of the Federal Tort Claims Act.

The advocate may sometimes find it helpful to urge resort to the choice of law rules of another state as an alternative route to a desired result. It may persuade a judge or two on an appellate bench. In Haumschild (Wis.1959; § 76), for example, a concurring judge went along with a choice of Wisconsin law not directly, as the majority did, but via California's conflicts rules, which he was convinced would apply Wisconsin law.

K. SPECIAL TORT CATEGORIES

§ 88. Choice of Law in Special Tort Situations

There are several categories of tort case that pose special issues in choice of law. One worth stressing is the defamation case in this age of instant worldwide communication. No matter where the defamatory words are first spoken or set to paper, they can be disseminated either instantly (a broadcast or via the Internet) or shortly (a periodical) across the planet. There are various suggested solutions to the issue of whose law should govern in such a case (see, e.g., Palmisano, SDNY 1955), but the Restatement (Rst.2d § 150), applying its most-significant-relationship approach, singles out the plaintiff's domicile at the time of the defamation, at least where the defamatory words reached into that state among others. This is sometimes known as the "single publication" rule, and it applies to one broadcast or to one edition of a book or magazine. Re-issuances or re-broadcasts under this rule can create new defamation claims, but only one substantive claim is recognized for the initial broadcast or publication (which is usually the only one). The theory behind choosing the law of the plaintiff's domicile is that in defamation cases the plaintiff usually sustains her primary injuries at her home base, where her reputation is presumably strongest.

This single-publication rule, whether leading in a given case to the law of the plaintiff's domicile or to some other place, has had impact in analogous cases. It was applied, for example, in Ralph Nader's right of privacy case against General Motors, the law of the District of Columbia (Nader's domicile) being chosen (Nader, NY 1970). And it was applied in Dale System (USDC Conn.1953) to a tort claim based on the defendants' statement that only X offered a certain service. The plaintiff offered the service, too, and so charged the defendants with a business disparagement claim. The law chosen to govern the claim was the law of the corporate plaintiff's principal place of business.

Unless the law of but one place, or at most of one or two select places, is plucked from the mass of states the defamation reaches into, the choice of law problem would be unmanageable. Shall the forum judge separately charge the jury on the law of each of the 20 (or 200) states in which the defamation was heard or read, as the rule applicable at common law would have required?

The fraud case can also pose a dilemma if the misrepresentation is made in one place but the plaintiff in reliance acts in another and suffers damages there or in still other places. The Restatement addresses this situation (Rst.2d § 148), and lists the various contacts that the court should review in determining which state has the most significant relationship to the particular issue raised.

The Restatement also lists various individual issues that can arise in tort cases, picking out the more frequently met among these and addressing a separate section to each of them (Rst.2d §§ 156–174). Many of these sections merely refer back to the basic choice of law position taken in the Restatement, which is the most-significant-relationship technique (Rst.2d § 145), but after each such separate section appear annotations that the lawyer will find of much aid.

§ 89. Workers' Compensation

Workers' compensation occupies a unique niche in the conflicts realm. The compensation acts of the states are not the same, either in the extent of the recoveries they allow or in their impact on other claims the injured worker may have in tort, such as against third persons other than the employer. The acts are theoretically supposed to afford a worker injured on the job a recovery without having to prove fault, but in a sum less than might be expected in an ordinary common law tort action, and to insulate the employer from such an action as long as he has obtained compensation coverage. Since the compensation acts of the several states involved in a given accident, if several there are, may differ, the lawyer's burden is to ascertain their respective advantages, determine which would be applicable, and then invoke from among the applicable the most beneficial.

When compensation cases are met in a conflicts setting, it is often because the claimant's lawyer—or the claimant without a lawyer—has too hastily applied for compensation in her own state without ascertaining and comparing other options and opportunities, both as to compensation and as to possible remedies against wrongdoers other than her employer. Different factors interact, and these, along with the peculiar position workers' compensation has in the "choice of law" realm in the first place, make the subject an involved one. This section may therefore come on a bit strong. A second reading will soften it measurably.

At the outset, two things must be observed about compensation acts in a conflict of laws context. The first is that there is seldom any "choice" of law for the forum to make. The claimant brings her claim in the state whose act she wants applied. The forum does not then decide "which" compensation act to choose, but rather whether the forum's contacts are sufficient to permit a recovery under the forum's own act, which is the only one the forum will apply. (If the forum's is inapplicable, the result is likely to be a denial or dismissal without prejudice rather than the choice of another state's compensation act.)

The second special point is that while some states permit a compensation recovery to be sought in a court action, most have set up a special administrative machinery for it, such as a board or commission.

The main inquiry then, when a claim is duly brought before the appropriate tribunal in the selected forum, is whether the contacts required by the forum's own compensation act are sufficient to invoke it. Of course, the contacts must also suffice to permit the application of forum law as a constitutional matter. The constitutional issue is discussed in the earlier section on "constitutional considerations in choice of law" (§ 56), a general discussion in which some of the major cases in fact involved compensation acts. As far as the constitution is concerned, a state is free to apply its compensation act as long as it has had significant contacts with the case. For compensation purposes this covers the state of the injury although it may not be the domicile of the parties (Pacific, USSC 1939), the state with the predominant contact with the employment relationship even though the injury occurred elsewhere (Alaska, USSC 1935), and states with yet other combinations of contacts (see Rst.2d § 181).

This answers what a state *may* do. The question of what the state *will* do is a matter of internal preference discernible only by studying its act and the case law on it.

Before seeking compensation under the law of a given state, perhaps chosen because the sum it allows for the particular injury is greater than elsewhere, there are other inquiries to make. Will invoking that law bar other remedies against third persons? One state's compensation act may make a compensation recovery the claimant's exclusive remedy, barring tort claims against third persons as well as against the employer. Another's may make it exclusive solely for compensation purposes, thus barring only a further compensation recovery under the law of another related state that the lawyer later learns awards more (Magnolia, USSC 1943), while allowing a regular tort action against a third party. These compensation statutes are seldom lucid by their own terms, and, requiring judicial construction, similar statutes can get different constructions. (Cf. Magnolia, supra, with Industrial Commission, USSC 1947.) A minority of the U.S. Supreme Court tried to overrule Magnolia in Thomas (1980). The overruling would have allowed a claimant, getting one sum from one state, to seek the difference to the greater sum another state would give under its compensation act even if the first state purported to forbid any further compensation. But Magnolia apparently stands, barring State Two from awarding more compensation if State One, to which the claimant first applied, makes its own award exclusive, though few states purport to make their awards exclusive. But we must distinguish between workers' compensation and regular tort claims.

Even if the obtaining of an award can bar further compensation elsewhere under the Magnolia rule, it cannot, even if it presumes to, bar a regular tort claim against a third party in another jurisdiction if the other, having contacts with the case, allows it. This is the holding of Carroll (USSC 1955), allowing R, injured on the job in Arkansas, to bring a common law tort action against a third party in Arkansas, permissible under Arkansas law, despite having sought and obtained compensation under the law of Missouri, which provided that the recovery shall be exclusive of all other remedies, compensation and tort alike.

In Carroll, Arkansas law allowed the third party action. Had Arkansas chosen to, it could have applied Missouri law and barred the tort claim altogether. This suggests how important it is to ascertain all available options in advance, before applying for compensation anywhere, and this means an inquiry into what the consequences of an award would be under the law of each state whose compensation act appears to be available, and into whether each state in which a tort suit might afterwards be attempted would be disposed to honor an exclusivity label appended by the compensation-awarding state. A variety of options may appear. In Carroll, Arkansas, where the injury occurred, allowed a tort suit against a third person (a person other than the employer) even though Missouri, which awarded compensation, said no to it. Another state, awarding compensation, might have a rule allowing a third party action but defer it to the compensation policies of the state of the accident, whose rule bars it (e.g., Wilson, NJ 1958). Research into the alternatives applicable to given facts may of course reveal no choice of forum advantage at all. But if the initial choice of one state's law can, through the interplay of these elements, offer the client more, the lawyer's obligation is to make that choice, and it may entail the retaining of counsel in another state if the choice points there.

The foregoing shows how the content of a given state's compensation act can create perhaps unexpected opportunities, such as where it is construed to be the exclusive remedy against the employer but does not bar ordinary tort or wrongful death actions against third persons who also contribute to the injury in some way, a frequent happening, for example, in construction accidents. In a state with such a law the lawyer combs through every on-the-job accident case for evidence of third party involvement, which, avoiding the compensation-exclusivity barrier, offers the promise of an increased recovery. Some states go even further, ironically, by permitting the third person, when sued by the employee, to implead the employer for contribution, thus indirectly exposing the employer to the tort recovery from which the employer is supposedly insulated for having obtained insurance coverage for workers' compensation. (Good advice to an employer client is to keep in force, whether in one or separate insurance policies, ample coverage for both compensation and tort.)

When there are several states involved, the internal idiosyncrasies of each of their compensation acts and the results when these acts are juxtaposed and compared must all be considered in advance of an application under any one of them. And their separate limitations' periods must also be assessed. What profit a soul to be guided in the straightest path if it has been barred by time?

L. GRATUITOUS PROPERTY TRANSFERS

§ 90. Gratuitous Transfers of Personal Property; Inter Vivos

The caption is a fancy name for a gift, including a gift in trust, but gifts take many forms and the law may have different things to say about them. We are concerned here with personal property. Real property is addressed in § 95.

By "gratuitous" we primarily mean to distinguish (and exclude) contract cases, which roam a broad range and are covered elsewhere. The Uniform Commercial Code governs in many if not most contract cases. If a chattel is sold, for example, it falls under Article 2 of the Code. If it is made the subject of a security interest, it comes under Article 9 of the Code. Choice of law in UCC cases is separately treated (§§ 71 and 72).

A gratuitous transfer may be made during the donor's life, in which case we call it an inter-vivos transfer. Or it may be made after death, either expressly, as by will, or by operation of law, as by an application of the intestacy laws of the appropriate place if there is no will. Inter-vivos and post-death transfers should be distinguished. We do the inter-vivos ones here.

In the case of an ordinary gift by a living donor, it is made by the donor merely giving the thing to the donee. The validity of the transfer will be governed by the law of the place where the transfer is made. The Restatement couches this in terms of the "most significant relationship" test, but points to the law of "the location of the chattel" as having the "greater weight" (Rst.2d § 244). It is also permissible to accompany the gift with a writing selecting the law to be applied, and the general rule here as in contract cases (§ 68) is that if the law selected is that of a reasonably related jurisdiction, the choice will be honored.

The rule that a gift of personal property will be governed by the law of the place where the gift is made is readily applied to tangible property, including interests embodied in written instruments when the instrument proper is deemed the property. Money itself is a tangible and subject to this rule (Cutts, NJ Eq.1938). Insofar as it lends itself to the particular case, the rule also applies to intangibles, but if the property is intangible it will usually take a paper of some kind to effect the gift, as where it consists of a patent right or the modest royalties called for on a Nutshell. If the interest is embodied in a more formal instrument, such as a check, note, bill, certificate of title or stock or the like, the instrument, as indicated, is likely to be deemed the property and a gift of it will be adjudged by the law of the place if its delivery. The Uniform Commercial Code and especially its Article 3 on commercial paper will be relevant even in gift cases and should reduce choice of law problems at least on the domestic scene. Whether a gift can be shown to be within the substantive reach of the UCC or not, however, the UCC is not everywhere applicable, nor necessarily given the same construction in states where it does apply, and so it does no harm to see that the method of a paper's transfer satisfies not only the law of the place where the transfer is made, but also the law of such other place as may have some say about the paper involved. If, for example, a share of stock in a State C corporation is transferred in State T, and they have different rules about what must be done to effectuate the transfer, steps that will please both should be taken.

If the transfer is made by a donor in State R sending the chattel to a donee in State E, and the donor is a competent adult and the transfer is clearly voluntary, the law of State E will usually govern if the laws of the two states differ, or—more than likely today in view of the apparent wishes of the donor to make a gift of the property—it will be sustained if valid by the laws of either place. This is known as the "rule of validation". It was previously met in discussing usury (§ 74). The principal cases manifesting circumstances like these involve trusts, but gifts in trust are gifts nevertheless, and, invoking essentially the same rules, supply answers applicable generally. Where, for example, a Canadian established a New York trust of property and the trust was invalid by Canadian but valid by New York law, it was sustained in Hutchison (NY 1933). This can be explained under the rule that a transfer from State R to State E will be measured for validity by the law of State E. But if the laws were reversed, and the transfer good by State R law but void by State E's, that rule would overturn the transfer. That a transfer in such a case was sustained only a few years later in Shannon (NY 1937) by the same court manifests the judicial favor shown for the "rule of validation" over other more arbitrary choices. In Shannon, a New Jersey settlor sent property to New York to be set up in a trust, the transfer valid by New Jersey law but void by New York law under its stricter rule about perpetuities (a phenomenon devised by old lawyers to minimize the competition of new ones). The transfer was sustained. The "rule of validation" can account for both cases.

If a transfer is made in State R, and the donee obtains good title to the property there, only afterwards taking it elsewhere, say to State X, the general rule is that the donee's title will be respected even though the original transfer in State R might not be valid as measured by State X's law. (See Rst.2d § 247.) Further transactions by the donee in State X will be measured by the usual rules, premised now on the donee's ownership. In other words, interests in a chattel perfect in State R before the chattel is carried into State X, persist in State X and will be recognized there. (Rst.2d §§ 247, 252.) While this rule presumably applies to property subjected to security interests in State R before removal of the property, the issues are never that simple in the "secured transactions" category, and some extra precautionary steps may be advisable (see § 72).

§ 91. Gratuitous Post–Death Transfers of Personal Property, Introductory

Choice of law rules on post-death transfers of personal property differ from the inter-vivos rules, in contrast with the situation obtaining when real property is involved (§ 95). While the situs of the personal property is usually the key place to look to for governing law for an inter-vivos transfer, the law of the decedent's final domicile will usually govern issues connected with post-death transfers.

If the decedent has left a will disposing of personal property in several states, issues may arise about whose law is to determine whether the will is valid (whether the decedent was competent, whether proper formalities of execution have been fulfilled, etc.). This subject is taken up in the next section, but we may note here that all of its lessons about whose law will be applied to govern the validity of an already executed will are good to keep in mind when first drawing the will.

If the will appoints a personal representative, we call the appointee an executor or executrix. If it does not, the personal representative appointed by the court is called an administrator or administratrix. An early job of the appointee, whatever his or her title, is to gather up the decedent's property, a procedure sometimes called "marshaling the assets". This involves a number of considerations and for convenience has been made the subject of a separate section (§ 94).

Intestacy, which results when there is no will or when the will fails for some reason, such as improper execution, also has a separate section (§ 93).

The premise of this and the next three sections is that a decedent has left some personal property in a state other than her own final domicile. This can present problems of estate taxes in addition to transfer issues. But here, too, the decedent's final domicile will usually be looked to for governing law, not only for resolution of the obvious issue of how much of a state estate tax there is to be, but also for incidental tax issues. In Doetsch (CA7 1963), for example, the corpus of an inter-vivos Illinois trust went to R, but its value was included in the settlor's estate and the whole brunt of the estate tax fell tentatively on W, the decedent's wife and sole beneficiary. Whether R had to contribute proportionately to the tax was held to be governed by the law of Arizona, the decedent's domicile, rather than that of Illinois, the situs of the trust.

§ 92. Post–Death Transfers of Personal Property by Will

When the decedent has left a will, the first question to ask is whether the will is valid, and this is true without regard to where the decedent's personal property may be located. But whose law will determine whether the will is valid? The most obvious place is the decedent's final domicile, and of course if the will satisfies domicile law in respect of execution and formalities and all of the decedent's personal property is located there, its instructions on distribution will be carried out. But what about property left elsewhere?

As elaborated later (§ 94), it may be necessary for the personal representative to go to the state (or states) in which personal property was left and perhaps even bring a court proceeding there to get possession of it. And it may be necessary to have "ancillary" letters (also discussed in § 94) issued there. Should such suit be necessary, and assuming that ancillary letters have been obtained if required, the validity of the will may come in issue in the foreign court. If it does, what law will the court apply to adjudge its validity?

If each state in which personal property has been left and in which a proceeding is necessary were to gauge the validity of the will by its own internal requirements for execution, a will valid when and where made might be rejected by another state, frustrating the testator's intentions entirely. To remedy this, most states have adopted one version or another of a uniform will code that recognizes a will as long as it is valid under the law of any of several likely places, including the decedent's domicile at the time of his death or at the time of the will's execution, the place of its execution, or the situs of the affected property. This is a fine safety valve, but if a lawyer drafting a will knows of the several states in which the client has or is likely to have substantial property, there is nothing wrong with quickly checking into the execution rules of such places and seeing to it that the will satisfies all of them. An extra witness or an extra ritual may prove all that is required.

If the will is valid under the rule being applied in the court that is hearing the issue, the transfer that it makes of the personal property will be upheld.

§ 93. Post–Death Transfers of Personal Property in Intestacy

If the decedent dies intestate, her personal property, wherever situate, will usually be distributed according to the laws of intestacy of her final domicile. (Rst.2d § 260.) So common is acceptance of this rule in our jurisprudence that it is sometimes deemed the product of a constitutional demand. It has no such force, however, and, indeed, a maverick state may sometimes adopt a different rule, such as one that orders distribution of locally found personal property pursuant to its own intestacy lists even though they differ from the domicile's. (E.g., Miss. Code § 91–1–1.)

The Restatement's position (Rst.2d § 260) is that a reference to domicile law for rules on the intestate distribution of personal property is intended to be to the domicile's whole law, including its choice of law rules. That sets the stage for renvoi (§ 18), but the point is not often at issue among American states because the ultimate stopping point, whether the trip is direct or indirect, is usually the domicile's internal law.

§ 94. Post–Death Transfers of Personal Property; Marshaling Assets; "Ancillary" Letters

Since the decedent may have left personal property in various states, an early job of the personal representative is to gather up that property from wherever it may be. If he has been duly appointed (granted "letters") by the probate or equivalent court of the decedent's domicile, where the estate will be administered, he may hope that this designation will serve him in other states when he goes there to get the decedent's property. If he can't get that property from another state without judicial aid, as where the person having possession or custody of it will not surrender it without a direction from the local courts, he may have to make an appropriate petition to those courts for what is generally called "ancillary letters".

"Ancillary" letters are issued by a court in a state where there is property of a decedent but which was not the decedent's domicile at the time of death. The domicile's probate court is the one that issues the "principal" letters appointing a personal representative, and another state in which the decedent left property may recognize that appointment and allow that representative standing to sue in its courts without having to petition the local probate court for special permission (see Ghilain, NH 1929) or for the appointment of some local person to act as representative. But some states do require such a petition. Those that do are requiring what we call "ancillary" letters.

It is not only the presence of tangible personal property in the nondomicile state that may warrant ancillary administration there. The presence there of a debtor of the estate, the asset in this case being a chose in action, can support it (Saunders, Me.1882), with the appointee then able to sue on the debt in the courts of that state. When a cause of action constitutes the estate asset, it is the amenability of the defendant (against whom the claim exists) to suit in the nondomicile forum that justifies its treatment of the claim as the equal of a tangible asset, supporting ancillary letters (Milmoe, CA D. of C. 1966).

A major aim of ancillary administration is to enable the state in which a nondomiciliary decedent has left property to apply that property to satisfy local debts the decedent may have left, before the property is removed from the state. This spares local creditors the burden of having to seek payment at their debtor's domicile. If the estate is insolvent, however, even a state entertaining only ancillary administration may consider the claims of out-of-state creditors as well, and try to adjust payments so that all unsecured creditors share ratably. (Hirsch's Estate, Ohio 1946.) (Secured creditors will of course look to the property that secures their debts, but they can line up with unsecured creditors if the security proves inadequate.)

§ 95. Gratuitous Transfers of Real Property; Inter–Vivos and Post–Death

While inter-vivos and post-death transfers of personal property are separately treated in the last few sections, they can be treated together when real property is the subject. The reason is that while domicile law usually governs post-death transfers of personal property (situs law governing only in inter-vivos cases), in matters affecting real property it is situs law that governs both in life and after death. The immovability of real property has given primacy to situs law, so that anything a lawyer does to effect a transfer of any interest in real property should satisfy the law of its situs first and foremost, and in respect of both form and substance. A deed to or mortgage or other lien on real property by way of inter-vivos gift (or any other dealing, for that matter) should be in the form the situs requires.

While the personal estate of a person dying without a will is distributed under the laws of intestacy of her last domicile, it is situs rather than domicile law that dictates the intestate succession to real property. Consistently with this rule, situs law also governs such inter-spousal land rights as dower and curtesy (Rannels, CA8 1908).

If the owner would devise the real property by will, he had best be sure that the will satisfies the situs in all respects (Freedman, Ga.1967). Insofar as execution is concerned, if the situs has the uniform will provision mentioned when we discussed personal property (§ 92), and is satisfied if the will conforms to the law of some other designated place, execution under such law will do the job. It nevertheless behooves the careful lawyer to take whatever additional steps will satisfy the internal rules of execution of the situs. The U.S. Supreme Court has held that title adjudications made by State F as to State S land need not be recognized by State S, elevating the issue to one of subject matter jurisdiction (Clarke, USSC 1900). Even if the Supreme Court were to retreat from that position today, it is a wise precaution to satisfy the situs's wishes.

And if the testatrix has validly executed a will devising real property, and would revoke it, she had best be sure to follow the revocation rules of the situs. In one well known revocation case, Barrie (Iowa 1949), an Illinois testatrix devised Iowa real property in a will executed to Iowa's satisfaction. She later changed her mind and wrote "void" on the will, which sufficed to revoke the will by Illinois standards but not by Iowa's. The devise of the Iowa land thus remained valid, obviously contrary to the testatrix's wishes.

Related questions affecting real property are also likely to be governed by situs law, whether respecting an inter-vivos or post-death transfer, such as the question of whether an equitable conversion (from real property to personal property) has resulted from a sale or other dealing affecting the land (Toledo, Tex.1953; Rst.2d § 255).

Does a reference to situs law mean the internal law of the situs, or its choice of law rules? Since the situs must as a practical matter be respected for almost anything concerning real property, it is appropriate—if the situs wants the law of some other place applied because of a given element present on the facts—to apply that other law. For this reason the Restatement's position is that for both inter-vivos and post-death real proper transfers, the whole law of the situs, including its choice of law rules, governs. (Rst.2d §§ 223, 236, 239.) The purpose is to have the forum court reach the same result the situs court would.

§ 96. Trusts

Trusts are not really a separate topic because they are governed by essentially the same principles that govern choice of law in gratuitous transfers generally. Indeed, many of the cases clarifying choice of law on gratuitous transfers involve gifts in trust (see § 90). (Only gratuitous trusts are the subject here. If there is a contract to establish a trust, it may of course also involve choice of law principles applicable to contracts [§ 68].) But it may be helpful to set forth a few principles by way of review.

If the trust is of real property, just about everything connected with it, from the execution of the instruments creating it to the details of its administration, had best satisfy situs law. The Restatement recognizes the settlor's right to designate governing law by including a choice of law provision in the will or inter-vivos instrument creating the trust (Rst.2d § 277), but says that absent such a stipulation situs law governs: the whole law of the situs, including its choice of law rules. This means that the forum should do just as a court of the situs would do, choosing the governing law of yet another place if it is shown that the situs would do so.

As to inter-vivos trusts of personal property, the Restatement again recognizes the settlor's right to choose governing law, provided that it is that of a state with "a substantial relation to the trust" (Rst.2d § 270[a]). Absent the stipulation, the Restatement reverts to its "most significant relationship" test (Rst.2d § 270[b]).

Courts favor a rule of validation, meaning that if of two related states the trust is valid under the law of one but invalid under the law of the other, the one that validates is chosen. One finds this rule applied to both inter-vivos trusts (Hutchison, NY 1933) and testamentary trusts (Chappell, Wash. 1923), and the rule is invoked even when internal forum law would invalidate the trust and the rule of validation points to the law of the other state, as occurred in Shannon (NY 1937), where, additionally, the instrument specifically chose the validating law. (That never hurts.) Implied in the rule of validation is that even a settlor who has made no choice of law in the instrument would choose the validating law if he thought about it.

If the trust is set up in a will—we call this a "testamentary" trust—among the basic questions to ask, once again, is whether the will is valid, an issue discussed in § 92. That discussion applies here as well.

Trust cases often involve a power of appointment, whose exercise determines who is to have the corpus of the trust at a designated time, or the continued income from it after a gift of the income of a prior period expires. A rule of validation would be appropriate here, too. The failure to apply it in Matter of Bauer (NY 1964) resulted in New York's prompt statutory overruling of the case. In Bauer, the settlor created an inter-vivos trust in New York with herself as beneficiary, reserving to herself the power to designate by will the later beneficiaries. Long afterward, having become an English domiciliary, she exercised that power by will. The court held the exercise to be governed by the New York law applicable years earlier when the original trust was created, and this had the effect of casting down the exercise of the power of appointment (which exercise was satisfactory to English law) and wholly undermining the intent of the testatrix.

Since a power of appointment is usually an adjunct of a trust, a rule of validation is just as appropriate to apply to it as to the basic trust document itself.

M. ADMIRALTY

§ 97. Admiralty, a Special Situation

Admiralty and maritime cases occupy a unique place in the law, requiring coordinated address to

jurisdiction and choice of law together. Roughly
speaking, admiralty or maritime—we will use the
terms interchangeably but there are technical differences between them—describes any case involving a claim arising on the high seas or navigable
waters or the carriage of goods or persons by sea. It
is a category of subject matter jurisdiction, one of
the items of permissible federal court jurisdiction
listed in § 2 of Article 3 of the federal constitution,
and it has from our national beginnings been exploited by Congress with a jurisdiction-giving statute, presently § 1333 of Title 28 of the United
States Code. The annotations on § 1333 in 28
U.S.C.A. are the place to look for specific answers
about the jurisdictional reach of admiralty jurisdiction.

Section 1333 presumes to give the federal district
courts "exclusive" jurisdiction of an admiralty
claim, but it qualifies the grant by "saving to suitors" (a famous clause to admiralty lawyers) the
right to bring the case in any court as long as the
relief sought on the claim is a category of remedy
known to the common law. Because most cases
brought under the "admiralty" banner do seek relief known to the common law, such as a simple
money judgment, few admiralty cases are "exclusively" federal. If a plaintiff seeks only a money
judgment on a maritime tort, for example, she can
bring her case in a federal court under the admiralty caption or in any state court having the appropriate monetary jurisdiction. The saving-to-suitors
clause, in other words, gives the plaintiff a choice of

forum. Of the few admiralty remedies that turn out to be exclusively federal, and hence beyond the reach of the saving to suitors clause, the best known is the action in rem against a vessel (§ 41).

Turning to choice of law, the first point is that the basic governing law in admiralty cases is a body known as the "general maritime law". It is a kind of common law of the seas, consisting of decisions handed down by the courts of maritime nations. It is essentially a federal possession in the United States today, much expanded by Congress with special statutes creating new claims and regulating old ones, and it must be applied to the rights of the parties whether the admiralty case is brought in a federal court or, under the "saving to suitors" clause, in a state court. If because of its subject matter it qualifies as an admiralty case, it remains one no matter where sued on and the state court must apply to it the same law that the federal court would.

Examples of legislatively created maritime claims are the Jones Act (46 U.S.C.A. § 688), the Longshore and Harbor Workers' Compensation Act (33 U.S.C.A. § 901 et seq.), and the Death on the High Seas Act (46 U.S.C.A. §§ 761–7). The last named was relevant in Moragne (USSC 1972), involving a problem area of admiralty: the death claim arising in the nation's territorial waters, where the Death on the High Seas Act does not govern. For a time the vacuum was filled by the application of the wrongful death statute of the adjacent state. Moragne obviated this by holding that the General Maritime Law recognizes a wrongful death claim; in effect, it creates a cause of action for wrongful death occurring in territorial waters. This removed the state death acts from that scene. A later case, Sea–Land (USSC 1974), elaborated some of the elements of the Moragne-devised claim.

Many an accident involving an airplane on a cross-country rather than oceanic mission occurs in the water simply because many an airport is built near water so as to minimize noise pollution by enabling aircraft to take off over, and to make their landing approaches by, sea. Resulting claims were often treated as admiralty cases until the U.S. Supreme Court in Executive Jet (1972) rejected a simple territorial test. If a plane is on an overland mission having no significant relationship to maritime activity when it goes down in territorial waters, admiralty jurisdiction is not invoked, held the court, and so admiralty substantive law would not be involved either. It would be strictly a state-law case to be governed accordingly, for choice of law as well as any other purpose.

The most typical admiralty "conflicts" case is where foreign nationals have had some involvement. Here choice of law problems are analogous to those met on the interstate level. The Supreme Court opted for a kind of most-significant-relationship test in its major pronouncement, Lauritzen (1953), involving a Danish plaintiff with a claim of maritime tort. He sued in a United States court hoping for a Jones Act application, but it appears that the only American contact was that he signed on to the vessel in New York. The ship was of Danish flag, registry, and ownership. The injury occurred in Cuban waters. The employment contract stipulated that Danish law would be applicable. An "overwhelming preponderance in favor of Danish law" was found by the court, and the Jones Act held inapplicable. When the contacts are not so one-sided and American involvement on the facts is greater, United States law will apply (Hellenic, USSC 1970).

This choice of law approach devised for admiralty cases must of course be used in whatever domestic court the case finds itself: a federal court, or, based on the saving to suitors clause, a state court.

N. FOREIGN NATION INVOLVEMENT

§ 98. Cases Affecting Foreign Sovereignty; "Act of State" Doctrine

When a choice of law competition is between the laws of two United States jurisdictions (states, territories, state law versus federal law, etc.), the federal constitution supervenes and everything that goes on has to satisfy it. The constitution acts as a kind of overseer, imposing uniform standards of fairness and balance. When one or more of the competing laws is that of a foreign country, however, perhaps not all of the elements will meet our domestic standards. If all do, the competition is likely to be resolved by the same choice of law principles applicable in domestic cases. But if some do not, there is difficulty.

A potential problem exists when a court is asked to apply domestic law to conduct occurring on foreign soil. The mere fact that an act takes place outside the country does not automatically insulate it from domestic regulation. A case in point is Timberlane (CA9 1976), involving the federal antitrust laws. It was a private suit against the Bank of America (among others) for conspiracy to prevent the plaintiff from milling Honduran lumber and shipping it to the United States. Elaborating the test to be applied to determine whether our antitrust laws can be allowed extraterritorial reach, the court held that they can as long as the conduct complained of has links to the United States strong enough to affect American commerce (and of course only if the persons aimed at are subject to local jurisdiction, which the Timberlane defendants were).

The main problem element in Timberlane was the contention that the Honduran government countenanced what the defendants did. To what extent does conduct on foreign terrain mandate a hands-off policy in American courts? This gets us to the so-called "act of state" doctrine, which at its most rigid recognizes what a foreign sovereign does on its own soil whether we like it or not, and accords it respect even if the doing has impact on people in this country. The Supreme Court is ambivalent about the scope of this doctrine. In First National (USSC 1972), the court said that it is just a rule of decision (rather than a mandate of the constitution or of international law) that precludes examining into a foreign nation's act on its own soil, but the court is not clear on when it should be applied. The massive property expropriations that followed the Castro takeover in Cuba occasioned much of the not very helpful case law. Much of the property taken belonged to United States citizens, or to Cuban aliens who fled here to escape Castro.

The root problem is that United States foreign policy can easily become involved in these otherwise private cases, because they may offend the foreign sovereign. The courts are willing to hear what the U.S. government's official position is, and for this reason the parties should make appropriate inquiries of the State Department. The Supreme Court in Am. Ins. Ass'n v. Garamendi (USSC 2003) invalidated California's Holocaust Victim Insurance Relief Act because it threatened to impinge on the Presidents ability to negotiate with the German government over the appropriate nature of a compensation fund for survivors. As the Cuban cases manifest, a disregard of the foreign act, i.e., a refusal to apply the "act of state" doctrine, is a good deal easier when we have broken off diplomatic relations with the country involved and hence care little about its sovereign sensibilities.

One thing clear about the act of state doctrine is that it is not for each state to interpret for itself. It is a federal matter to be uniformly shaped based on national rather than local considerations (Banco Nacional, USSC 1964), but those considerations require a sui generis balancing in all cases and it is hard to predict the outcome in most of them. It is also clear that the presence in the United States of property that the foreign government or its agents claim (such as that resulting from an expropriation) and as to which local companies or persons make conflicting claims (perhaps as victims of the expropriation) is what gives the court a domestically relevant controversy and the parties a stake worth pursuing.

In Bi (CA2 1993), the well known Bhopal gas leak disaster case injuring numerous Indian citizens, India enacted a statute making itself the sole representative of all its citizens' claims and then settled the entire dispute. When some of the claimants then tried to get out from under the settlement in an action in this country, the court, describing the case as one of first impression, held the settlement binding. Its holding that the claimants lacked standing to sue here was based on the act of state doctrine and the doctrine was held binding on federal and state courts alike.

If no act of state doctrine or equivalent federal policy intervenes, domestic criteria for the validity of the acts involved are likely to govern. Here the bottom line is that a foreign act on foreign soil can find itself disregarded in deference to our domestic concepts of due process and equal protection, although it might have avoided that confrontation, or at least stood a better chance, had the foreign government troubled itself to maintain friendly relations with the United States. When diplomatic ties remain, the foreign nation's pleasure, if not served blindly by a domestic court, will at least be examined with solicitude and with deference at the ready should sovereign feelings really be involved. The Timberlane case (above) shows this in its inquiry into whether Honduras commanded the defendants' acts, or merely tolerated them (only the commanded ones get the deference).

§ 99. Treaties; Warsaw Convention

Since under the supremacy clause of the federal constitution (Article VI) a treaty to which the United States subscribes becomes the supreme law of the land, a treaty and its implementing legislation is the source of the governing law in any situation it addresses. The subject matter of most treaties affects the ordinary citizen little or not at all in her daily rounds, but one that crops up more than others and deserves at least passing mention is the Warsaw Convention (see 49 U.S.C.A. § 40105 note). It applies to international travel and while it provides (among other things) for liability without fault in tort cases against air carriers, it sets money limits on that liability. These limits were initially so low that the United States came under pressure to renounce the treaty, to which it had duly subscribed in the 1930s. Instead, a meeting took place in Montreal in the 1960s involving many of the signatory nations, and from it emerged the Montreal Agreement (see Rosman, NY 1974) to which most international air carriers subscribed, which increases the limit to $75,000 per passenger if the flight involves the United States. Airline passengers can often find an additional stub on their tickets warning of the gist of these limitations.

Not only may the coverage be unduly low, at least as measured by American expectations, but there may be areas of liability covered by state law but not covered at all under the convention, and for that reason not compensable under it. It was held in Rein (CA2 1991), for example, that only compensatory damages may be considered under the convention; punitive damages are barred. And in Eastern Airlines (USSC 1991), the U.S. Supreme Court held that psychic injury is not a compensable item under the convention when not accompanied by a physical injury.

The numerous cases on the convention—too numerous to treat here with their myriad distinctions—are more often than not efforts by plaintiffs to avoid the limits, including even the more generous ones applicable when the United States is involved. Sometimes the plaintiffs do avoid them through one route or another, but a far healthier lesson to the lawyer, which takes almost no space to mention, is to advise clients to take out hefty insurance (see § 78). This can be done on an individual-flight basis. There are often insurance counters at airports. A better idea to put to a client who flies often, or who travels a lot even if not always by air, is to keep in effect a regular accident policy paid by annual premium. The cost is relatively low and it can avoid the perils of last-minute errors or oversights at airports as well as the unrealistic limitations of the Warsaw Convention. And it will cover not only air travel, but all other kinds.

CHAPTER V

ERIE DOCTRINE

§ 100. Erie Doctrine, Introductory

One of the most influential cases ever handed down by the U.S. Supreme Court is Erie Railroad Co. v. Tompkins (USSC 1938). It overruled Swift v. Tyson (USSC 1842) of almost a century earlier. Both concern choice of law in a federal court and involve a federal statute that has been on the books since 1789: the "Rules of Decision" Act, presently 28 U.S.C.A. § 1652. It provides that

> The laws of the several states, except where the Constitution or treaties of the United States or Acts of Congress otherwise require or provide, shall be regarded as rules of decision in civil actions in the courts of the United States, in cases where they apply.

When federal jurisdiction is based on a federal cause of action ("arising under" jurisdiction), of course federal sources, whether statutory, constitutional, or otherwise, will govern the case substantively. But what law is to govern when diversity of citizenship is the basis of federal jurisdiction? The diversity case is the theater of Erie's operations.

If a local statute were in point, Swift agreed that under the Rules of Decision Act it was applicable.

This included state case law construing the statute and well as cases in matters regarded as being inherently "local", such as real estate matters. But when there was no local statute and the case was governed by the "general" common law, Swift held that "general" (or as we sometimes refer to it, "federal") rather than state common law was to govern.

After some 96 years of this (actually longer, for the Swift decision was hardly the first of its ilk), the Supreme Court acknowledged the unfair choice of forum this gave the plaintiff in a case governed by general rather than local law merely because the plaintiff and defendant happened to come from different states. Reconstruing the Rules of Decision Act, the Supreme Court in Erie overruled Swift and held that state law governs in the common law as well as in the statutory situation. Subsequent cases clarified that this means forum law: the law of the state in which the federal court is sitting.

The result is that the federal court in a diversity case sits in effect as just another state court, seeking out forum state law for all substantive issues. The Rules of Decision Act does not apply to procedural matters, however; for matters of procedure a federal court, sitting in a diversity or any other kind of case, applies its own rules. This has been so since 1938, when, coincidentally (Erie was also decided in 1938), the Federal Rules of Civil Procedure arrived on the scene.

It takes little imagination to guess that the problem of Erie lies in determining whether in a diversity case a given issue is substantive, which requires reference to state law, or procedural, which does not. No simple formula has ever been devised to determine with certainty what's substantive and what's procedural, however. Many an issue that might fit under a "procedural" label in some other context has been in effect labeled "substantive" in a diversity case so as to assure recourse to state law. Many courts have in fact determined that very often labels can't be used at all.

It will always help to remember that the policy of the Erie doctrine is to achieve a basic uniformity of result between state and federal court when the coincidence of diversity happens to offer a litigant a choice of forum. If lawyers confronting a new issue keep that in mind, they will be able to guess whether Erie applies to require its resolution from state law. But while this is often so, it is not always so. With a certain small proportion (but fair number) of issues, other considerations come into play. These are the ones that have sent some special trains down the Erie Railroad track, and earned for the Erie doctrine this separate chapter.

After Erie, is there a federal "common law"? There is, and Erie never said there was not. All Erie said is that there is no "general" federal common law. But there are a significant number of instances in which the governing rule of law in a federal court (and sometimes even in a state court) should logically come from federal sources and there is no federal statute in point. The federal courts in such cases may be called on to devise a body of governing law through the decisional route, and these devisings qualify as "federal common law". A few well known examples are Textile Workers (USSC 1957), involving a labor dispute under the Taft–Hartley Act; Ivy Broadcasting (CA2 1968), involving the standards to be applied to interstate telephone service; Illinois (USSC 1972), involving interstate pollution; and perhaps principally Clearfield (USSC 1943), concerning the rights of the United States on federal commercial paper. Whenever such a federal common law takes over (and assuming that it is not itself preempted by federal legislation afterwards), it will usually preempt state law, which may have been allowed some governing role before the takeover (Carlson, USSC 1980).

With Erie's rejection of Swift, however, the main "common law" opportunities of the federal system—those that had obtained for almost a century in diversity cases under the Swift decision—are indeed withdrawn. With the withdrawal, although there will always be many factors to consider when determining whether to sue in a federal or state court (of course assuming that a choice exists), a different substantive law will not be one of them.

§ 101. Erie and the Statute of Limitations

The statute of limitations posed some special problems for the Erie doctrine. (The statute of limitations poses problems for anyone who trifles with it.) Early in Erie's life the Supreme Court held that in a diversity case the federal court must measure the timeliness of the action by the same yardstick the forum state court would use. (Guaranty Trust, USSC 1945.) This merely means that the basic period that the state court would apply to the particular kind of action must be applied by the federal court as well.

A more difficult question was how far this statute-of-limitations deference had to go. In Ragan (USSC 1949), the Supreme Court said that it had to go far; that the moment that the action is to be deemed "commenced" for statute of limitations purposes must also, in a diversity case, be governed by state law. Under the Federal Rules, commencement is deemed to occur when the complaint is filed rather than when the summons is served (FRCP Rule 3). Summons service in a federal action can come quite a bit later on, and, when it comes, it is deemed to relate back to the filing of the complaint for a limitations measure. If the state practice requires that the summons be served, and is not content with the mere filing of the complaint within the applicable time, the diversity plaintiff who files in time but serves afterwards is, in two ugly words, too late. The plaintiff in Ragan was too late.

After Ragan came the Hanna case (USSC 1965; § 102), which was thought in some quarters to overrule Ragan. It did not. The Supreme Court held in Walker (1980) that Ragan is still good law. The lesson to the diversity plaintiff is to take such steps as will satisfy state as well as federal law in respect of the "commencement" moment. As has been pointed out elsewhere (§ 58), the statute of limitations can be as fatal to the plaintiff as an adverse judgment on the merits, and with much less trouble for the defendant.

The statute of limitations is usually regarded as a "procedural" item. It is regarded as procedural for other purposes, in any event. (Many a state lists its limitations periods in its procedure act, for example.) But it strikes so swiftly, and so finally, that the Supreme Court had no difficulty in Guaranty Trust in disregarding its traditional "procedural" characterization and requiring that it be treated as substantive for Erie purposes. Guaranty Trust announces what is known as the "outcome determinative" test: that if it can be shown that the outcome of the case would change if federal rather than state law were applied to the issue at hand, then Erie governs to require that the state law be used. This test is still the best around—surely better than any substance-versus-procedure niching—but that it, too, has its shortcomings is evident in the Hanna case, treated in the next section.

§ 102. Erie; Substance Versus Procedure

The Guaranty Trust and a number of other cases in the Supreme Court and below teach that an attempt to determine whether Erie (and thus state law) applies to a given issue in a diversity case merely by categorizing the issue as one of "substance" (state law applies) or "procedure" (state law doesn't apply) is simplistic and often will not work. This is called "characterization" and it can too easily avoid a reference to state law in a case in which the underlying policies of the Erie case would want state law applied. Guaranty Trust and its statute of limitations issue, treated in the prior section, is an example of that.

Another example is Bernhardt (USSC 1956), involving an issue of arbitrability arising in a federal court in Vermont. The federal arbitration act (§ 75) was by its own terms inapplicable so that the field was open in this diversity case to look to state law. But isn't arbitrability a "procedural" question, so that no state law reference under Erie would be called for? It was shown that Vermont, with an anti-arbitration attitude, would not have enforced the agreement to arbitrate. Under Erie, said the Supreme Court, neither should the federal court in this diversity case. With a "characterization", an arbitrability issue would almost certainly end up on the "procedural" side. But it would undermine Erie's policy if a federal court in a diversity case were to order arbitration when the state court sitting next door would not. Ergo, Erie applies, and never mind characterizing the issue, which is just a form of judicial name-calling.

Of course, the state's choice of law must be a constitutional one, i.e., the law chosen must be that of a state having sufficient contacts with the case to make the choice of its law a fair one (§ 56), but that was clearly the case in Bernhardt. A more interesting question arises when the federal judge, asked to apply a certain law because it is shown that the state court would, feels that the state law would be a constitutionally impermissible choice (§ 104).

Burden of proof cases can also illustrate how categorizing an issue may have to be avoided in order to do Erie's proper bidding. In Sampson (CA1, cert. den. USSC 1940), a Maine accident was the subject of a Massachusetts federal diversity suit. Maine had a rule putting the burden on the plaintiff to prove freedom from contributory negligence. Under Massachusetts law the burden was on the defendant to prove any negligence on the part of the plaintiff. The court held that Massachusetts law must govern even though it was shown that Massachusetts itself regards the issue as a "procedural" one. Had the federal court accepted this Massachusetts characterization for the Erie purpose, Massachusetts law would not even have been looked at. In other words, had captions carried the day, the only thing the federal court would have learned by looking to Massachusetts law is that it was in error for looking to Massachusetts law.

Burden of proof can become substantive, indeed, especially when all first-hand witnesses to the event in issue are dead. When access to proof is impeded for both sides, the party with the burden of proof will usually be the loser. Hence burden of proof deserves an Erie trip to state law, rather in contrast with the mere burden of pleading, which requires only a verbalization on a piece of paper. Hence a nice line has been drawn between the burden of pleading, where Erie does not necessarily govern, and the burden of proof, where it does (Palmer, USSC 1943).

The effect of a judgment (i.e., its res judicata impact) is also sufficiently "substantive" that state law must govern it, said the Supreme Court in Semtek (USSC 2001). A California federal court sitting in diversity dismissed the case on statute of limitations grounds and purported to make the dismissal "on the merits". California law, however, treats limitations dismissals as non-merits dismissals. The plaintiff refiled in Maryland where the statute had not yet run and now came the question of whether the purported "merits" dismissal in the California diversity court could preclude Maryland from proceeding to the merits. It could not, said the Supreme Court. A federal diversity judgment is subject to the same res judicata rules that govern a state court judgment, and since the California state court here would not deem the claim barred substantively, the plaintiff was free to pursue it in another forum.

Probably the principal pronouncement on the Erie doctrine since Erie itself is Hanna v. Plumer (USSC 1965). The case was against an executor in a federal court in Massachusetts. Massachusetts had a statute requiring that service on the executor be made by "delivery in hand". Service was instead made by delivery to the defendant's wife at his residence, precisely as authorized by the federal rule applicable at the time, Rule 4(d)(1) (now

4(e)(2)) of the Federal Rules of Civil Procedure. The district court dismissed for failure to follow the state service method, and the dismissal was affirmed at circuit. In that posture did the case reach the Supreme Court. For relying on a federal rule in this diversity case, the plaintiff was punished with a dismissal too late to start the action over. The Supreme Court realized that if this result were to be affirmed, it would be dangerous for any party to rely on the Federal Rules of Civil Procedure for procedural instruction, even for something as mechanical as summons service, in a diversity case. Thus the Federal Rules faced an onslaught from the Erie doctrine, which could have seriously curtailed their utility in diversity cases. The Supreme Court, unanimously reversing and sustaining the service in Hanna, held that anything contained in the Federal Rules of Civil Procedure is presumptively "procedural" (even for Erie purposes), and that it takes some heavy doing to rebut the presumption. The very placement of an instruction in the FRCP is evidence that the Advisory Committee of distinguished lawyers, which drafts the provision, the Supreme Court, which promulgates it, and Congress, which must be given a chance to veto it before it becomes effective, all deem it procedural.

After Hanna, parties could presumably turn with safety to the Federal Rules of Civil Procedure in a diversity action as in any other federal action.

The main potential casualty of the Hanna case was Ragan (USSC 1949), which held that Erie governs to require that state law be applied in a diversity case even to determine the moment that the action is deemed commenced for purposes of the statute of limitations. (See § 101.) Because FRCP Rule 3 provides that the action is commenced when the complaint is filed, Hanna's indication that state law is preempted for matters addressed by the FRCP was thought to overrule Ragan, but it did not. The Supreme Court later held (Walker, 1980) that one must still examine the scope intended to be accorded a given rule, and that the scope of Rule 3 is not so broad as to require it to dictate the moment of "commencement" in diversity cases when state law prescribes a different time. The Semtek case (noted above) faced a similar question of scope, this time with regard to FRCP 41, which governs dismissals. Arguably, the rule might be read to create a federal law on the effect of judgments, but the court decided that this was too much substance to pour into a procedural vessel.

Hanna also demonstrates that the "outcome determinative" test, while probably the best around, is not perfect. Had state law rather than federal law governed the service method in Hanna, there would indeed have been a different outcome: the action would have been dismissed for improper service. On this summons service issue, with state law the case was dead; with federal law, it was very much alive. Hence "outcome determination", held the Supreme Court, can't be the ultimate test. Even a rule as unambiguously mechanical and "procedural" as one that says how to serve a summons must be backed by a sanction when it is disobeyed, and that sanction can climb up to the ultimate disaster that can visit a plaintiff: a dismissal of the case. Thus the simple fact that the "outcome" may differ when federal rather than state law (or vice-versa) is applied to an issue is never final proof that Erie wants state law applied. The policies of the Erie doctrine must be investigated. (It is doubtful that the Erie panel itself would have thought so piddling a matter as how to present a summons to the defendant needs federal deference to state law.) And countervailing policies coming from other sources may be relevant and ultimately decisive against a choice of state law. (See § 104).

If the lawyer is faced with an issue that has not yet undergone an Erie test, so that there is no case to suggest whether Erie refers this issue to state law, a wise lawyer may prefer, if the consequences are great enough, to take steps that would satisfy both federal and state law with respect to the particular issue met. It will not be a frequent prospect, but when the bet can be fatal there is no harm in hedging.

§ 103.   Erie and Choice of Law

When the diversity case in federal court involves contacts with more than one state, and a choice of law problem is presented, the federal court must choose the same law that the forum state court would to govern the issue. (Klaxon, Griffin, USSC [both 1941].) In other words, Erie applies to choice of law rules.

This has been criticized as requiring the federal courts to abdicate an opportunity to resolve choice of law issues with less bias than state courts would presumably have. The premise of the criticism is that state courts are usually too forum oriented in their own interest. But the other side defends the rule by pointing out that although it does not deter forum shopping between one state and another when several states are available, it at least takes the juice out of shopping between a federal and state court within the same state. The Supreme Court was given the benefit of both views, and decided to adhere to the rule that requires a federal court to apply state choice of law rules (Day, USSC 1975).

§ 104. Erie; Constitutional Considerations

The Erie doctrine has constitutional auspices, but of a somewhat equivocal variety. The Supreme Court was at pains in Erie not to declare the Rules of Decision Act (28 U.S.C.A. § 1652) unconstitutional. It was the construction given the act in Swift v. Tyson that Erie found unconstitutional. Erie implicates the 10th Amendment, which reserves to the states matters not governed by federal sources, and holds that it would violate the amendment to exclude state law—common law or whatever—from a case on the mere coincidence of diversity of citizenship. The Erie bench also mentioned equal protection as being violated by the Swift approach, suggesting 14th Amendment involvement as well. However this may be, the federal courts including the Supreme Court itself have over the years treated Erie as just an authoritative case construing an influential statute.

In most cases it does not matter much whether Erie rides a constitutional or mere statutory train: it applies in either instance. But place Erie on a single track riding towards state law, and face it head-on with an engine going the other way, seeking application of federal law, and it starts to matter. If the opposing engine is built of constitutional material, and Erie is mere statutory fabric, Erie will be derailed and federal law will govern, which is in effect what happened in Byrd (USSC, 1958).

In Byrd, P sued D for personal injuries. A defense to D under state law was that P was an employee and workers' compensation was therefore the exclusive remedy. State law also provided, however, that this particular defense, although presenting a question of fact, must be passed on by the court rather than by a jury. Erie's pressure, if it had any to apply, was to have the federal court do the same thing, i.e., follow the state rule. But the federal constitution's 7th Amendment, guaranteeing trial by jury in money cases (which this was), came down the track pointing to federal law, and prevailed over Erie. The court held that the 7th Amendment requires retention of the same distribution of function between judge and jury that existed when we became a nation; that it could not be neutralized by a state statute attempting to redistribute those functions in a federal court. Erie had to give way, either because it had no real constitutional underpinning or because whatever it had was too weak to face up to a challenger from a different part of the constitution with a stronger sense of mission. Erie might have given way even if it had its own fully furnished constitutional car, but the collision would have been louder.

Byrd's 7th Amendment rationale showed up again in Gasperini v. Center for the Humanities (USSC 1996). There the court faced the applicability of a New York "tort reform" statute that gave New York's intermediate appellate courts the power to set aside jury verdicts that "deviate materially from what would be reasonable compensation". The common law standard for setting aside a jury verdict on the grounds of excessiveness is that it must "shock" the court's conscience. Gasperini involved a $450,000 verdict in a diversity case that was apparently "deviantly" high, but not shockingly so. The question was what to do with the New York statute in diversity cases. The court held that the difference between the common law "conscience" rule and the New York rule was sufficiently substantive that failure to apply it could lead to forum shopping in violation of the policy of Erie. However, the 7th Amendment's "re-examination" clause limits the ability of federal appellate courts to order new trials. So, in a Solomonic decision, the court decided that federal trial (i.e., district) courts should apply the New York statute, but that federal appellate tribunals would continue to exercise only common law "abuse of discretion" review. Byrd, now with Gasperini at its side, show that the 7th Amendment continues to have some influence on the allocation of authority within the federal court system, though not over the application of substantive rules of law.

A different constitutional issue can also arise in an Erie setting. When we say that a federal court must apply state choice of law rules in a diversity case (§ 103), the assumption is that the choice the state would make is itself a constitutional one. Indeed, the same would be true of a non-conflicts diversity case in which the federal court is merely looking to the forum's internal substantive law: it had better be constitutional in the judge's eyes. If the state courts, and even the state's highest court, have passed on a given law or choice of law rule and found it satisfactory to federal constitutional standards, the finding will of course be persuasive to a federal judge facing the same issue, but it is not likely to be decisive.

Take, for example, the Doggrell case (CA6 1953). Arkansas law imposed personal liability on shareholders of Arkansas corporations if certain papers were not filed in a designated office. A creditor of the corporation sued some Tennessee shareholders to collect under this liability in a federal court in Tennessee. The shareholders' defense was that the Arkansas statute was penal (§ 51) and thus should not be enforced in Tennessee. The Sixth Circuit rejected the defense on a 2–1 vote. The majority of two held that the statute was not penal and was thus enforcible in Tennessee. Shortly after that the Supreme Court of Tennessee in a different case held that the same Arkansas statute was indeed penal, and not enforcible in Tennessee. Now a reargument motion was made to the Sixth Circuit in the earlier case and the court reversed itself, one judge switching to make for a 2–1 majority for the defendant, upholding the defense. The switching judge apparently found no constitutional impediment in Tennessee's refusal to apply the Arkansas law; in his view there was sufficient room for Tennessee to say, constitutionally, that the statute was "penal" and that Tennessee thus did not have to enforce it. So for that judge this was strictly an Erie case, with the federal court required to do the state's bidding, whatever it was.

The judge who did not switch, but dissented on the reargument, held on both votes that the Arkansas statute was not penal. The first time around he may have assumed that Tennessee would so hold as well. Thus on the first vote he could merely have cited Erie. But now that the Tennessee Supreme Court had come down with the holding that the statute was penal, a judge refusing to follow that holding would have to have some reason besides Erie. The judge had. In his view, there was nothing in the Arkansas statute that left room for another state to refuse it application on the ground of its being a "penal" law. Tennessee's refusal thus amounted to a denial of full faith and credit to the Arkansas law—a federal constitutional violation that left Erie no room for maneuver. This judge was holding that he could not make the choice of law the state would make when the choice would violate the federal constitution.

Erie or no, federal judges are not terribly deferential to state courts on matters of federal constitutional law.

§ 105. Erie and the "Door–Closing" Cases

What the usual diversity case expects to find when it turns to state law is a governing rule that disposes of the case on the merits, either directly, the forum being the only state concerned with the case, or through the forum's choice of law rules leading to the substantive law of some other state. But suppose, in a given case, it appears that the forum would not reach the merits at all; that it would dismiss the case on some ground short of the merits. Cases like this are known as "door-closers" rather than "merits-reachers".

Woods (USSC 1949) is a good example. A state statute prevented a foreign corporation from suing in its courts if it failed to qualify to do business in the state. When such an objection is present, this kind of statute dismisses the case at the threshold, without reaching the merits. Woods holds that a federal diversity court must apply such a statute. Were the rule otherwise, the policy underlying a legitimate state statute could be undermined by a plaintiff's merely invoking federal rather than state jurisdiction. The purposes of Erie would not be fostered by such permission.

Angel (USSC 1947) is an even more intriguing example. A deficiency resulted after the in rem foreclosure sale of mortgaged land in Virginia. The defendant was from North Carolina and the plaintiff sued him for the deficiency in a federal court there. North Carolina had a moratorium statute barring its courts from entertaining deficiency actions. The statute operated not to adjudicate the merits in the mortgagor's favor, but merely to bar the entertainment of "jurisdiction". It was argued that it was therefore a mere procedural instruction for which a federal court did not have to look to state law. The argument did not prevail. The facts of Angel were more complicated, but the question that evolved on the bottom line was whether a moratorium statute (we assume a valid one) which carries out its aim not by awarding the mortgagor judgment on the merits, but by merely barring the exercise of jurisdiction, must also be applied by a federal diversity court. It must, held Angel.

The Supreme Court has yet to offer a satisfactory discussion of whether federal diversity courts are to apply state forum non conveniens rules. These are rules designed to keep out of a state court cases that lack local contacts and are therefore rejected by the state as unjustified impositions. (See § 53.) It can be argued that if the matter is merely one of convenience, then the federal court's entertainment of a case that the state court would not entertain does nothing to undermine state policy, and, hence, that the state's conveniens rules need not be adopted under Erie. To buttress this, the availability of a cross-country transfer within the federal system under 28 U.S.C.A. § 1404(a) is cited, a transfer power that a state court can't match. If a state court finds another place more convenient for a case, the best it can do is stay or dismiss it without prejudice to the plaintiff commencing a fresh action in the other state's court. In a federal court, on the other hand, a mere transfer is available, and the transfer is preferred as a conveniens cure. That is said to be a further reason for not having a federal court resort to state conveniens rules, which can result in a dismissal for want of an option to transfer.

The foregoing is applicable in diversity cases, in any event. Forum non conveniens may sometimes be applied to dismiss even a claim arising under federal law (see § 56). The U.S. Supreme Court has held that if such a dismissal does come about in a state court, however, and a federal court in the same state is the tribunal to which the plaintiff now turns, the state court's earlier conveniens ruling is not binding and the federal court can apply § 1404(a) unimpeded by it. (Parsons, USSC 1963.)

Section 1404(a) assumes that there are several permissible districts that would be a proper venue for the federal action, and authorizes the court in the district in which the action was commenced to transfer it to another district if it appears to be the more convenient one. It is required that the proposed transferee district, in addition to being a proper venue under federal statutes (e.g., 28

U.S.C.A. § 1391), also be a district in which the defendant would have been amenable to personal jurisdiction (Hoffman, USSC 1960). Section 1404(a) of course poses the issue—should a federal diversity case be transferred from one state to another on its authority—of which state's law governs the transferred case under Erie. The Supreme Court held in Van Dusen (1964) that transferor state law accompanies the transferred case; that the change under § 1404(a) is merely one of courtrooms, not of law, and that the federal judge in the transferee district is for Erie purposes to deem herself sitting in the state in which the action was commenced.

In Van Dusen, it was the defendant who moved for the transfer. In Ferens (1990), the U.S. Supreme Court held that the same rule applies—the § 1404(a) transferee must apply transferor law under the Erie rule—even when it is the plaintiff who moves for the transfer. The plaintiff in Ferens brought a personal injury action in Pennsylvania. One of the counts was in tort, however, and the Pennsylvania statute of limitations on it had expired. So the plaintiff brought the tort count in a federal court in Mississippi, which had a much longer statute of limitations (and no borrowing statute that would have selected some other state's statute of limitations on the facts), and then moved to transfer the case to Pennsylvania under § 1404(a). It worked. The plaintiff was able to keep his favored forum (Pennsylvania) while securing the more favorable choice of Mississippi law on the limitations issue. It is doubtful that § 1404(a), or the Erie panel, ever intended this kind of blatant forum shopping, but the Supreme Court countenanced it in Ferens, albeit only on a 5–4 vote. (The root of the problem may be laxness in putting constitutional restrictions on a forum's choice of a statute of limitations in a multi-state setting. See § 61.)

Assuming a substantial difference in the law of two states on a given issue, return now—in light of the Van Dusen/Ferens rule—to the question of whether a federal diversity court should apply a state conveniens rule, and dismiss, or instead apply § 1404(a), and transfer. If the case is dismissed in the federal court in State X, and is commenced afresh in the federal court of State Y, the latter's state law governs under Erie. But if it is transferred from X to Y, X law presumably accompanies under Van Dusen/Ferens. Perhaps the Van Dusen/Ferens rule should be adjusted to except a case which (it is shown) the original state court would have dismissed under a conveniens rule.

Van Dusen led some courts to assume that when only a dismissal can implement a conveniens objection even in a federal court, as when a foreign-country court, to which a facile § 1404(a) transfer can't be made, is the more appropriate one (§ 53), it can't be granted if it is shown that on the merits the foreign court would apply law less favorable to the plaintiff. The Supreme Court rejected that idea in Piper (1981), holding the dismissal permissible nevertheless, but treated the issue as if one of federal law without addressing Erie.

§ 106. Finding State Law

Neither a state nor a federal court has difficulty finding the applicable rule of state law when it is contained in an unambiguous statute or a recent all-fours precedent of the state's highest court. Any court may experience difficulty, however, when the point is novel, an undecided matter of common law or the subject of an unclear statute. But while a state court's determination of the matter can afterwards be taken along an appellate path that will lead to the ultimate authority on the point—the state's highest court—the federal court has no access to that oracle and must do the best it can without it. (Some states have a certification procedure permitting at least some federal courts to obtain an advisory opinion on state law from the state's highest court [see Clay, USSC 1964]. Many states forbid advisory judicial opinions of this kind, however.)

What is a federal court to do in a diversity case when the state law that it must apply is not clear? While the decisions of the highest state court (assuming of course that they satisfy the federal constitution) bind the federal court, is binding effect also to be accorded the decision of an intermediate appellate court? a trial-level court?

The major Supreme Court address to this matter is in Commissioner of Internal Revenue v. Estate of Bosch (USSC 1967), reviewing earlier cases. The decisions of state nisi prius tribunals, while entitled to "some weight", are "not controlling", holds the court. The decision of an intermediate appellate court is "a datum ... not to be disregarded", unless the federal court is "convinced by other persuasive data that the highest court of the state would decide otherwise." It boils down to the federal court's making the best effort it can to predict what the highest court of the state would hold today on the point at issue. Lawyers often brief these issues mightily in a federal court in an endeavor to persuade about what the highest state court would do.

It may be that while the state's highest court has not decided an issue of state law, the federal court of appeals for the circuit embracing the state has. Other federal courts are likely to deem themselves bound by that decision. (Factors, CA2 1981.)

When a state choice of law rule has to be applied in the federal court, a problem of broader dimensions can arise. If the forum's (State F's) choice is that of the substantive law of State X, and that law is unclear, the perception of State X law that the federal court must pursue is not its own direct analysis, or that of State X's highest court directly, but that of State X's highest court as the federal court thinks the highest court of State F would perceive it. The tools of the search for State X's law are likely to be identical whether the federal court is going to State X law on a line, or through State F's choice of law rules, but the situation is fanciful enough to have prompted Judge Henry Friendly in such a case (Nolan, CA2 1960, afterwards set aside and remanded, USSC 1961) to note that his task was "to determine what the New York courts would think the California courts would think on an issue about which neither has thought."

§ 107.   Erie in Non–Diversity Cases?

Practically speaking, the Erie doctrine applies only when the basis of federal subject matter jurisdiction is diversity of citizenship. But Erie is a construction of a statute—the Rules of Decision Act—that applies in all situations in which a point of law arises not governed by federal law. Even when there is no diversity, therefore, and the federal court is hearing a case "arising under" federal law, it will sometimes happen that an issue arises having no federal source for resolution. Here, too, the Rules of Decision Act may apply and require recourse to state law. This happens, for example, when, in an otherwise federal context, an issue of a family relationship arises. There is no federal body of family law and the issue may therefore have to be resolved by reference to state law. De Sylva (USSC 1956) is an example. Federal law listed those entitled to succeed in interest to a federal copyright, and "children" were on the list. Whether an out-of-wedlock child would be embraced among "children" was found to be an issue whose resolution would have to come from state law.

One sometimes hears the Erie doctrine credited (or blamed) for such a reference to state law in a non-diversity context. The description is harmless enough, but Erie's primary arena remains the diversity case.

CHAPTER VI

JUDGMENTS

A. INTRODUCTION

§ 108. Recognition of Judgments, Introductory

The third and last of the three major conflict of laws realms is the recognition of judgments. It is often studied before choice of law in law school curricula, but its more logical place is after. It can then build on principles studied during choice of law, as it often has to do.

Judgments must be divided into two categories: those of American courts and those of foreign countries. Only the former get full faith and credit, as elaborated in § 110. The judgments of foreign countries can at best expect only what we call "comity", which is a voluntary giving of recognition, whereas full faith and credit, when applicable, is mandatory. Perhaps ironically, awards of arbitration panels of most foreign nations come in for mandatory recognition in the United States. This is because of a treaty to which the United States has subscribed (§ 120). But absent a treaty—and a treaty is seldom present when the judgment of a foreign court is involved—"comity" is what applies. It is taken up in § 109.

Some terminology should be noted. Since we will almost invariably be addressing the situation in which the judgment of one court is asking recognition of another, reference is facilitated by calling the first court to render its judgment "F–1". "F–2" will be the court called upon to recognize the F–1 judgment. Occasionally an "F–3" may appear. The "F" of course stands for "Forum".

The question also arises at the outset as to why it should be necessary, especially within the United States, for a party with a judgment from one state to take any additional steps in order to have it enforced in another. The answer is that the states are sovereign, and the enforcement officer of F–2 will not take any steps to enforce an F–1 judgment until it has been duly converted into an F–2 judgment. The process of undertaking that conversion is one of the contexts in which the parties meet issues of recognition.

One way, and the traditional way, to convert an F–1 judgment into that of F–2 is to bring a plenary action in F–2 based on the F–1 judgment. Often today F–2 will have an even more expeditious procedure available for something as presumptively meritorious as a claim already reduced to judgment elsewhere. It may provide something as fast as a mere registration procedure. A federal judgment, for example, once rendered in any district, can be transmuted into a judgment in any other federal district through a mere filing procedure (28 U.S.C.A. § 1963).

The mechanics of the conversion are for F–2 to determine. The main question we meet in the ensuing materials is the more substantive one of whether F–2, through whatever procedure, must recognize and respect the F–1 judgment.

B. COMITY

§ 109. "Comity"; Foreign–Country Judgments

There are so many things to be said about judgments that get full faith and credit and so few to be said about those that do not, that "comity", which describes those that do not, should be treated first and put aside. Black's Law Dictionary describes "comity" as "a willingness to grant a privilege, not as a matter of right, but out of deference and good will." That serves well here. Nothing in the federal constitution compels a state to recognize the judgments of a foreign country, and, absent a treaty so requiring, the states are on their own. Thus each state decides for itself how far it will go in recognizing a foreign country's judgment. In general, the judgment will be recognized if it appears to have resulted from procedures compatible with domestic American concepts of due process: fair notice, appropriate jurisdictional basis, fair hearing, etc. (Cowans, NY 1927; Rst.2d § 98.)

There is seldom any reciprocity requirement, that is, a showing that the foreign country would recognize a given state's judgment before that state would recognize the foreign one. The point is relevant chiefly because the U.S. Supreme Court, in opting for a rule to be applied in the federal courts, did settle on such a reciprocity requirement. In Hilton (USSC 1895), the court refused recognition to a French judgment against a United States citizen because it appeared that if the tables were turned France would not have recognized ours; France would have permitted relitigation of the merits. With the advent of the Erie rule of 1938 (§ 100), requiring a federal court to apply the state rule of decision at least when the federal court's jurisdiction is based on diversity of citizenship, which is usually the case when a recognition situation appears in a federal action, there is little left of Hilton. Over half the states have adopted the Uniform Foreign Money Judgments Act, which does not require reciprocity. A few states, however, have added a non-uniform reciprocity provision.

The bottom line for the lawyer who seeks recognition for a foreign country judgment and with whom the initiative lies is to bring an action on the judgment in the courts of the state her research determines to have (1) jurisdiction, (2) property of the defendant, and (3) the most congenial "comity" doctrine.

The doctrine of "comity", understood mainly as affecting the recognition of judgments, sometimes interplays with the "act of state" doctrine (§ 98), which requires recognition here for acts taken by a foreign sovereign within its own precincts. In the Bhopal case (Bi CA2), for example, India enacted a statute making itself the sole representative of all its citizens and then settled all their claims. The settlement was held binding: claimants trying to avoid it in litigation in this country were held to lack standing under the Indian legislation.

C. FULL FAITH AND CREDIT

§ 110. Full Faith and Credit, in General

Section 1 of Article IV of the federal constitution provides that

Full faith and credit shall be given in each state to the public acts, records and judicial proceedings of every other state.

As discussed at some length in § 56, this clause plays little role in choice of law. It plays a major role, however, in the recognition of judgments. It is with respect to "judicial proceedings" that the U.S. Supreme Court has given the clause full sway, requiring every American court to recognize every judgment duly rendered by every other American court.

Note that the full faith and credit clause in the constitution refers only to "states", presumably referring, therefore, insofar as judgments are concerned, only to the judgments of state courts. But Congress has by statute, 28 U.S.C.A. § 1738, extended it (or its equivalent) to federal, territorial and District of Columbia courts as well, with the result that they and the state courts all come under the full faith and credit umbrella and the term

"American" courts is used in this book to refer to all of them collectively. It is through a variety of other constitutional provisions that Congress derives authority to extend the recognition requirement to these other courts, including its constitutional powers over the District of Columbia (Article I of the federal constitution), the territories (Article IV), and the federal courts in general (Article III). The supremacy clause (Article VI) then alights on the statute to make its mutual recognition requirement binding on all courts, including those of the states.

At root, full faith and credit as applied to a judgment is a doctrine of interstate, mandatory res judicata. As long as the judgment has been duly rendered by any American court, every other must recognize it, i.e., must accept what it has done on the merits without relitigation. And by "duly" the only thing meant is that the rendering court (F–1) had jurisdiction, a matter elaborated in the next section.

A proviso is that the judgment be a final one. An intermediate order rendered during the housekeeping phase of a litigation will not ordinarily invoke full faith and credit. Nor will an interlocutory judgment (Crayne, Nev.1932), of the kind met often but not exclusively in marital actions, for the reason that it still contemplates some further doing at home before the home forum deems it final, and if it is not final at home it has no call on recognition elsewhere.

§ 111. F–2's Inquiry Into F–1's Jurisdiction

In determining whether full faith and credit applies to the F–1 judgment, F–2 may inquire into whether F–1 had jurisdiction (Thompson, USSC 1874), and, at least at the outset, only that. If the inquiry reveals that F–1 did have jurisdiction, of both subject matter and person (or res, if in rem jurisdiction is involved), F–2 must discontinue the inquiry and honor the judgment.

We must distinguish here between a default judgment and a contested judgment. Both get full faith and credit but different rules apply about the jurisdictional inquiry. If D never appeared in the F–1 action, and the merits judgment against him therefore came about by default, D is entitled to have the F–2 court make a determination of whether F–1 had jurisdiction. Here F–2 may examine into all of the due process ingredients that go into jurisdiction: did F–1 have a jurisdictional basis and give D adequate notice and opportunity to be heard? But F–2 may not apply its own internal requirements to judge F–1's jurisdiction; only into the elements of federal due process may F–2 look, because it was only those elements that F–1 had to satisfy to obtain jurisdiction. Was the jurisdictional basis one that due process, as interpreted by the Supreme Court, recognizes (§ 24)? Did the method of service also comport with due process? Here F–2 must be careful. F–2 can't insist that F–1 be shown to have used only a jurisdictional basis or only a method of service that F–2 recognizes as an internal matter. Due process sets broad standards and is content with any of a wide variety of bases and methods (§§ 24, 47). Each state is free to choose its own as long as it meets those standards. If F–1 used a basis and method satisfactory to due process, although not the same as F–2 itself uses, F–1 obtained jurisdiction and F–2 must acknowledge it.

When in this default situation it was longarm jurisdiction that F–1 relied on under one of its statutes, F–2 will be in the position of having to determine the scope of the F–1 longarm statute as well as whether its application to the facts satisfies federal due process. This is not an infrequent situation in our mobile society. The reason for F–2's being able to look into these matters at all when D has defaulted in F–1 is the general rule in this country that a defendant is entitled to one day in court on a jurisdictional issue and that if he has not appeared in F–1 he has not yet had that day and is entitled to it when the matter of F–1's jurisdiction arises in a recognition context in F–2.

But when D has appeared in F–1, and has raised the jurisdictional issue there and it has been adjudicated against him, i.e., the F–1 court upheld its jurisdiction, full faith and credit works a bit of additional magic. D has now had his day in court on the jurisdictional point in F–1 itself and hence whatever F–1 judgment now eventuates on the merits, whether after contest or by default (as where D refuses to participate on the merits after losing on the jurisdictional point), is entitled to full faith and credit along with the jurisdictional determination itself. In other words, the fact of D's appearance in F–1 means that not only are the merits beyond F–2's review, but so is the issue of F–1's jurisdiction. As soon as F–2's inquiry reveals that D appeared in F–1, F–2's inquiry must cease and it must recognize the F–1 judgment.

These are clearly the conclusions when D, appearing in F–1, has specifically raised the jurisdictional issue and lost on it (Baldwin, USSC 1931). And the objection need not necessarily have been raised during the F–1 action. If, for example, D did not initially appear but only raised the jurisdictional issue after a default judgment was rendered against him, as where D made a post-judgment motion to the F–1 court to vacate the default judgment and the motion was denied (jurisdiction being sustained and the default standing), that also used up D's day in court and requires F–2 to respect F–1's jurisdictional adjudication as well as the merits.

Likely to surprise the lawyer, and especially the student, is that this hands-off rule apparently binds F–2 to recognize F–1's jurisdiction not only when D has specifically raised the jurisdictional issue in F–1, but even when he appears in F–1 without raising it (see Cook, USSC 1951). The theory is that with his appearance in F–1, D had the opportunity to raise the point, and, failing to, concedes F–1's jurisdiction and can't contest it elsewhere. Some states hold that D's appearance need not even have been in person; that it suffices if D, even though not domiciled in F–1, merely signs a writing purporting to appear in F–1 (e.g., Boudreaux, La.1966). Other states won't go that far, permitting themselves, when they are F–2, to examine the paper by which D presumed to "appear" in the F–1 proceeding, and, gauging its validity by the law of some other related jurisdiction (usually F–2), finding it void (e.g., Day, Md.1965). Most cases on this point are in the matrimonial realm, which is the subject of a separate chapter later (Chapter VII).

Up to now we have been discussing only an issue of personal jurisdiction. The same rules can be said to obtain when it was only in rem jurisdiction that F–1 was asserting, in which event the jurisdictional elements that F–2 must consider are of course those applicable to in rem jurisdiction. Differences between in personam and in rem judgments are more pronounced when we examine the scope of the recognition they are entitled to on their merits, a point treated in the next section.

The appearance of D in F–1 forecloses not only the issue of F–1's personal jurisdiction, but, if the point is raised in F–1, of F–1's subject matter jurisdiction as well. The Supreme Court has so held not only in a matrimonial context (Sherrer, USSC 1948), but in a land dispute as well (Durfee, USSC 1963). The concept is a bit rough. How can a court that lacks competence to adjudicate, which is what subject matter jurisdiction is all about, adjudicate itself into a competence that it lacks the competence to adjudicate? The point is a neat one, but even issues of subject matter jurisdiction need repose—repose being the aim of res judicata and the full faith and credit notion that embraces it—and hence can't be kept open indefinitely. The Restatement of Judgments 2d (Ch. 2, § 12) takes the position that F-1's adjudication of its own subject matter jurisdiction—even an implicit adjudication to that effect embodied in the simple fact of a judgment rendered by F-1 on the merits—must be recognized in F-2 except in certain designated situations, one of which is where subject matter jurisdiction was "plainly" lacking. This would at least cover the situation in which a town or village magistrate with no civil jurisdiction in F-1 purports to grant a divorce, or pass on title to the Mississippi River.

Assumed throughout the foregoing is that if the jurisdictional point adjudicated in F-1, in respect of any kind of jurisdiction, was appealable, then it was either duly appealed or the time for its appeal expired under F-1's practice. Implicit is that when F-2 gets the question it has at least been finally determined under F-1's practice.

§ 112. F-2 Bound by Merits

Seldom today, even in the choice of law realm (where no judgment has yet been rendered), will a state refuse to entertain a sister state's law on the ground that it violates the forum's "public policy" (§ 57). But there is in that instance at least some room for a refusal. Once a judgment has been rendered on the claim by an American court with jurisdiction, however, then neither public policy nor much of anything else can be used to deny it recognition. In fact, the Supreme Court said so explicitly in Baker v. General Motors (1998) where it specifically rejected the idea of a "roving" public policy doctrine to reject a sister state judgment. This is so in any event of the money judgment, the most common of all.

A cause of action on a judgment is different from that upon which the judgment was entered. In a suit upon a money judgment for a civil cause of action, the validity of the claim upon which it was founded is not open to inquiry, whatever its genesis. (Milwaukee, USSC 1935.)

In the Milwaukee case the F–1 judgment was for F–1 taxes. Had F–2 been the initial forum, it might have refused to entertain a direct suit for F–1 taxes (see § 52), but the F–2 option to refuse exists no longer when what F–2 has before it is a judgment that F–1 itself rendered for its taxes. The full faith and credit clause in effect puts blinders on F–2's eyes. All F–2 can see is a judgment. As a general rule, what lies behind the judgment becomes invisible.

If there was any error in the F–1 proceedings on the merits, it should have been corrected by appeal in F–1. As with jurisdiction (§ 111), so with the merits: there is only one day in court for them. If the judgment is final in F–1, it binds in F–2. (Emery, NH 1931.) F–2's distaste for the underlying claim is of no moment. Hence Illinois could not refuse to entertain suit on an Alabama judgment merely because it was rendered on an Alabama wrongful death cause of action that Illinois would not have entertained directly (Kenney, USSC 1920). (Illinois later learned that it could not even refuse a direct suit if Illinois contacts made Illinois an appropriate forum. See the discussion of the Hughes case in § 56.)

F–2 may sometimes have to swallow hard. Highwater mark in this area is Fauntleroy v. Lum (USSC 1908), an opinion by Justice Holmes in which F–2 was required to recognize an F–1 judgment that involved F–2's own law and was in error on it. Involved was a Mississippi gambling transaction void under Mississippi (F–2) law, the only relevant one. P happened to find D in Missouri (F–1) and sued him on the gambling claim there, deliberately seeking to avoid Mississippi law. Missouri was evidently in error on the merits when it allowed the recovery (Missouri had assumed that a Mississippi arbitration award on the claim was valid when it was not), but error on the merits is no ground for refusing full faith and credit. Missouri, as F–1, had jurisdiction, and Mississippi, as F–2, had to recognize the judgment.

Even a merits error of federal law, or of federal constitutional law, is no ground for F–2 to refuse recognition to an F–1 judgment, as long as F–1 had jurisdiction. Even if Missouri in the Fauntleroy case could be shown to have applied her own law, irrelevant to the case, to gauge the legitimacy of the Mississippi transaction, and the situation was one in which due process would insist that only Mississippi law could govern because only Mississippi had the requisite contacts (§ 56), Mississippi would still have had to recognize the Missouri judgment. Missouri had jurisdiction, and that settles the matter. The "due process" objection, just mentioned, if such it was, was due process in its substantive phase, not its procedural one, and only a procedural due process violation has the ability to undo F–1's jurisdiction and thereby cancel the full faith and credit obligation.

Another swallow-hard situation appears in Roche (USSC 1928). A judgment was rendered in Washington and then duly converted into an Oregon judgment. Now an action was brought in Washington on the Oregon judgment, which Washington wanted to reject as untimely by applying its statute of limitations and measuring it from the time of the entry of the original Washington judgment that underlay the Oregon judgment. This Washington could not do. It had before it an Oregon judgment and could not look behind it, even though what lay behind it was Washington's own original judgment.

Equity decrees, though falling within the command of full faith and credit, can sometimes be rejected as representing an impermissible interference with another state's affairs. This was apparently the rationale for the decision in Fall v. Eastin (USSC 1909), where it was decided that a Washington state court decree could not transfer title to Nebraska real property. More recently, in Baker v.

General Motors (USSC 1998), the court considered a Michigan injunction purporting to forbid a former employee of the defendant from testifying in cases against the defendant. The court held that a Missouri court need not bar his testimony because the question of whether to allow him to testify was merely a question of the "enforcement" practices of the rendering state. To allow that state to dictate enforcement practices to another would be to "interfere" in a matter over which the rendering state has "no authority." Of course, the rendering states (Washington in Fall and Michigan in Baker) might have held the parties in contempt for defying their decrees, and in that lies an inconsistency that has yet to be resolved by the Supreme Court.

A similar rule applies to a federal judgment rendered in F–1 and then converted into an F–2 judgment pursuant to the registration procedures of 28 U.S.C.A. § 1963. If later enforcement of the F–2 judgment is sought within F–2's statute of limitations, albeit beyond the time period that F–1 would have allowed, the effort is timely. Stanford (CA8 1965).

Perhaps the closest that the present state of the law comes to allowing F–2 to reject an F–1 judgment is where the latter is based on a penal law. But even there the F–1 judgment probably has to be the product of an outright criminal prosecution in F–1. A judgment from the civil side of the court, notwithstanding some ostensibly "penal" element in the underlying claim, may not be turned down. Hence a New York judgment against an incorporator based on a statute imposing personal liability on him for a corporate debt for having filed a false certificate could not be denied recognition by Maryland under a "penal" label (Huntington, USSC 1892).

Because the merits adjudication binds F–2 only to the extent that F–1 had jurisdiction to address the merits, an in rem judgment in F–1 will bind with respect to parties in F–2 only to the extent of their interests in the res of which F–1 had jurisdiction. Extended to the realm of quasi in rem jurisdiction, in which property of D is seized in connection with an unrelated money claim in F–1 and F–1 lacks in personam jurisdiction of D, the judgment will bind D in F–2 only to the extent of D's interest in the seized property (Benadon, NY App.Div.1960). This quasi in rem jurisdiction has of course been much curtailed by the U.S. Supreme Court decision in Shaffer (§ 44).

If the F–1 disposition was not on the merits, it does not get full faith and credit. An important example of this is where F–1 has dismissed the action because brought too late under F–1's statute of limitations, or because barred under F–1's application of the doctrine of laches. If F–2 has a longer period, still alive when P sues in F–2, the F–1 untimeliness disposition will not bind F–2. (Warner, CA2 1933.) The result might be different if F–1

measured timeliness not by its own statute, but by
F–2's, as might happen if F–1 has a "borrowing"
statute or makes an equivalent borrowing under its
decisional law (§ 58). In that instance the timeliness of an F–2 action under F–2 law would be an
issue that F–1 disposed of by applying that very
law, and, even should F–1 have been in error in the
application, its holding on the point would presumably have to be deemed dispositive by F–2 under
general full faith and credit principles.

A myriad of other F–1 dispositions not reaching
the merits will enable F–2 to go forward unimpeded
by the F–1 judgment. Among these non-dispositive
adjudications (non-dispositive in the sense that they
do not preclude a new action) are F–1 dismissals for
want of jurisdiction, failure to join a proper party,
improper venue, prematurity, pendency of a prior
action on the same cause, failure of an infant or
incompetent plaintiff to bring suit through an appropriate representative, and the like. (The common
law called these things pleas in "abatement" as
opposed to pleas in "bar".) The common sense of
the situation is the primary source of guidance.
Common sense will similarly manifest dispositions
that are the equivalent of merits adjudications—
even if made on motion at the threshold rather than
after trial—and which would therefore bar a new
action. Among these would be F–1 dismissals based
on payment, release, settlement, res judicata, discharge of the claim in bankruptcy, etc.

D. EXTENT OF REQUIRED RECOGNITION

§ 113. Persons Affected by Judgment

The F–1 judgment will bind in F–2 only with respect to parties of whom (or with respect to whom, in the case of in rem jurisdiction, to which we turn in a moment) F–1 had jurisdiction. Indeed, if F–1 lacked jurisdiction of a given person, not only is recognition by F–2 not required as to that person under full faith and credit; it would be prohibited by due process (an interesting interplay of the two clauses).

Privity may of course spell out a binding effect for the judgment. Where, for example, an F–1 judgment was rendered against X with jurisdiction, and X then dies, her personal representative, R, would be bound by the judgment.

If some category of in rem jurisdiction was relied on in F–1, and D, although beyond F–1's personal jurisdiction, was duly notified of the action, F–1's adjudication of D's interest in the res on which F–1 jurisdiction rested binds in F–2, but has no in personam effect beyond that.

If on close analysis it turns out that F–1 had no kind of jurisdiction with respect to X, its judgment can of course have no binding effect on X at all. In Riley (USSC 1942), for example, Georgia (F–1) in the equivalent of probate proceedings presumed to adjudicate who was entitled to certain shares of stock. Georgia had all of the interested parties before it except N, a New Yorker. In Delaware (F–2), the issue arose as to whether the Georgia judgment could bind N. Since in personam jurisdiction over N was lacking in Georgia, in rem jurisdiction was investigated. The shares involved were conceded to have had a Delaware situs at all times. Hence Georgia had neither in personam jurisdiction of N nor in rem jurisdiction of the shares so as to be able to adjudicate with respect to N's interest in them. The result was that the Delaware court was free to adjudicate the merits afresh with respect to N, and did, and found for N.

As long as a given person or his privy was before the F–1 court, the extent to which the F–1 judgment will bind that person, i.e., the res judicata effect of that judgment on that person, will be governed by the law of F–1 (Rst.2d § 94).

A judgment in a class action that satisfies the demanding standards of class form under prevalent American concepts can constitutionally bind the members of the class (Hansberry, USSC 1940), and will if the law of class actions of F–1 so provides and meets constitutional criteria. And it has been established that a court can exercise jurisdiction over nonresident members of the class even though the forum lacks a nexus with them; that the opting-out procedure applicable in class actions, under which each class member must be notified and given a chance to demand exclusion from the class, satisfies due process requirements. (Phillips, USSC 1985.) (Choosing local substantive law to govern the non-

resident parties is a different matter entirely. See
§ 85.)

§ 114. Scope of F–1 Judgment; Issues Disposed of

The doctrine of res judicata ("claim preclusion"
in the terminology of the Second Restatement of
Judgments) and its diverse family members, including collateral estoppel ("issue preclusion"), election
of remedies, splitting, merger, bar, and perhaps still
others, all have the general aim of precluding a
second forum from relitigating something disposed
of in the first one. But the states can and do differ
on how far the doctrine (or doctrines) may go, i.e.,
how much a judgment disposes of. One state may
give broader scope and influence, for example, to a
contested judgment than to one taken by default;
another may treat them the same. One may give its
judgment effect only as to issues actually litigated;
another may give equal effect to matters not actually addressed at the trial but nevertheless put in
issue by the pleadings. One may retain to one
extent or another the so-called "mutuality" doctrine that prevents X from using a judgment
against Y unless it is shown that Y, had he won,
could have used it against X. Another may have
overruled the mutuality doctrine. "Privity" may
come into the picture in some form, describing, or
trying to, the link that must be shown between a
nonparty and a party to the F–1 action before use
may be made of the judgment by or against the
nonparty in the second action. The states may differ

on whether and how to apply this "privity" concept. Given all of these possible differences, and still more that anyone who has ever tackled a thorny res judicata problem can easily attest to, whose law is to govern these issues?

All of this has to do with the scope and effect of the F–1 judgment. The general rule is that its scope and effect is governed by F–1 law (Rst.2d § 95), and that F–2 must determine F–1's wishes in this regard and honor the judgment accordingly. The nagging question of what F–1's "law" is in diversity cases in federal courts was answered by the Supreme Court in Semtek (2001). The court there reaffirmed its old decision in Dupasseur v. Rochereau (1875), which held that in diversity the effect of a judgment "is such as would belong to the judgments of the State courts rendered under similar circumstances". So the old answer is the new answer: in diversity cases the federal judgment is to be deemed a state court judgment.

The main proviso, as discussed in the prior section, is that the person against whom the F–1 judgment is being used was duly brought within F–1 jurisdiction or bore a relationship to an F–1 party such that she can constitutionally be bound through that party.

Thus the question of how far the judgment goes is a matter of F–1's intent, not F–2's (McCune, CA2 1975). F–2's burden is to seek out F–1's preferences.

§ 115. F–2 Can Exceed "Full" Faith and Credit

Full faith and credit is what might be termed a minimal doctrine. It requires F–2 to give the F–1 judgment at least as much effect as F–1 does. But it does not stop F–2 from giving it more, as long as no other constitutional doctrine intervenes with some objection.

Suppose, for example, that a hundred people are injured or killed in an airplane accident. The families of 30 sue and win in F–1, establishing the airline's liability. Assume that the law of F–1 does not give the other 70 a "free ride", i.e., does not permit the 70 to use the doctrine of collateral estoppel in their later F–2 suits against the airline. But assume that F–2 does. Since the airline had a full hearing on the issue of its liability in the F–1 suit by the 30, it would seem that nothing in the constitution prevents F–2 from visiting an estoppel on the airline in the F–2 action, thus establishing the airline's liability in the F–2 action and dispensing with relitigation of that issue. (Hart, NY Sup.Ct. 1969.) Due process would have prevented an airline victory in F–1 from being used against the F–2 plaintiffs, for the reason that they would as yet have had no day in court on the issues. But when the one against whom the estoppel is sought in F–2 did have a full F–1 hearing, the fact that the F–2 party who would make use of its result was not also an F–1 party poses no constitutional issue. The doctrine that prevented (and in some places still does) such estoppel use by an F–1 nonparty, which is called "mutuality of estoppel", is not of constitutional dimension and has been abandoned by many courts (United States v. United Air Lines, D.Nev. 1962).

A similar conclusion can be reached when F–1's judgment purported to be only in rem but F–2 wants to give it in personam effect. Harnischfeger (Miss.1939) is a well known case in point. P sued D in Louisiana (F–1) to foreclose a mortgage on a machine. D defended in full and all of the issues between the parties were litigated, P winning. The Louisiana Supreme Court held on appeal, however, that the proceedings were only in rem. Then P sued D in Mississippi (F–2) for the sum still due after applying to the debt the money that the sale of the machine brought in in the Louisiana action. Mississippi, with in personam jurisdiction of D, held that P was entitled to an estoppel against D on the issues. D was barred from relitigating them. Perhaps the result would have been different had it been shown that D entered the Louisiana (F–1) proceedings only on the assurance that no in personam judgment would be entered against him (this is sometimes called a "limited appearance"). There was no such showing in Harnischfeger, which is an example of F–2 giving in personam effect to an F–1 in rem judgment. What is to stop F–2 from doing that? If D was heard on all of the issues in F–1 and was under no misleading impressions about F–1's jurisdiction at the time, due process would seem to tolerate F–2's extra recognition. And unless due process or some other constitutional provision restrains F–2, F–2's sovereignty would seem to let it do as it chooses.

As will be seen in the matrimonial realm (§ 129), where this matter takes on its greatest importance, the rule that permits F–2 to exceed full faith and credit also allows F–2, if it is willing to, to "adopt" an F–1 alimony or support decree as its own. That enables F–2 to entertain modifications of the F–1 decree in behalf of a family that has since changed roots from F–1 to F–2 and spares the family the expense—which can be prohibitive—of having to go back to F–1 with modification requests.

§ 116. Attacks on F–1 Judgment in F–2

A state usually has rules allowing an attack on its judgment on any of several grounds, even when jurisdiction is not disputed. These rules may allow the judgment to be set aside for fraud of some kind, for example, such as the perjury of a witness or the bribery of a juror. They may allow it to be reopened on the discovery of a new piece of relevant evidence, or on a showing that the judgment was rendered on the defendant's default and that the default is excusable. These and yet other grounds may exist under F–1 law to vacate or modify the judgment.

To what extent may F–2 entertain an attack on the F–1 judgment? The rule is that F–2 may entertain an attack on any ground that F–1 recognizes. This is consistent with full faith and credit. F–2 need not give the judgment more credit than it has at home, and preventing F–2 from entertaining an attack that F–1 would itself recognize amounts to requiring more credit to the judgment than F–1 accords. Hence where it was established before F–2 that P and D met after the F–1 action began and settled it, but that P then pursued the action in violation of the understanding and that F–1 would deem this a fraud sufficient to vacate the judgment, F–2 looked into the fraud when the F–1 judgment came before it, and denied the judgment recognition on the fraud ground (Levin, No.Car.1906).

The form that the attack takes in F–2 will be determined by F–2 procedures, however, a point that becomes important if in one of the states there has not been a merger of law and equity and separate courts are maintained for each. Fraud, for example, is generally deemed an "equitable" defense. At common law, a law court could not entertain the fraud defense against a "law" judgment. It took a separate action in chancery to enjoin the enforcement of the law judgment based on the fraud. If F–2 retains the separation of courts, it may require D, when sued on the F–1 judgment in an F–2 law court, to bring a separate equity action in F–2 to enjoin the enforcement in order to take advantage of the fraud defense that F–1 allows (see Christmas, USSC 1866, where D did not do that and thus failed in the F–2 attack). Conversely, where it is F–1 that maintains the separation of law and equity but F–2 has merged them, a showing that F–1 would entertain a separate equity action to enjoin its law judgment on the fraud ground establishes that fraud is an available objection in F–1. This does not mean, however, that such a separate action is necessary in order to assert the objection in F–2 when the F–1 judgment asks for recognition there. Since F–2 has a merged system, the fraud objection to the F–1 judgment can be interposed as a defense in the F–2 law action that is looking into the F–1 judgment.

Other vacatur or modification grounds that F–1 recognizes, such as newly discovered evidence, may also be entertained by F–2 in respect of the F–1 judgment. But it is important to note on all of these grounds, fraud included, that although F–2 has the power to entertain them, it will not necessarily do so. F–2 may instead take the position, if it finds the tendered objection at least tenable, that it should be submitted instead to F–1, such as by a motion to the F–1 court to vacate the judgment, with the F–2 action being stayed while that is done. F–2 may be especially prone to follow that tack when the objection, if sustained, would require a retrial of the claim on the merits.

§ 117. "Direct" Versus "Collateral" Attack

These terms are often bandied about. They have precise meanings. A "direct" attack on an F–1 judgment is one made in F–1 itself, either by appeal from the final judgment or by a motion to vacate the judgment made to the very court that rendered it. Whenever a different court (or even the same court in a different action) is asked to reject the judgment, we call the attack a "collateral" one. All endeavors to get F–2 to refuse to recognize an F–1 judgment are "collateral" attacks.

As long as F–1 had jurisdiction, a collateral attack in F–2 is limited, as the prior section discusses, to only those objections that F–1 recognizes for the undoing of its judgments. If F–1 lacked jurisdiction, F–2 need not recognize the F–1 judgment at all.

When fraud is the ground on which an F–1 judgment is attacked in F–2, the case may come close to the jurisdictional line, beyond which no recognition need be given at all. A given piece of fraudulent conduct can be perceived by some as affecting jurisdiction itself, but by others as affecting only the merits and not undoing jurisdiction. The fraud that goes to jurisdiction is sometimes referred to as an "extrinsic" fraud, the other kind being "intrinsic". Under which category shall we put the subornation to perjury of a witness? the bribery of a judge or juror? the forgery of a judgment? While theoretical considerations can gratify either side, they do not gratify the F–2 judge who has to decide whether or not to recognize the F–1 judgment. If the issue is a close one, it is probably within the judge's discretion to remit the parties to F–1 to have the point decided, especially when F–1 is near at hand and the parties are not without means to travel to it. Remitting the parties to F–1 to resolve the fraud issue with a direct attack has the additional merit of obviating a finding about which "trinsic" the particular fraud falls under.

§ 118. Equity Judgments

It is perhaps fortunate that most of the judgments that seek full faith and credit are judgments at law, where the rules are relatively clear. They are not clear on equity judgments, especially those granting injunctions. The ugly counter-injunction goings-on in the James case (§ 54) illustrate. But what about other equitable dispositions, such as those affecting land elsewhere? Fall v. Eastin (USSC 1909) is a leading case. For a while it seemed that Fall had lost its luster, but it was restored by a favorable discussion and citation in Baker v. General Motors (USSC 1998). Fall seemed to permit Nebraska (F–2) to deny full faith and credit to a Washington (F–1) judgment. The Washington action was for a divorce between W and H and presumed to award to W some land of H in Nebraska. H meanwhile transferred the land to others, apparently relatives. P afterwards brought an action in Nebraska to test her right as against these others, and the others won.

The issues on which Washington had concluded that as between W and H, W had the right to the land, do bind when the land jurisdiction gets the question, or at least there seems to be weighty authority to that effect today (including Nebraska itself, see Weesner, Neb.1959). So it just seems to be a matter of moving as quickly as possible to convert a court victory in F–1 into an appropriate judgment in the land jurisdiction, F–2. At worst, P should, on winning in F–1, file in F–2 a lis pendens (a paper used in conjunction with a real property action to put the world on notice that P has a claim affecting the land) or equivalent. Indeed, if the land jurisdiction (F–2) allows it, P might consider filing the lis pendens in F–2 while the F–1 proceeding is still pending.

Arranging for an appropriate proceeding in F–2, where the land is, after succeeding in a litigation in F–1, is necessitated by the common understanding in this country that one state cannot directly affect land title in another. A deed to F–2 land made by a court-appointed person in F–1, such as the clerk or a sheriff or referee or the like, apparently need not be recognized by F–2 even if F–1 had in personam jurisdiction of the owner of the land (see § 42). This is a curiosity, because a deed made by the owner himself (assuming always that it is in the form that F–2 requires) would apparently be valid in F–2 even if made in F–1 under the threat of a contempt sanction (Deschenes, NY 1928).

Building on the land cases, the Supreme Court in Baker (1998) returned to the issue of full faith and credit for equity decrees. The Court made clear that equitable decrees are not immune from the full faith and credit clause's demands. In that case, the court confronted a Michigan injunction that purported to prevent an employee of the defendant from testifying in lawsuits against the defendant. When the employee testified anyway in a Missouri case, the defendant tried to have the judgment reversed on the grounds that the Missouri court had denied full faith and credit to the Michigan injunction. While the court held that the injunction was subject to full faith and credit, it did not reverse the Missouri court's judgment. It held that the question of whether the defendant's former employee should be allowed to testify was simply a matter of the method of enforcement of the judgment and that allowing Michigan to dictate to Missouri on this would amount to improper "interference" with Missouri's right to handle its affairs. The court analogized to Fall because allowing a court in one state to transfer land directly in another would amount to a similar "interference."

The practical lesson here may be that one is better off returning to the court that issued the injunction to get it enforced. In Fall the husband could have been held in contempt by the Washington court for refusing to transfer title. In Baker the defendant's employee could have been held in contempt for agreeing to testify. As noted earlier (§ 112), conflicts perceivable in these alternatives have never been resolved by the Supreme Court.

The absence of guiding rules about full faith and credit in equity cases creates special embarrassments in custody cases, especially when the parents, now residing in different states, each obtains an injunction from the local forum purporting to restrict the activity of the nonresident parent. This subject, to which both federal and state statutes are now addressed, is left to a separate section (§ 130) that treats jurisdiction in custody cases together with the recognition aspects of custody decrees.

§ 119. Inconsistent Judgments

If two or more judgments between the same parties and in respect of the same subject are outstanding, and they are inconsistent, the rule is that the last in time prevails. The theory is that whatever error F–2 may have made in not recognizing the F–1 judgment, even if the F–1 judgment was an American one and called for full faith and credit and the point was duly brought to F–2's attention, should have been corrected by appeal in F–2—including a petition to the U.S. Supreme Court if necessary—and not by asking yet a third forum, F–3, to ignore the F–2 judgment. Note that the judgment that gets F–3's recognition is not necessarily that rendered in the last commenced of the earlier actions, but in the last to go to judgment.

The major case is Treinies (USSC 1939). Mr. Pelkes and Mrs. Mason were vying for certain shares of stock. F–1 was a Washington state court. It found for Pelkes against Mason after upholding its jurisdiction against Mason's attack, which she made in an appearance in that action. Idaho was F–2. With jurisdiction of both parties, Idaho refused, despite Pelkes insistence, to recognize the Washington judgment. Directly contra to what Washington itself had held, the Idaho court said Washington had no jurisdiction. It then gave judgment for Mason. The company whose shares were involved then brought an interpleader claim against both parties in an Idaho federal court, and that was F–3. The U.S. Supreme Court said that F–3 had to recognize the F–2 judgment even if F–2 was in error for not recognizing F–1's; that if F–2 (Idaho) denied full faith and credit to F–1's judgment, that was an issue of federal law that should have been taken to the U.S. Supreme Court within the F–2 proceedings. (In fact, Pelkes had sought Supreme Court review of the Idaho [F–2] proceedings, but his certiorari petition was denied. Reminded of this in the Treinies case, which was the F–3 proceeding, the Supreme Court held that the earlier petition for certiorari in F–2 was premature; that the Idaho Supreme Court's determination contemplated further proceedings and that it was only at the conclusion of those further proceedings that the case would be ripe for review by the U.S. Supreme Court. One would need more than a Nutshell to respond to that. Putting a party to the economic and emotional burdens of two certiorari petitions to the Supreme Court on the same matter may qualify as an advanced form of cruel and unusual punishment.)

E. QUASI–JUDICIAL DETERMINATIONS

§ 120. Administrative Determinations and Arbitration Awards

The general rule is that an administrative determination is entitled to recognition like a judgment. (Magnolia, USSC 1943.) Given the bureaucracy by which the states and the nation are governed, things would be at an impasse if the determination of an administrative agency rendered with all requisite jurisdiction could be ignored by a subsequent tribunal, whether a court or another agency.

The same may be said of an arbitration award. If the award is that of an arbitration panel duly constituted under the law of the place where it sits, and the parties have submitted to arbitration voluntarily (or, today, if they have been submitted to it by state law in one of the burgeoning areas of compulsory or semi-compulsory arbitration, such as certain labor situations and some no-fault cases in tort), the resulting award, if recognized at home, must be recognized elsewhere. (See Rst.2d § 220.) Indeed, some states will voluntarily recognize arbitration awards rendered in a foreign nation (and therefore not even within the reach of the full faith and credit clause, e.g., Gilbert, NY 1931).

A state will often supply a procedure whereby an arbitration award rendered locally can be converted into a regular court judgment, thereby being entitled to exploit the enforcement devices applicable to judgments. It is a good idea to invoke such a procedure, if available in the rendering state, before going outside for recognition and enforcement elsewhere. A second forum unwilling to recognize or enforce an arbitration award coming directly out of F–1 may be of a different mind if it is presented in the form of a duly rendered F–1 judgment.

In some contexts, like a federal civil rights action, the Supreme Court has refused preclusive effect to an unappealed arbitration award, perhaps by indirection reenforcing the difference between an "unappealed" award and one that has been duly converted into a court judgment. (See McDonald, USSC 1984.)

On the international scene, a treaty to which the United States and a number of other nations are parties calls for the mandatory recognition of arbitration awards rendered in a signatory nation. This treaty, which may be found with its implementing legislation in Chapter 2 of 9 U.S.C.A., applies to commercial disputes. It is also written in Internationalese, which means that it contains a number of openings whereby recognition can be refused if the award violates some basic policy of the forum in which it seeks enforcement. (See § 75 on the general subject of arbitration.)

CHAPTER VII

FAMILY

A. PRELIMINARIES

§ 121. Family, Introductory

Under the heading of "family" comes marriage as well as the actions that dissolve or annul it. The law respecting marriage is briefly stated in § 122. The rest of this chapter is mainly devoted to the myriad aspects of breaking the marriage up—"matrimonial" actions, which have a far greater hold on the conflict of laws.

The ingredients that go into the matrimonial actions in some measure overlap those met previously in this book, but the matrimonial action poses special problems in both kind and degree, and hence we have saved it to do last so that it can build on everything that has preceded. Jurisdiction in matrimonial actions was briefly discussed earlier in § 43 (on the use of the marital status as a "res" for "rem" jurisdiction). There will be much more to say about that here. Choice of law in marital cases has been entirely deferred to this point because of unique factors applicable to it. These are reviewed in § 123. And despite a whole chapter devoted to judgments and their recognition, the recognition elements that go into matrimonial (notably divorce)

379

decrees are numerous enough to merit separate treatment, including the distinctions between "bilateral" and "ex parte" divorces and sister-state and foreign-country divorces. The incidents of alimony, support, maintenance, marital property, and child custody are also the subject of much case law. Hence their separate treatment here.

B. MARRIAGE

§ 122. Marriage

The validity of a marriage is as a rule governed by the law of the state in which the ceremony takes place. (Ommang, Minn.1931.) If the marriage is valid there it will usually be recognized everywhere. The Restatement's position is that this issue like most others in choice of law should be governed by the state having the "most significant relationship" to the issue (Rst.2d § 283[1]), but it goes on to note that this is usually the state of the ceremony unless the marriage "violates the strong public policy of another state" and it is the other that has the predominant contacts with the parties when they marry (Rst.2d § 283[2]). This is an accurate reflection of the way things stand.

The domicile of the parties has the dominant if not the sole interest in the marriage, at least if it is also to be the state of the matrimonial domicile. Thus, if the parties go to a state that would permit a marriage that their own domicile would not, whether the domicile, when it gets hold of the issue in some appropriate context later, will uphold the marriage will turn on how deeply the domicile is offended by the other's law. If the place of ceremony permits polygamy, for example, or marriage between infants younger than the domicile wants married, or siblings, it is likely to displease the domicile and result in an annulment. In Wilkins (NJ 1958), for example, New Jersey annulled a marriage of two of its young people even though it was valid under the law of Indiana to which they eloped just for the ceremony.

But if the law of the ceremony state, although different from the domicile's, is not so different as to shock the domicile's sensibilities unduly, the domicile is likely to uphold the marriage when it gets the question, as New York did in May's Estate (NY 1953). Cousins could marry in New York but not uncle and niece. The one degree difference was not enough in Mays to undo an uncle-niece marriage that took place in Rhode Island where it was valid. It was also significant that 40 years had passed since the marriage. One of the children was trying to get herself appointed representative, which she could do only by showing that her mother's marriage to her father was no good, else her father, who was still alive, would get the appointment. He got the appointment. The Rhode Island law was not so offensive that New York felt bound to disregard it, especially after 40 years. This is not to say that if the New York test was prompter New York would not have gone the other way. When the marriage, however questionable at first, endures for years, naturally the judges are going to be less anxious to shoot it down with choice of law weapons.

Indeed, they may even go to some lengths to find inapplicable an invalidating statute of the state whose law they do choose. In Lenherr (Pa.1974), for example, H and W were Pennsylvanians. They had intercourse with each other while married to others and after divorcing their spouses they married each other in 1932 in West Virginia, where the marriage was valid. But Pennsylvania had a statute barring the intermarriage of adulterers (perhaps in fear that the affliction was hereditary?) during the life of the innocent spouse, and since they came back to Pennsylvania promptly and lived there happily ever after, or at least until 1971 when H died, it was urged that Pennsylvania law should govern. The court applied the most significant relationship test and found Pennsylvania to have it. But it found the Pennsylvania statute inapplicable on the facts. The suit tested whether W was a surviving spouse for a marital tax exemption and the statute was found to have no purpose to deny her the exemption.

A sometimes-unspoken factor in these cases that tests the validity of marriages is the identity of the party challenging the marriage. Note that in Wilkins it was a party to the marriage who tried to be freed of its bonds. In that case, the court was probably sympathetic to the young wife trying to extricate herself from what may have been a foolish mistake. But in May's Estate and Lenherr, it was a third party (in May's Estate the child and in Lenherr the tax collection authorities) trying to benefit by invalidating the marriage. A third party apparently bears a heavier burden in that effort.

A "common law marriage", in which the parties live together and agree to be husband and wife but do not go through a ceremony, will become a valid one as soon as the couple establish their domicile together in a state that recognizes common law marriages. Thus, if they so cohabit at first in a state that does not recognize the marriage, but later establish domicile in a state that does, they will be deemed married as of the latter moment and other states will recognize the marriage as of that time. (Boykin, Oreg.1960.)

The current furor in the field of marriage conflicts surrounds same-sex marriage. Massachusetts by decree of its Supreme Court now recognizes such unions, and Vermont allows a sort of parallel institution of "civil unions" for same-sex couples with essentially all the legal attributes of a marriage. States that do not favor such arrangements can apparently refuse to recognize them, presumably on "public policy" grounds. (See the general discussion of public policy in § 57 above.) But just to make the matter clear, all but about a dozen states have enacted statutes specifically forbidding their courts from recognizing same-sex unions. Congress also stepped into the fray and enacted the Defense of Marriage Act (28 U.S.C. § 1738C), which explicitly authorizes states to refuse to recognize the same-sex unions of other states. This subject, current and controversial, will doubtless be getting some heavy judicial attention.

Even in light of these recent developments, marriage is not as often a problem in conflict of laws as is divorce. Marriage—for heterosexuals, anyway—is easy and divorce is hard, rather the reverse of the way a lot of thoughtful people think things ought to be. The situation has made for a fascinating aggregate of divorce cases. Their study is next.

C. DISSOLUTION OF MARRIAGE

§ 123. Matrimonial Actions, Generally

A matrimonial action as generally defined is an action for divorce, separation, or annulment. If the marriage is "void" it technically need not be "annulled", but a judicial decree announcing the nullity, which a party may want, may usually be obtained through the expedient of an action for a declaratory judgment. The declaratory action may also be used to declare a marriage valid, if that's the spouse's purpose.

Some preliminary ABC's. A divorce action assumes the validity of the marriage but dissolves it. An "annulment" determines that the marriage never was; it is a kind of nunc pro tunc dissolution. A separation of course concedes the marriage's validity. Since the parties do not need a decree to live separately, a separation decree is usually sought only when money, property, or custody is disputed, or to set up a divorce ground.

Several bases exist for matrimonial jurisdiction. In personam jurisdiction over both spouses will of course suffice for a matrimonial decree of any kind, but so will "in rem" jurisdiction. If either party is a domiciliary of the forum state, its courts have jurisdiction of the marriage itself—sometimes called the "matrimonial res"—and can render a marital decree without in personam jurisdiction of the other spouse (§ 43). This is called an "ex parte" divorce and is the subject of § 125. The divorce is called "bilateral" when the divorcing court has in personam jurisdiction of both parties. The bilateral divorce and its incidents are taken up in § 124. Both of the cited sections are concerned with the recognition of a marital decree rendered by an American court. One rendered by the court of a foreign nation, since it does not get full faith and credit, is treated separately in § 126.

On choice of law, there are several fundamentals to note. Since an annulment action seeks to have the court hold that the marriage never came into existence at all, the basic issue in an annulment action is the validity of the marriage itself (Rst.2d § 286). Choice of law on that subject was treated in § 122. The court in an annulment action may indeed put the issue through a choice of law test, and the general rule is that the law applicable to whether the marriage is valid is that of the state where the marriage was contracted (Whealton, Cal.1967). Hence, if a marriage takes place in State X, the court in an annulment action in State F will ordinarily apply the annulment grounds recognized by State X.

Divorce (and separation, a way station on the way to what may become a divorce) is a wholly different matter. In a divorce action there is no law-choosing process in the sense that it exists in the usual contract, property, or tort action, or, indeed, in the annulment action just mentioned. While it is occasionally suggested that a divorce action should be put through the same choice of law process that seeks out the appropriate governing law in other cases (see Alton, CA3 1953 [dissenting opinion]), in divorce the forum looks only to its own law to determine whether grounds for divorce exist. The phenomenon that makes this constitutionally permissible is the commonly accepted rule in this country that rests jurisdiction in a divorce action on the forum domicile of either or both of the spouses. The very requirement that the forum be shown to be the domicile of at least one spouse simultaneously gives the forum contacts with the marriage itself that permits the forum's law to be chosen to determine divorce grounds.

Usually a state will insist that one of the parties be shown to have been a local domiciliary for a particular period of time as a condition precedent to the entertainment of a divorce action in its courts. A one-year requirement was upheld as constitutional by the U.S. Supreme Court in Sosna (1975), for example. Some states require less. Differences in durational residence requirements account for the popularity of the states with the shortest periods as divorce meccas for out-of-staters.

Note that "domicile" rather than mere "residence" is the jurisdictional touchstone here (Williams II, USSC 1945). Often the state statute imposing the requirement will say "residence", but it is usually construed to mean "domicile" (e.g., Williams I, USSC 1942). It is the intention to make the place home (§§ 12, 15) that changes a residence into a "domicile" and satisfies this requirement, a subjective thing that can sometimes jeopardize an ex parte divorce (§ 125) but rarely a bilateral one (§ 124).

Because a person can change domicile readily and need then only await the "residency" period imposed by the new domicile state, a spouse who comes from a state with restrictive divorce laws can, by changing domicile, "shop" for the more liberal divorce grounds available elsewhere. The preference is usually for a forum in which marriage alone is deemed ground for divorce, or where, less facetiously, incompatibility is the ground specified in the forum's statutes, or where the grounds stated, whatever they are, are generously applied in the particular state to facilitate divorce.

Were it not for this forum-shopping potential offered by the variety of divorce laws of the several states in our federal system, states with restrictive divorce laws might have been pressured long ago into a liberalization. Some legislatures have been able to indulge the luxury of continued internal restrictions, thereby avoiding sensitive moral and religious issues that could have political repercussions, only because the huddled masses of their oppressed spouses were able to find ready relief across state borders. Their seeking of this relief by the hundreds of thousands has generated a big body of case law on the recognition requirements applicable to divorce decrees. The ensuing three sections separate these into sister-state bilateral divorces (§ 124), sister-state ex parte divorces (§ 125), and foreign-country divorces (§ 126).

§ 124. Mandatory Recognition for Sister–State "Bilateral" Divorce

When the F–1 court has in personam jurisdiction of both parties, the resulting divorce is called "bilateral". The bilateral divorce rendered by a sister state is a prize. Either spouse can safely remarry on the strength of such a divorce because every other state must recognize it. A showing that the defendant spouse appeared in the F–1 action, moreover, forecloses F–2 from even examining further into F–1's jurisdiction. Thus, if spouses domiciled in a state with restrictive divorce grounds agree to divorce, they can readily arrange for a divorce under the more liberal laws of a sister state.

Assume, for example, that wife W is to be the plaintiff and husband H the defendant. To exploit this sister-state divorce possibility, W goes to the other state (F–1) and remains as long as necessary to satisfy its "residence" requirement. Assume it is six weeks, as it is in Nevada, reputed to be the nation's divorce capital. H appears in person on the trial day and after whatever hearing F–1 requires, a divorce is granted. This divorce carries full faith and credit not only for the merits, but for the very fact of F–1's jurisdiction. If anyone, including either of the spouses, should afterwards contest the F–1 divorce in F–2, F–2 must discontinue its inquiry as soon as it is shown that H (the F–1 defendant) appeared in F–1, and must recognize F–1's jurisdiction as well as the validity of the divorce. This is so even if F–1 required "domicile" rather than mere "residence" and neither party had become an F–1 domiciliary, or ever intended to. It all has to do with F–1's jurisdiction: the mere fact of H's appearance in F–1 puts the matter beyond F–2's review, even if F–2 is the real domicile of the parties both before and after the divorce. This is so regardless of the jurisdictional category to which this issue of F–1's jurisdiction, all related to the "domicile" question, may be assigned. Whether it relates to subject matter or to personal jurisdiction, says the U.S. Supreme Court, the defendant's appearance in F–1 requires F–2 to keep hands off the issue of F–1's jurisdiction. (Sherrer, USSC 1948.)

The rule obtains not only when the defendant has physically appeared in F–1 and litigated the jurisdictional issue and lost on it (Davis, USSC 1938), or merely contested it in the pleadings without pursuing it at the trial (Sherrer, USSC 1948), but also when the defendant appears without raising the issue at all. The fact of the defendant's appearance means that he had the opportunity to raise it and uses up the one day in court to which he is entitled on a jurisdictional issue as a matter of constitutional law (§ 111).

Nor need the defendant's appearance in F–1 be in person. An appearance through an attorney of his or her own choice apparently suffices even if the defendant stays at home (see Johnson, USSC 1951), although there may be some state resistance on this point, especially if F–2 can find some taint in the papers whereby the defendant deputized an F–1 attorney to appear for him. No F–1 appearance of any kind would be required of the defendant in order to invoke these rules if it can be shown, simply, that the defendant was personally served with process in F–1, for that alone would establish F–1's jurisdiction sufficient to put the merits beyond F–2's review. (See Cook, USSC 1951.)

High-water mark for how far F–2 must go in recognizing an F–1 bilateral divorce is Boxer (NY 1959). Boxer involved a so-called "quickie" divorce in which a one-day physical stay by the plaintiff combined with a mere paper appearance by the defendant through an F–1 attorney sufficed for a divorce under F–1 law. Alabama, F–1 in the Boxer case, offered such divorces for a time, and H and W, New Yorkers, got one. H was the plaintiff and went to Alabama for the day. W appeared through an Alabama lawyer to whom she sent an authorization by mail. In a later action in New York (F–2), the validity of the Alabama divorce came in question. Both parties admitted on the F–2 record that neither ever intended to become an Alabama domiciliary; that their conduct was in effect a fraud on the Alabama court (which presumably required domicile even though it was willing to wink at what the parties before it might attest to in that respect). New York held that under full faith and credit Alabama had obtained jurisdiction, and so New York could permit the decree to be attacked only on such ground as Alabama would itself recognize. Then, finding in Alabama law no authority for undoing the divorce, New York deemed itself bound by full faith and credit to uphold it, and did.

Note the point that an attack on an F–1 decree is permissible, but, when F–1 is found to have had jurisdiction, only on such ground as F–1 recognizes. The spouses are of course bound by this rule, but so is every other person in "privity" with one of the spouses (Rst.2d § 73). This means that the question of who may attack the F–1 judgment is also to be determined by F–1 law. In Johnson (USSC 1951), H and W–2 (wife number two) got a Florida divorce. H then married W–3. Endeavoring to show that this third marriage was no good, a child of H's marriage with W–1 (the child stood to gain more from H's estate if there were no third marriage) tried to attack the Florida divorce of the second marriage in a New York proceeding (a reinstatement of the second would void the third). Whether she could, held the court, had to be determined by Florida law. Since Florida law said she could not, New York could not entertain her attack.

Apropos of the Alabama "quickie" divorce mentioned above, it may occur to the reader to ask why anyone from a restrictive divorce state who is looking to the law of some other should turn so often to Nevada, which has a six-week residence requirement, when a state with as short a requirement as one day is available. The financial difference is great. The answer is that no state today offers a one-day "quickie" divorce. If one did, it would quickly become a divorce magnet, as Alabama did for a while. (Alabama closed its doors to the quickie divorce several decades ago with internal law changes. Today the quickie is primarily the business of the Dominican Republic, after Mexico's brief reign, but their judgments do not get full faith and credit, as Alabama's do. See § 126.)

A state like Nevada, where divorce is a business, while it may wink or laugh outright during discussions of when and how a plaintiff becomes a "domiciliary", has no sense of humor in the application of its durational residency requirement of six weeks. The plaintiff stays the six weeks and only then becomes entitled to a Nevada divorce. Reduced to lowest terms, Nevada is exacting six weeks of contribution to its economy as the price for a divorce binding (as long as the defendant appears) on all other American states. Implicit in this is also some tolerance for perjury should the plaintiff spouse swear that he or she plans to remain in the state indefinitely—the "domicile" showing—while holding in purse or pocket a ticket home for a day or so hence. This cynicism is no compliment to the system, but on some moral scales these doings may stand a mite higher than legislative lethargy in another state which, by refusing reasonable divorce grounds locally, forces great unhappy numbers of its citizens to seek relief elsewhere. In that light, perhaps Nevada's is just an understanding grin beside her golden door.

An interesting two-wives situation can arise when an F–1 divorce is afterwards vacated in F–1 at the behest of one of the original spouses. H and W–1 go to F–1 and get a divorce. On the strength of it H marries W–2 in F–2. After that W–1 goes back to F–1 and gets the divorce vacated, popping the first marriage back into existence, to the chagrin of W–2. New York in such a case (New York was F–2) declared H to be the lawful husband of both wives, W–1 for monetary purposes only, W–2 for all purposes. (DiRusso, NY Sup.Ct.1968.) This may mean dual support obligations. A problem may also arise later, when H dies. Which wife gets the right to elect against a will, for example, if such there be, or to take in intestacy if there be no will? Presumably the suitable result is that they share in those respects as well.

Parties agreeing to a bilateral divorce in a sister state (or, for that matter, in a foreign country) must be sure to consult their attorneys about the impact that they want the divorce to have on existing agreements between the parties, such as a separation agreement respecting their property. They may provide that the agreement be incorporated into the decree, which will then give its provisions the force of a judicial judgment and entitle it to be treated as such. Doing so, they may provide that the agreement be "merged" in the decree, in which case it will lose its separate identity as a contract, or that it instead be "incorporated but not merged" in the decree, in which case the agreement will survive as a contract and impose its obligations on the parties distinct from the decree. Depending of course on the laws of F–1 and F–2 as they apply to these matters and interrelate under full faith and credit principles, this may enable one spouse to call on another for the fulfillment of the contractual agreement to the letter despite modifications made in the decree that purported to incorporate it.

§ 125. Jurisdictional Problem With "Ex Parte" Divorce

There is sometimes a tendency among students and perhaps even among some lawyers to equate "ex parte" with "invalid" in the marital sphere. There is no relationship. An ex parte divorce may be a valid one, indeed, as long as F–1 had jurisdiction. The rub is that the question of F–1's jurisdiction to grant an ex parte divorce may be open to F–2's independent investigation, which is not so in the "bilateral" divorce situation treated in the prior section. There, the fact of the defendant's appearance in F–1 gives the F–1 court in personam jurisdiction of both spouses; this makes the divorce "bilateral" and binds F–2 to recognize F–1's jurisdiction.

In the ex parte divorce situation, F–1 does not have jurisdiction of both spouses, but of only one of them. That one is usually the plaintiff (and that will be our assumption in this discussion), who has gone to F–1 for the divorce, presumably because of restrictive divorce laws back home.

An ex parte divorce is based on the in rem jurisdiction that F–1 gets over the marriage when the plaintiff spouse becomes an F–1 domiciliary. The marriage itself is the "res" that supports this "in rem" jurisdiction, and it is the plaintiff's domicile in F–1 that brings the marriage there (§ 43). At no time does F–1 obtain in personam jurisdiction of the defendant. F–1 lacks basis, and process in its divorce action is served on the defendant by substituted means or by service outside F–1. At no time does the defendant appear in the F–1 action. (If he were to appear, in personam jurisdiction would result and the divorce would be a bilateral one.) This is the classic fact pattern of the ex parte divorce.

The court in F–1 grants the divorce on the defendant's default. The issue of its validity arises in an action in F–2. W, the F–1 plaintiff, claims full faith and credit for the F–1 decree. H, the F–1 defendant never subject to F–1 in personam jurisdiction, says that jurisdiction in F–1 was lacking. This turns on whether W became a domiciliary of F–1. She says she did and points to the F–1 decree holding jurisdiction present. H says that F–2 is entitled to decide for itself whether W became a bona fide F–1 domiciliary. H is right. The famous Williams cases in the U.S. Supreme Court establish the rules.

If W became an F–1 domiciliary, the ex parte divorce is valid and must be recognized in F–2. (Williams I, USSC 1942.) But whether W became an F–1 domiciliary is an issue that F–2 may examine into. (Williams II, USSC 1945.) F–2 must give at least prima facie respect to the F–1 finding of W's F–1 domicile, but is not bound by it. If the proof adduced before F–2 warrants it, F–2 can conclude that W never became an F–1 domiciliary, and down tumbles the jurisdictional foundation of the F–1 judgment. The want of domicile means that the marital "res" never got into F–1's hands. Since the "res" was not there, F–1 never got the "in rem" jurisdiction it was relying on, and had no other. F–1 having no jurisdiction, F–2 need not recognize the F–1 divorce. And as Williams II manifests, this means that the F–1 party who remarries on the strength of the F–1 divorce can be prosecuted for bigamy in F–2 for doing so. Uneasy lies the spouse with an ex parte divorce, unless he or she so clearly became domiciled in F–1 as to put the matter beyond question no matter who looks into it.

Suppose, for example, that W leaves F–2 (assume it's the marital domicile) and goes to F–1 and stays just six weeks, satisfying F–1's residency requirement and getting an ex parte divorce on constructive service on H outside F–1. H never appears. When the divorce's validity later arises before an F–2 court, H shows that shortly after the divorce W surrendered her apartment in F–1, closed her bank account there, and returned to F–2, where she resumed domicile. With this proof, including facts only coming into existence after the F–1 divorce, F–2 can hold against F–1 jurisdiction and refuse to recognize the divorce.

Hence the jeopardy of a sister state's ex parte divorce, in contrast with the security of a bilateral one. A spouse seeking a divorce elsewhere and unable to obtain the consent of the other spouse must either sue that spouse where in personam jurisdiction of him or her is available, or else move— genuinely change domicile—to the state where the divorce is sought, with all that entails. Only with an outright move will proof of domicile result such as will preserve an ex parte divorce.

In some situations a spouse may be estopped from attacking an ex parte divorce, even if it is an invalid one. The party who obtained the divorce, for example, may be estopped from later trying to derive some advantage by attacking it, as happened in Krause (NY 1940). H got an ex parte divorce from W–1 in F–1 without becoming an F–1 domiciliary. He then married W–2. When W–2 later sued him for a separation (which is of course premised on a valid marriage), H tried to show that he was never married to W–2 because the ex parte divorce he had himself obtained from W–1 was invalid. He was estopped from pleading that the F–1 divorce was invalid.

§ 126. Foreign Country Divorces

Whether to recognize a divorce granted by a foreign country is for each state to decide for itself. Full faith and credit is no more applicable to this than to any other judgment of a foreign nation. Hence, if a would-be plaintiff thinking about obtaining a foreign-country divorce has domiciliary roots in a state and is likely to return to that state after the divorce, it is important for him or her to take note of whether that state will recognize the divorce, and what the consequences of non-recognition may be.

An ex parte foreign divorce has little chance of state recognition. The states are even divided on the bilateral one, at least when it is of the voluntary one-day "quickie" variety in which the plaintiff goes to the foreign country for a day and the defendant appears through an attorney but not necessarily in person. Mexico specialized in these quickies for a while and tens of thousands of Americans obtained them. New Yorkers appear to have relied on them more than others (up until 1967 adultery was the sole ground for divorce in New York) and New York, after some lower court resistance, finally recognized them (Rosenstiel, NY 1965), to the great relief of many. Other states did not (e.g., Meeker, NJ 1968; see Boyter, US Tax Ct., 1980).

Mexico left the "quickie" business and Hispaniola (the Dominican Republic and Haiti) rushed in to pick up what it hoped would be a booming trade.

Lawyers there sometimes send solicitation letters to American lawyers in states with likely candidates for foreign divorces, offering personal (travel, hotel, etc.) as well as legal services, and quoting bargain rates. These one-day divorces are ostensibly "bilateral" by analogy to the full faith and credit divorce, because the defendant puts in an appearance, but because they do not get full faith and credit it is imperative that the parties determine where they will be going after the divorce, and whether the place of their respective post-judgment domiciles will honor it. Bigamy can become a problem if they remarry without that investigation. An adultery charge may also be in prospect, especially in a state that still thinks hormonal activity can be regulated by statute.

D. PROPERTY INCIDENTS

§ 127. Marital Property

As any matrimonial lawyer will attest, especially in states with community property or equitable distribution laws, the resolution of property questions between divorcing or separating spouses can be a considerable problem within the confines of but a single state's law. It expands when two states are involved. Agreement between the spouses, at or after estrangement if not before marriage (pre-marital property agreements are not uncommon) is a welcome relief to divorce court judges.

The parties, with or without estrangement, can stipulate to a choice of law to govern the nature of their ownership of specified property. This has been upheld, especially when the law stipulated to is that of the state to which the property has in fact been transferred. (Wyatt, NY 1965.) When there is no such stipulation (and there usually is not), the best that the body of conflict of laws can manage when multi-state contacts are present is a few general rules.

The effect of marriage on interests in land acquired during the marriage is governed by the land's situs (Hammonds, CA10 1939), as the Restatement acknowledges (Rst.2d §§ 233, 234), but for the effect of marriage on personal property the Restatement reverts to its "most significant relationship" test, pointing to the parties' domicile as ordinarily having the most significant contacts (Rst.2d § 258; Crichton, NY 1967). Hence the state of the matrimonial domicile will usually determine one spouse's interest in personal property acquired by the other during the marriage, no matter where acquired.

The comment on § 258 of the Second Restatement states that the rule applies to both tangibles and intangibles, and to property interests embodied in a document. Once an interest in personal property is obtained by virtue of the marital relationship, it adheres even if the property is then removed to another state (Rst.2d § 259).

If the property is acquired while the parties are domiciled in a state that follows the common law rule (which is that each spouse can obtain and own property individually), and they then remove to and become domiciled in a state with community property rules (under which each spouse has an interest in property acquired by the other), they can be held to have subjected themselves in one degree or another to the community property rules of their new domicile should they then divorce there. (See Addison, Cal.1965.) This is not always so far removed from a strictly common law situation. If common law rules at all times obtained during the marriage, but under the domicile's divorce laws the parties' property can be equitably apportioned between them without regard to who owns what (see, e.g., NY Dom.Rel.L. § 236), the apportionment can reach similar results even though the spouses had no contact with a "community property" state.

If a chattel is acquired while the spouses are domiciled in a community property state, the rule that it remains community property even after being removed from the state can result in its being traced into property, including land, purchased elsewhere if such a tracing is needed to preserve the community right of a spouse (Rozan, Cal.1957). Since the property belongs to H and W under the community property rule of their domicile, and the rule would be defeated if one spouse could remove the property and sell it and pocket the money, it is understandable that a court in the community property state would be receptive to evidence tracing the proceeds of the chattel's sale into the property bought by the wrongdoing spouse elsewhere. If the newly acquired property is land, the usual problem (see § 118) arises about how to convert an in personam adjudication in State F into a meaningful land disposition in State L (where the land is). Proceedings in State L may be necessary (see Rozan, No.Dak.1964, the follow-up on the California Rozan case cited above).

A related problem concerns a spouse's right to elect against a will. If of the several related jurisdictions some confer such a right and others do not, or confer it in different measures, whose law governs? Here an analogy lies to the usual post-death rules of property distribution. For land, situs law governs. For personal property, the law of the parties' domicile governs. The domicile would have the predominant interest in whether and to what extent a surviving spouse should have a right of election against the decedent-spouse's will. In Clark (NY 1968), the right-to-elect law of Virginia, the domicile, was applied despite the testator's placing the subject personal property in New York and stipulating in his will to have New York law apply. Should the spouses have different domiciles at the time of the death of one of them, a logical choice of law for an election problem, should there be a conflict, is that of the state in which the couple last cohabited as spouses (the final "matrimonial" domicile), at least as to personal property acquired during marriage.

§ 128. Jurisdiction for Alimony and Support

In personam jurisdiction of both spouses will give the court jurisdiction to affect their money obligations to one another, by way of alimony, support, or other maintenance. Hence a court rendering a bilateral divorce can also provide for alimony or support. Since the court has in personam jurisdiction, it can, alternatively, absolve one spouse of an obligation to support the other. (Rst.2d § 77[2].) An F–1 in personam judgment has even been allowed to bar child support that F–2 tried to award after the father had paid a lump sum for child support pursuant to an F–1 decree. In Yarborough (USSC 1933; § 129), the court upheld F–1's jurisdiction of the child based on the father's F–1 domicile and an F–1 rule which said that the child's domicile is always with the father, and then held F–2 bound by the F–1 determination that the lump sum terminated the father's support obligations. It precluded F–2, in which the child lived, from awarding any further support against the father.

It would not be so clear today that a child's domicile is with the father if the child has in fact been removed, lawfully (no "child snatching" involved), by the mother to the state of her present domicile. But even if the child's domicile is found to be with the mother, the idea that this will by itself give the mother's state child-support jurisdiction over the father has been rejected by the Supreme Court. In Kulko (USSC 1978), the court said that not even the father's consent to the child's living in that state would confer such jurisdiction on its courts if the father was never domiciled in that state and did not otherwise have substantial contacts with it. Hence the influence of the child's domicile or presence for support purposes does not weigh as heavily on the jurisdictional scale as it does for custody purposes, although it is not decisive in that instance either (§ 130).

This does not necessarily mean that a nondomiciliary spouse or parent is beyond the reach of the court. It merely means that the forum must have appropriate longarm contacts before exercising extraterritorial jurisdiction. With a proper longarm statute, support jurisdiction is of course available against a spouse or parent who is no longer a local domiciliary, and perhaps never was (§ 37).

Assuming properly based in personam jurisdiction, the court can order support for the children, or between the spouses themselves, and this of course includes a divorcing court if the support claim is made as part of a matrimonial action, as it often is. If the monetary disposition is adjudicated in the form of periodic payments, the next conflict of laws realm that the judgment will meet, if any, is likely to concern F–2's recognition obligation, a matter addressed in § 129. The F–1 judgment will at least be able to approach that meeting with the sturdy credentials of a "bilateral" decree, the in personam jurisdiction of F–1 having made it that.

Jurisdiction to touch monetary obligations is a more difficult question in ex parte divorce situations. Here the court lacks in personam jurisdiction of the defendant spouse. Assume that the defendant is H, the husband. If H has property in the divorcing forum, the property can be seized by appropriate process (attachment, sequestration, garnishment, or whatever else the forum may call it) and made to serve as a "quasi in rem" basis for a monetary award. This means that the court can render a support judgment, in a lump sum or in installments, but that it will be effective only to the extent of the local property seized and will lose all force and effect when that property is used up (Rst.2d § 77[1]). There is some question whether the U.S. Supreme Court's decision in Shaffer (1977), which curtails quasi in rem jurisdiction in ordinary money actions, would also bar its use in the matrimonial context under discussion. A strong argument can be made for its continuing use there (see § 44).

While an ex parte divorce can't adjudicate as to property rights of the absent spouse directly, the very fact that it can dissolve the marriage can affect something like a dower or curtesy right, which comes into being only at the time of the spouse's death. Hence, if a valid ex parte divorce has dissolved the marriage so that the marriage no longer exists when the spouse who obtained the divorce dies, the surviving spouse, even though never within the in personam jurisdiction of the divorcing court, will nevertheless lose all future rights of dower or curtesy (Simons, USSC 1965).

This is accounted for by the inchoate nature of these rights. They don't come into existence until death, by which time the divorce decree, by dissolving the marriage, has also dissolved rights that depend on there being a marriage at the time of death. But rights of alimony, support, and maintenance exist during life and it takes in personam jurisdiction to affect them. What happens to the support right, then, when a valid ex parte divorce is obtained by one spouse, say the husband, against the wife? Can the divorce, because valid, cut off the wife's support? It cannot. This involves the doctrine of "divisible divorce" discussed at the end of § 129.

§ 129. Recognizing Alimony, Support and Maintenance Judgments

Because many alimony and support provisions (sometimes referred to as "maintenance" today) in matrimonial decrees call for periodic payments under F–1 law, special questions arise about F–2's recognition obligations. If the F–1 judgment is of that kind, and F–1 has itself entered a judgment for accrued arrearages under its own decree, the result is a money judgment entitled to recognition in F–2 by the same standards that govern any other (Lynde, USSC 1901), at least where the F–1 judgment in that respect is deemed final by F–1 standards. Since an arrears judgment adds up the accrued installments and gives a single judgment for the whole sum now due, such a judgment is commonly deemed a final and enforcible one among American jurisdictions and thus demands full faith and credit (Barber, USSC 1944).

But full faith and credit does not require F–2 to "adopt" the F–1 decree as its own, that is, convert it into an F–2 judgment to such an extent that the obligation to pay the periodic installments called for by the F–1 judgment would now be deemed an F–2 obligation. So says the U.S. Supreme Court in the Lynde case, noted above, basing its holding on the fact (applicable in many states) that the periodic payments obligation can be modified (even retroactively) from time to time and that the very fact of modifiability divests the decree of the finality it needs in order to invoke full faith and credit. This is an unfortunate view produced during an earlier era when travel was slow and families stayed put. Today divorced spouses in F–1 can each cross the country in different directions on the same day and settle elsewhere. If the F–1 divorce decreed weekly or monthly alimony or support, and with the passage of time the dependent wife's or child's needs increase, or the father's ability to pay declines, so that a modification of the F–1 decree is in order, must the party seeking the modification always return to F–1 to get the modification? F–2 can apparently put the parties to that burden if it wishes; full faith and credit tolerates that.

But while the full faith and credit clause does not require F–2 to go so far as to "adopt" the F–1 decree, neither does it prevent F–2 from adopting the decree voluntarily (People ex rel. Halvey, USSC 1947). Many an F–2 has so adopted it (e.g., Worthley, Cal.1955), which means that F–2 will also entertain modifications on grounds F–1 recognizes (e.g., Salmeri, Wyo.1976).

Into this breach, however, stepped two important pieces of legislation. One is a uniform enactment called the Uniform Interstate Family Support Act ("UIFSA"), now in force in all states. Another is a federal statute (28 U.S.C. § 1738B). Although different in some respects (the federal statute only applies to child support, while UIFSA applies to spousal support as well), they generally require that credit be given even to modifiable awards. Modifications, as contemplated by the original tribunal (F–1), are then made by F–2, the forum now required to recognize the award. So, although it took the better part of a century, Lynde (USSC 1901) was eventually overruled legislatively.

Throughout the foregoing it has been assumed that F–2 now has jurisdiction of all the interested parties. If the support obligor (usually the husband/father) now lives in a state other than that of his dependents, posing jurisdictional problems, and they can't for economic or other reasons pursue him to his own state, they will find aid in UIFSA. UIFSA (like its predecessors the Uniform Reciprocal Enforcement of Support Act (URESA) and its revised version (RURESA) allows for a "two state" proceeding in which the obligee (mother in our example) can bring an action in her home state and enlist the cooperation of a court or enforcement agency in the obligor's (father's) state. If the mother's home state courts have longarm jurisdiction over the father (thus allowing a "one state" proceeding) then she has other enforcement options, dispensing with the two-state procedure, including sending notice to the father's employer (even though in another state) to garnish his wages.

Discussion up to now has assumed that F–1 rendered its monetary decree with in personam jurisdiction of both spouses. Suppose that F–1 lacked in personam jurisdiction of one of the spouses; that its divorce decree was ex parte only. Suppose further that the decree was obtained by the spouse who would ordinarily have had the support obligation. For example: Husband H goes to F–1 and becomes a domiciliary there, thus giving F–1 sufficient in rem jurisdiction to dissolve the marriage. Wife W, duly notified, defaults; she does not appear and is at no time brought within F–1 in personam jurisdiction. F–1 renders an ex parte divorce, a good one. Now W sues H for support in F–2, where both parties are within in personam jurisdiction. H argues that since he is not W's spouse because of the valid F–1 divorce, F–2 cannot impose a support obligation on him. H is wrong. The recognition required for the divorce, for which F–1 had adequate in rem jurisdiction, does not extend to any monetary right of W. For that, in personam jurisdiction was needed and F–1 did not have it. F–2 is thus entitled to go forward with an alimony or support disposition unfettered by the fact of the F–1 decree even if it presumed to address the money matter. (Estin, USSC 1948; Vanderbilt, USSC 1957.) This is known as the "divisible divorce" doctrine. It separates the monetary issue from the marital-status issue and, while requiring recognition for the status, permits fresh address to the monetary matter.

E. CUSTODY

§ 130. Child Custody

Emotions are at their highest in custody cases. It has not been uncommon for the noncustodial parent to steal the child from the other's legal custody. Our language ought to have a better word for this than the one that also describes stealing a child for ransom, but "kidnapping" applies to both acts (albeit with different zeal about prosecution). One also hears "child snatching" as a euphemistic substitute. When the parents now reside in different states and pull the child back and forth, each one seeking an injunction in his or her own state to stop the other from taking the child back or otherwise to dictate to the nonresident parent, the problem is at its sharpest and the courts sometimes at their most helpless.

A good example of this bad situation is Kubon (Cal.1958). First Nevada, with the requisite in personam jurisdiction, awarded custody to W, with visitation rights in H, who also had a monetary obligation under the decree. While the children were with H in California he got from a California court an injunction restraining W from taking them back to Nevada. She took them back anyway and then got Nevada to modify its decree to allow H visitation only in Nevada. In retaliation, H stopped payments. W then got an arrears judgment from Nevada and took it back to California and sought full faith and credit for it. The California court held that W's disobedience of the California injunction restraining her from removing the children was a defense to H and the court therefore refused to recognize the Nevada money judgment. What a mess! May we not at the very outset conclude that the Nevada judgment is just a money judgment, and that since it was rendered with jurisdiction it is entitled to full faith and credit (as Justice Traynor concluded in his dissent in the California case) on that ground alone (§§ 110, 111)? And why should the California judges be so sensitive to W's disobedience of a California injunction when the injunction was really only an incidental product of H's disobedience of Nevada's custody decree?

The field was open to these goings on, and they took place by the thousands, because of the absence, until the very end of 1980, of any full faith and credit requirement for custody decrees, notwithstanding that the decree was made with all requisite jurisdiction. As a matter of constitutional law, the U.S. Supreme Court never applied the full faith and credit clause to custody decrees (see Justice Frankfurter's concurrence in May, USSC 1953), and many states took the position that the clause was not operative in the custody sphere at all (e.g., Bachman, NY 1956). And even if a court in F–2 were prone to give res judicata effect to the facts underlying F–1's custody adjudication voluntarily, the F–2 court could then go on to find changed circumstances since the F–1 decree was made, and on that basis make a custody determination afresh (e.g., Sayler, So.Car. 1972). This could even be done consistently with F–1's own law, which almost always authorizes modifications of custody decrees, thus enabling F–2, in modifying, to say that it is doing no more than F–1 itself would have done. Nothing in the way of full faith and credit, remember (§ 115), stops F–2 from going so far as to "adopt" an F–1 decree to such an extent as to permit the F–2 courts to entertain modifications on grounds that F–1 recognizes (People ex rel. Halvey, USSC 1947).

Some courts came closer to recognizing that this was mere lip service, and they adhered to the F–1 disposition in full, unless, for example, it were shown that keeping custody in the person who was awarded it by the F–1 court would "jeopardize or seriously endanger the child's health or safety" (Ferreira, Cal.1973).

A Uniform Child Custody Jurisdiction Act (UC-CJA) met some of these interstate recognition problems, but it of course depended on uniform interpretation of the statute by all the state courts, a goal that proved elusive. The UCCJA has been replaced in some states by the Uniform Child Custody Jurisdiction and Enforcement Act (UCCJEA), which does cure some of the original statute's difficulties, but the UCCJEA has not been adopted in all states.

Onto this chaotic scene stepped § 1738A of Title 28 of the U.S. Code on December 28, 1980, entitled "Full faith and credit given to child custody determinations" and better known as the Parental Kidnaping Prevention Act. Section 1738, recall, is the general full faith and credit statute, broader in demand than is the constitutional clause that it implements (§ 110). Section 1738A, by its very placement, thus establishes Congress's intent to obtain mandatory recognition for custody decrees akin to the recognition required for judgments generally by § 1738. It might have been simpler to merely amend § 1738 to add a specific reference to custody decrees, but there was too much to say. Hence the distinct § 1738A and its more extended prescription. It provides that F–2 "shall enforce according to its terms, and shall not modify" an F–1 custody determination unless F–2 now has jurisdiction and F–1 now lacks it, or, if F–1 has it, declines to exercise it (subdivision [f]).

The key question under § 1738A, therefore, is whether the first court had jurisdiction to award custody. In this regard the statute seems at first to permit the state to base jurisdiction on its own law (subdivision [c][1]), but it goes right on to require a showing of certain additional contacts or conditions before the court may proceed (subdivision [c][2]), which also boil down to jurisdictional prerequisites. Among these additional contacts, which are in the alternative, are that the state is the "home" state of the child (which the act defines), or that the child is physically there after having been abandoned, and yet others that include forum contacts with the parents or other persons contesting for custody.

In the further hope of discouraging abductions, F–1's jurisdiction is deemed to be of the "continuing" variety (see § 40 in this book) as long as the child or any of the contestants continue to reside there (subdivision [d])—thus telling the would-be absconder that even if he takes the child out of F–1, F–1's jurisdiction will not be divested; that as long as F–1 has and is exercising jurisdiction, every other state's court is directed to keep hands off even though the child may now be before it (subdivision [g]).

Communication between states is encouraged. Congress's message accompanying enactment of § 1738A includes a wish to "promote cooperation . . . and expand the exchange of information". Some states, having adopted the uniform act previously mentioned, got started on court-to-court communication without awaiting this Congressional invitation (e.g., Vanneck, NY 1980).

Because § 1738A requires that a court, before acting at all, must have jurisdiction under its own law (in addition to satisfying the requirements prescribed by the act specifically), the jurisdictional standards for custody decrees predating the act continue to be relevant. The conventional rule here is that a court has jurisdiction to determine custody if it has in personam jurisdiction of the contestants (usually but not always the parents), or if the child is domiciled in the state or merely physically present there. (Sampsell, Cal.1948; Rst.2d § 79.) Although it may be a bit crude to articulate it so, this domicile or presence basis is a kind of in rem jurisdiction, with the child acting as the res. Indeed, in custody disputes the child is often the pawn.

Once a court has jurisdiction, whether F–1 originally and continuingly, or F–2 in the situation in which F–1 now lacks jurisdiction or declines to exercise it, the standard that will govern the award will presumably continue to be what it always has been: whatever is currently in the best interests of the child. Section 1738A seems to base just about everything on the presence of jurisdiction. This is consistent with the full faith and credit approach to judgments generally: that as long as F–1 had jurisdiction, F–2 must recognize the F–1 judgment, but that if F–1 lacked jurisdiction, F–2 can address the merits unimpeded. The wrinkle here is that it is not just a question of what jurisdiction F–1 had to begin with, but also a question of whether F–1 still has it and wants to continue to exercise it. Custody is a continuing issue until the child is of age (age under the act is 18), and if F–1 once had jurisdiction and still has and wants to retain it, F–2 is foreclosed from interfering even if, by the traditional measures of custody jurisdiction, F–2 could now claim jurisdiction, too.

Section 1738A is a just a law-dictator; it tells F–2 what it must or may do when confronted with F–1's custody decree. It is not a claim-creator or jurisdiction-giver. Hence it may not be used as a predicate for subject-matter jurisdiction in a federal court on the theory that it creates a federal cause of action. (Thompson, USSC 1988.) If its prescription is violated after the issue under § 1738A is pressed through a state court system, review of it may then be sought from the U.S. Supreme Court through a petition for certiorari.

The custody dispute will often arise within a matrimonial action, but that is by no means its sole context. The procedures to be used in taking on a custody case as a matter of subject matter jurisdiction are for each state to decide for itself. But insofar as the merits of recognition are concerned, § 1738A, as a uniform federal requirement, governs and must be followed.

§ 131. Adoption

Related to custody is the subject of adoption, a procedure governed by individual state statutes. Courts apply their own law to determine whether one person can adopt another (Rst.2d § 289). And as long as the state granting the adoption has jurisdiction, which is based on contacts similar but not identical to those on which custody jurisdiction rests (Rst.2d § 78), the adoption decree can usually expect recognition elsewhere as a matter of comity, if not formal full faith and credit. But even in recognizing the F–1 adoption, F–2 apparently need not accord all the rights to an adopted child that F–1 would (Hood, USSC 1915), an awkward notion that would seem to remove the benefits of recognition at the same moment that it purports to confer them. The Restatement's position is that F–2 will accord the F–1 adoption at least the same effect it would accord an F–2 adoption (Rst.2d § 290), a conclusion with which language in the Hood case is not (though it ought to be) entirely consistent.

INDEX

References are to Pages

417

INTANGIBLES
Transfer of, choice of law in, 295

INTER VIVOS TRANSFERS
See Personal Property Transfers; Realty; Trusts

"INTEREST ANALYSIS"
Choice of law, modern approach to, 240–242
Contract cases, 210
Tort cases, 250–254, 260–261

INTERNAL LAW
Choice of law rules, distinguished from, 28–29
"Municipal" or "local" law as synonyms, 32

INTERNATIONAL LAW
"Private", 2
"Public", 2

INTERNATIONAL SHOE CASE
See Longarm Jurisdiction

INTERSTATE COMMERCE
Dismissal of action for interfering with, 147

INTESTACY
Personal property, choice of law, 302
Real property, choice of law, 306

ISSUE PRECLUSION, 364

JONES ACT, 311

JUDGMENTS, 345 et seq.
    See also Full Faith and Credit
American courts, recognition of, 345
Attacks on in second forum, 368
    Form of, 369
    Merger of law and equity, effect of, 369
Converting one state's into another's, 346
    Mechanics of, 347
Evidence, vacating for newly discovered, 370
Foreign-country courts,
    Comity, 10, 347–349
    No full faith and credit, 347
    Reciprocity requirement, 347
    Recognition of, 345
    Where to sue on judgments of, 348

"PROCEDURE" LABELING
Choice of law avoidance with, 189, 236–237, 270–271

PROCESS SERVICE
Federal court methods, 126, 128
Foreign nation or subdivision, service on, 127–128
Methods,
    Federal courts, 126, 128
    Persons and entities, service on various, 127–128
    States free to devise own, 125–126
No constitutional formula, 125
Outside state as giving jurisdiction, 47
Publication, frowned on by Supreme Court, 126
States free to devise own methods, 125–126
Transient, service on as giving jurisdiction, 47
Within state as giving jurisdiction, 46–47

PROOF, BURDEN OF
Choice of law treatment, 193
Diversity cases, Erie doctrine in, 327–328
Pleading, distinguished from burden of, 194

PROPERTY
See Chattels; Personal Property; Realty

PROPERTY, SITUS OF
Chattels,
    Fraudulently brought into state, 117
    In transit, 117
Corporate securities, 119
Debtor–location, 122
Documents, property represented by, 118–119
Escheat cases, 120
"Garnishee", 122
Intangibles, 116–117
    Debts, 116, 122
    Liability insurance, 116
Money documents, 119–120
Rem jurisdiction, need to determine for, 117
Security interests, 121–122
Uniform Commercial Code cases, 121

PROPERTY TRANSFERS
See Personal Property Transfers; Realty; Trusts

PUBLIC POLICY
Analog, not violated by want of, 172

WARSAW CONVENTION, 317

WILLS
Personal property bequests, 300
Revocation of, law applicable, 305–306
Spouse's election against, 402
Validity,
    Personal property transfers, 299–300
    Realty transfers, 305

WORKERS' COMPENSATION
    Generally, 289–294
Administrative machinery for, 290
Analyzing options in advance of selecting, 294
Award as barring tort claim, 164, 291
Choice of forum, 290
Choice of law, 290
Contacts needed for recovery of, 290
Described, 289
Recovery, effect on third-party actions, 291
Third parties, suit against after recovery of, 164, 291
Tort action as barred by recovery of, 164, 291

WRONGFUL DEATH ACTIONS
Choice of law on damages, 161, 236–237, 247, 250–252, 258,
    273–274, 281–282

†